The Courage of Blackburn Blair

Eleanor Talbot Kinkead

THE COURAGE OF BLACKBURN BLAIR

BY

ELEANOR TALBOT KINKEAD

Author of "The Invisible Bond"

O for a living man to lead!
That will not babble when we bleed;
O for the silent doer of the deed!

—*Stephen Phillips.*

NEW YORK
MOFFAT, YARD & COMPANY
1907

GO

Published September, 1907

The Winthrop Press, New York, N. Y., U. S. A.

TO
THE MEMORY OF MY FATHER
WILLIAM BURY KINKEAD
WHO MORE THAN ANY OTHER REVEALED
TO ME THE FULNESS OF MEANING
CONTAINED IN THE TERMS
GENTLEMAN AND PATRIOT

AUTHOR'S NOTE

"THE Courage of Blackburn Blair" is the second book in the plan of a thought triology in which the three great fundamental relations of life are severally presented as the viewpoint from which the love theme is evolved. In "The Invisible Bond," the first of the series, emphasis is given to the marriage relation—the relation of man toward woman. The central thought is the idea of the sanctity of the marriage bond, leading up to a larger idea: the sanctity of the marriage relation, out of which alone, in the author's opinion, is to develop the solution of the problem of divorce. In "The Courage of Blackburn Blair," the emphasis is upon the fraternal relation—the relation of man toward humanity, the central thought here being the sacrifice of individual privilege for the sake of the good of the many. And it is the relation of the individual toward the divine—toward those mystic revelations that are the God-given things of the spirit—which is to be set forth in "The Vision Splendid," the third of the sequence, now under construction.

CONTENTS

BOOK I

BOOK II

BOOK III

BOOK IV

THE COURAGE OF BLACKBURN BLAIR

CHAPTER I

IN A ROSE GARDEN

"I THINK you mighty funny little boy, Blackburn Blair—Blackburn B-l-a-i-r."

The young person addressed looked up quickly from his book—an old leathern-bound volume with yellowed leaves—and a flush of indignant protest mounted hotly to his temples. There are some things a boy can't stand.

He was a handsome lad of fourteen, or thereabout, with a fine head and brow, and wide brown eyes that touched one by their wistful pleadings. And it was a singularly earnest face that a moment before had bent above the ancient book—a face grave, though healthful, and cast in a certain picturesqueness of mold that gave an impression of noble strength and beauty.

His glance swept the length of the long porch with its four great pillars and finally rested upon a tiny creature, that seemed all eyes and hair and audacity happily combined, standing a few yards away, and just outside the gate.

"See here now, Cicely," he demanded, stoutly, "can't you go back home and leave a fellow alone?"

Apparently Cicely found this a wholly impossible thing to do. She stood stock-still, swinging her little white-frilled, pink-lined sunbonnet by the strings, and staring calmly.

The boy resolutely turned a page.

With a shrug of her slim little shoulders, the child moved a step nearer and peered a trifle dubiously through the spokes of the tall iron fence, at the same moment breaking forth into ripples of mocking, irresponsible laughter, which, under the circumstances, were not calculated to soothe. It was very tuneful laughter, delicious as the bubbling of a forest spring—and quite as innocent of offense.

But Blackburn was not inclined to relish a merriment directed against himself—and by a girl at that.

His lips closed firmly, and his dark eyes scanned the page with severe determination. At that moment he was oddly suggestive of certain dim old portraits of individuals in high stocks and ruffled shirts that hung on the walls of his father's home. Presently he looked up.

"Cicely, if you won't go away and leave me alone, won't you come in?" he proposed, unconsciously resorting in his helplessness to an expedient which older and wiser heads than his have been known to turn to under similar stress. However, Cicely would neither go away nor come in.

"I think you mighty funny little boy, Blackburn Blair," she repeated loftily. The small person fixed her eyes significantly on the unsightly volume in the hands of the youthful student—so different from her own delightful picture books filled with tales of fairy enchantment and beautiful golden-haired princesses—and openly scoffed.

In the face of such persistent disdain there wasn't much for a boy to say, but Blackburn found a thing to do.

He closed the book, having first placed a small bit of folded paper between the leaves to mark the place, and then laying it down carefully—very carefully—on the settee beside him, he rose and crossed the long vine-shaded porch that ran the full length of the old house on one side.

Generations of courtly, high-bred men in him, were compelling him to a course of generous self-restraint, just as generations of beautiful high-bred women in her were compelling her to a coquettry, the arts of which her baby breast had never even dreamed of. but which she could no more fail to practice than a kitten could forget to purr.

"Cicely," inquired the boy, with a sort of quaint stiffness of speech that was yet neither priggish nor shy, "won't you come into the garden and let me fill your lap with roses?"

Cicely declined.

"Uncle Scip won't mind; he gives them to me all the time."

Cicely was firm. But the corners of her mouth were twitching; secure in her triumph she could afford to delay.

"Don't you want me to swing you for a while?"

Again that sweet, mocking overflow of wholly exasperating glee.

"Cicely Overton, if you aren't the—" he was beginning hotly, when there occurred to him the advantage that might be gained by a diplomatic change of base.

"There's a lot of awfully nice cherries up in the cherry tree," he suggested in a tone of nonchalance.

For a moment Cicely wavered. Then the shower of golden-brown curls began to glint and gleam in the merry June sunshine as the small head moved slowly and stubbornly from side to side.

The boy went back to the settee and opened his book. A moment afterward he was again deeply absorbed in its contents—and as wholly unmindful of the small person outside the gate as if she had never been born.

Seeing that her presence was no longer indispensable, or even desired, Cicely softly opened the gate and entered the yard.

She had crept quite close to him before he looked up, and when he did there was on his face a glow that lent a strange seriousness to the boyish features—the look of one who dreams of ancient prowess and renown, of savage wrong, and mortal foe, and

> "......old, unhappy, far-off things,
> And battles long ago."

In that moment Cicely seemed very far away. The child regarded him with a kind of awe.

"What make you read that dull old book, Blackburn?" she asked, opening her blue eyes very wide.

"This is no dull old book," retorted Blackburn, valiantly, "it's the nicest book you ever saw. It's 'Marshall's History of Kentucky,' that's what it is, and it beats any book *you* ever read."

"Mine's got lots of nice pictures in it—ladies with crowns on they heads and in pink silk with lace all about 'em *ever'where.* Major Wise brought it to me last night when he came to see my grandfather. Want me go and get it?"

"Pooh! who cares for pictures. Listen to this," and Blackburn turned to a favorite passage. "It's about Kentucky."

"'Here it was,'" he began in a voice which he vainly strove to render deep and impressive, 'here it was, if Pan ever existed, that without the aid of fiction, he held his sole dominion, and Sylvan empire, unmolested by Ceres, or Lucina, for centuries.'"

"Cicely," he demanded severely, pausing abruptly and with quite an air, "who were Ceres and Lucina, do you know?"

Cicely hung her head in ignorance and shame.

"Great big girl, ten years old, and never heard of Ceres and Lucina! Well, I declare!"

"I don't care," said Cicely, goaded to defiance.

"I'd think you'd be ashamed."

"I don't care," repeated Cicely in dogged desperation.

"Well then, listen, and I'll tell you. Ceres and Lucina were— were— Ceres and Lucina were—"

But Cicely unwittingly saved the situation from utter confusion and ignominy by suddenly breaking in.

"I know meningitis," she declared eagerly. Blackburn proceeded grandly.

"'The proud face of creation here presented itself, without the disguise of art. No wood had been felled; no field cleared; no human habitation raised: even the red man of the forest, had not put up his wigwam of poles and bark for habitation. But that mysterious Being, whose productive power we call nature, ever bountiful, and ever great—had not spread out this replete, and luxurious pasture without stocking it with numerous flocks and herds: nor were their ferocious attendants, who prey upon them, wanting to fill up the circle of created beings. Here was seen the timid deer; the towering elk; the fleet stag; the surly bear; the crafty fox; the ravenous wolf; the devouring panther; the insidious wild-cat and the haughty buffalo; besides innumerable other creatures, winged, four-footed or creeping. And here, at some time unknown, had been, for his bones are yet here, the leviathan of the forest, the monstrous mammoth whose trunk, like that of the famous Trojan horse, would have held an host of men; and whose teeth, nine feet in length, inflicted death and destruction, on both animal and vegetable substances—until, exhausting all within its range, itself became extinct.'

"There!" exclaimed Blackburn, triumphantly, "have you got anything in *your* book that can beat that?"

Cicely's piquant little face had paled, and her lips trembled. Her eyes were fixed on Blackburn's face in actual terror.

"You're a horrid, mean boy, and I don't like you one bit," she broke forth with a sob—"to come tellin' me 'bout that great big thing what eats people up, with his long teeth, and horns, and whiskers, and—*ever'thing.*"

Cicely's mastodon, a sort of hideous combination of man and beast, would doubtless have provoked but little fear in a mind already stored with tales of genii and giants, and hobgoblins of every kind, if only it had not been quite so definitely localized, and in her own Kentucky, the latter end of that mighty mammal having wholly escaped her in Blackburn's pompous reading. From the "surly bear," the "ravenous wolf," the "devouring panther," the "insidious wild-cat," the "haughty buffalo," and the rest—all of which she doubted not were still proudly parading the Kentucky woodlands—she hoped, through the intervention of a wise and merciful Providence, somehow, to compass an escape, but the *leviathan of the forest* was more than she could stand. She was therefore about to beat a hasty retreat, when Blackburn came bravely to the rescue.

"Cicely," he said, "you little goose, what are you crying about? The thing's dead, (gerimini, don't I wish he wasn't!) he's dead, I tell you, been dead—oh, a long, long time—a hundred and forty or fifty years, may be. Here, Cicely, please don't cry—*don't* cry."

Cicely looked up through her tears.

"Blackburn, are you sure he's dead, quite, quite sure?"

Blackburn hastened to declare that upon that point he was in no uncertainty whatever; whereupon, Cicely slightly mollified, announced that in that case she would stay a little—a *little* longer, not however, without a due sense of her own gracious condescension in the matter.

"Let's go into the garden," she proposed.

The garden began a few yards away from the low steps of the great side porch, and ran a considerable distance to the rear of the house—a huge buff-coloured structure with a Grecian portico in front and a long rambling wing at the back, that looked out upon the street. The old mansion, being one of the early landmarks of the town, doubtless had often furnished to the superstitious, sure and ready confirmation of the ancient prediction of disaster regarding the inmates of a corner house: sorrows manifold certainly had befallen its owners, if one has a mind to dwell upon such to the exclusion of happy things. But it is equally true that they had had their days of feasting and their nights of revelry too, when the great rooms were wont to take on a gracious, gala look and to ring with music and laughter, and when the fall of the Christmas snowflakes outside was only a little softer than the steps of the dancers within. Even Blackburn could recall a time when everything had been far different under the sway of a radiant presence, that had passed like the sudden fading of sunshine out of his life. There was no one now but his father and himself, and his father was broken in health and already grown old.

The two children had paused beside a damask rose bush in full bloom.

"Wait a moment till I get the shears," said Blackburn, eager to atone. "Uncle Scip has them over there," and he darted off in the direction of an old white-haired negro who was trailing a honeysuckle vine over a trellis at the extreme end of the garden and muttering low, disjointed sentences to himself, as his watchful eye traveled slowly from time to time toward the two childish figures in the distance.

"What dem chillun up to *now?*" he was saying, a look of quizzical good-humour resting upon the fleet-footed runner approaching.

"Bless Gord," he broke forth indignantly an instant afterward, "ef dat boy ain' come an' purloined my shurs right under my ve'y nose!"

But when Blackburn returned from his errand, Cicely had moved away from the damask roses. She had remembered that all the flowers of the garden had been freely hers save the roses from a single bush. These, for some reason unknown to her, had always been silently and persistently withheld; and it was upon these particular roses that now her gaze was fixed. Was she about to lose her Eden?

"I'll have *these*!" she exclaimed, pointing a small forefinger at a bush thickly laden with delicate white blooms; "they're almost as pretty as snowballs. I won't have any of those old red ones, and yellow ones, and pink ones. I want these!"

Blackburn's face suddenly paled. He stood speechless, looking from the child to the white rose bush in dismay.

"Cicely," he gasped at last, in a voice which he tried his best to make steady and natural, but which would grow husky in spite of him, dying away into something very like a sob, "you—you can't have any of those roses; there's—there's a reason. But there are loads of others," he added quickly, "just bushels of 'em. Here, hold your apron!" and he began to cut away with reckless prodigality, brandishing the shears, but all the while keeping his face steadfastly turned from her.

Cicely was beginning to cry. "You — never — do — what — I — ask," she wailed.

The boy's expression grew very grave and troubled, and again he pressed the despised blooms upon her.

"I — told — you — I — didn't — want — any — old red ones, and yellow ones, and pink ones. I — want — these!" she insisted wrathfully, being wilful, like most young things.

Blackburn paused. He stood a moment looking steadily at her, his back always turned to the beautiful white rose bush. Presently his gaze was caught by the flash of a blackbird's wing far in the deep blue of the soft Southern sky. Out in the street an ice-wagon moved noisily past, and then everything was still, save for the low hum of bees among the garden sweets, for it was four o'clock of a warm summer afternoon and the neighborhood was peacefully slumbering, preparatory to the drive that would follow later into the cool country lanes. Then his eyes wandered back to the shadowy garden, with its delightful little nooks covered over with grapevines and clematis and wistaria. Just a few steps away there was a mighty elm under which the two children used to play—before Blackburn became an absorbed student of Kentucky history, and inclined to neglect his more youthful associate for intellectual pursuits. There was a long bench under the tree, and it had been a favorite resort during the two or three preceding summers, as soon as Cicely arrived from Louisville for her annual visit. The last six months, however, had brought a wondrous rousing to the boy's latent powers—the first dawn of that great eagerness for knowledge and for work which was soon to possess him with a passionate energy and zeal.

"I am going to tell my grandfather on you, Blackburn Blair," said Cicely, at length, putting on her bonnet deliberately, and tying the strings with certain vicious little jerks indicative of her displeasure.

The picture of a little old gentleman, very queer and very stately, with an uncomfortable way of peering at small boys over his gold-rimmed spectacles, suddenly rose before Blackburn's mental vision.

"Don't go, Cicely," he pleaded quickly, "let's go over into the summer-house and get Uncle Scip to bring us some cherries."

Cicely's firm little chin was resting in one palm, the elbow of which was grasped tightly by her other hand. There was a judicial sternness in her attitude that would bear no trifling. The boy was on trial, and he knew it.

"Once more I ask you, Blackburn Blair, will you give me these roses — these?"

Blackburn turned and looked upon the beautiful, wilful little creature quivering with excitement, and a kind of pitying tenderness, a great longing to do what she wished, seized him all at once. The feeling was so new and strange and unexpected he stood helpless and bewildered in the presence of some mystic force which he was unable even dimly to comprehend.

For fully five-and-twenty seconds the struggle lasted. Then he looked her calmly in the eyes, and his lips closed firmly. With a pang, the meaning of which was deeper than she knew, Cicely saw that his decision was fixed.

"I can't let you have any of the white roses, Cicely," he said at length, very gently. "There's — there's a reason."

CHAPTER II

UNCLE SCIP

Under the shade of an old apple tree, a robin singing overhead, and a fine little breeze a-stir, Uncle Scip sat taking his ease after the heat and labour of the long summer day. His garden implements, like the arms of the faithful soldier, lay on the ground at his side; and his eyes, lazily wandering from time to time past shadowing vine and cool retreat to the sunnier portions of the little plot, rested complacently upon the results of his own skillful handicraft.

His rude wooden bench had been placed close to the bole of the tree, and against the dull gray bark the old negro's head showed white as cotton. He was of a familiar type, albeit one that is rapidly disappearing — the old-time Southern darky who is a droll imitation of his old-time Southern master in attire and in bearing, and who in donning the cast-off garments of his model sometimes takes on also a stately picturesqueness of demeanor that is always touchingly suggestive.

He had a lean, powerful form, a dark-brown skin, wrinkled and weather-beaten, like a russet leaf after the rains and winds of autumn, a scraggy gray beard, and an expression that was at the same time comical and appealing.

His head was thrown back, and his long bony hands lay peacefully folded in his lap — the hands of the humble toiler, pathetic in their brief idleness, while his whole being voiced a repose that had been earned by patient service and a fine intention.

Seeing him under the apple tree, Blackburn moved slowly across the lawn, a dull pain still tugging at his heart. From his babyhood the boy had looked upon the old negro as his special comrade and friend; and in this moment his childish steps instinctively turned toward the solace that had never failed him in all his young life.

Uncle Scipio's eyes were closed, though he appeared not to be sleeping, but rather to be indulging in one of those strange day-dreams of his declining years in which his spirit sadly wandered amid the scenes and recollections of a long-vanished past. As Blackburn drew nearer he roused himself with a start.

"Who dat?" he exclaimed, peering with a bewildered look into the boy's face. "Lawd, ef you ain' de ve'y spit o' yo' ma!" he added quickly, in a kind of awkward shame for his momentary lapse into uncertainty. "Honey, seem lak sometimes you got all de symptoms of Miss Mandy, tubbe sho."

Blackburn sat down on the bench by the old man's side. At the mention of his mother's name the boy's face changed, and the wistful look in the brown eyes deepened.

"Uncle Scip," he said at length in a low voice, "do you remember? It's the day."

Uncle Scip's head solemnly nodded. "Yas, honey, hit's de day; I ain't fergit."

There was a long silence. Somewhere in the garden, remote amid leafy inclosures, a dove was cooing with insistent moan, the plaintive note blending oddly with the buoyant song of the robin overhead. Presently Blackburn looked up.

"Uncle Scip," he said, with a little tremor in his voice, "four years is a mighty long time, isn't it?"

"Hit's a long time — a mighty long time, tubbe sho. But we's all in de han's of a onscrupulous Providence," said Uncle Scip, devoutly. "Some days seem lak 'tain' no time sence I seen her movin' roun' 'mongst dem flower-beds lak a queen an' smilin' jes ez soft."

The old negro's eyes suddenly dimmed. He was looking straight ahead of him with that deep, far-seeing vision that excludes all nearer objects.

"Seem lak I sees her now," he continued presently, "an' 'tain' no more'n yistiddy sence we planted de white rose bush. I dunno what mek her tek a noshun she wan' plant dat bush herself; but she wuz out in de gyardin *all* de time, an' I ain' nuver knowed what she gwine do nex'. She'd been laughin' an' talkin' to de flowers same ez they wuz people, an' she wuz kneelin' down by de side of de white rose bush we jes planted, an' all at oncet she stop, an' her face got white ez de roses bloomin' on dat bush to-day. 'Uncle Scip,' she say, standin' up an' fixin' her big eyes on me right stiddy, 'I dunno why 'tis, but I feels so strange.' I says, 'Miss Mandy, honey, when you feels lak dat,' I says, 'hit's caze some pusson's a-walkin' ober yo' grabe.'"

The old darky paused abruptly. "Hit wuz de ve'y' day we got news dat young marster wuz done drown*ed*; an' hit wan' but little better'n two months befo' she deceas*ed*," he added gravely.

Blackburn leaned down and plucked a bit of periwinkle that grew about the tree. "Tell me," he said at length, "tell me again about the first time father ever saw her."

Uncle Scipio stretched his legs and settled himself more comfortably.

"Hit wan' to say de ve'y fust time, honey, caze he done seen her befo' when she wan' nothin' but a little long-legged gal; but I reckon 'twuz de fust time all de same. Dat so. Hit wuz in de summer time, an' we wuz all livin' out on de old plantation, an' ole marse (dat yo' pa's pa) he owned all de lan' on one side of de road, an' yo' ma an' her ma an' pa, dey owned all de lan' on de urr side de road. We wuz all gran' people den. Dem slave times wuz heap better times," he broke off, falling into a confession. "But don' you nuver say nothin' lak dat to yo' Aunt Huldy," he added, quickly. "Huldy done jined de Society for de Promoshun of de Ladies of Colour, an' she ain' gwine stan' no talk lak dat. She say she gwine tek a broomstick to de haid of de nex' nigger she find blasphemin' an' puttin' a stumblin'-block in de way of de progress of de race. But dem wuz heap better times. Well, you know, ole marse (dat yo' pa's pa) he done gimme to yo' pa de day yo' pa wuz bawned, for a body-servant, an'——"

"Uncle Scip," interrupted Blackburn, suddenly recalling his Kentucky history, "did you use to help to fight the Indians?"

Uncle Scip stared. "Lawd, honey, no, I ain' nuver fit no Injuns. How ole you think I is?"

"I thought," suggested Blackburn a little doubtfully, "you must be pretty near a hundred, Uncle Scip."

"Heish! I ain' no hund'ed! How ole you think yo' pa is?"

"Father is sixty-one."

"Den dis ole nigger jes seven year older'n yo' pa. What dat make? Go long boy, come heah axin' me ef I ain' a hund'ed year ole, an' ef I ain' holp to fight de Injuns!"

It was evident that, in spite of the assumed severity of his manner, Uncle Scip was complimented in the extreme. "What I tellin' you?" he asked presently, endeavouring to gather together his scattered wits.

"You said that grandfather gave you to father for a body-servant," prompted Blackburn, deeply interested in the oft-told tale.

Uncle Scip bowed his head in stately affirmation. "On de day yo' pa wuz bawned," he concluded.

If it occurred to Blackburn that the youthful body-servant at such an early stage in his father's career might have been a somewhat superfluous possession, he wisely refrained from all heterdox expression, and Uncle Scip continued.

"Yo' pa wuz mighty high-sperited little boy, an' he jes shot up faster'n dem weeds I'm allus tryin' to keep track of. 'Twa'n' no time 'fo' he wuz goin' to school an' to de circus an' *ever'whar.* Ole marse (dat yo' pa's pa) used to say, 'Scip, don' you wa'n' go to de circus? Yo' young marster's goin to de circus,' an' we'd bofe go to de circus; an ever' day I'd go over to de schoolhouse an' tek him he victuals in a little baskit, an' on de way home we used to climb up in de tall trees an' git wild-grapes an persimmonses an' chincapins an' hawses. Dem wuz heap better times."

Uncle Scip seemed lost hopelessly in reminiscence,

but Blackburn still waited patiently, his grave, handsome face aglow with attention.

After a while the soft, droning voice began again. "Soon ez yo' pa got ole nouf, ole marse sint him to town to de University, an' nothin' would suit ole miss 'ceptin' fo' me to go long an' tek keer o' him, caze yo' pa allus totin' a book 'roun; but he bleeged to have he boots blacked. Arter we done learned all dey knowed at de University, he sint us up to de Norf somewhars, an' we staid long time. Arter we done learned all dey knowd thar, ole marse (dat yo' pa's pa) sint us to Yurrup; an' arter we done learned all dey knowed *thar*, by an' by we come home. Yo' pa wuz a tall black-hyared young man, head up, rared back, an' jes a-bowin' an' a-scrapin' *all* de time. He wuz a mighty peart lookin' young gemman, tubbe sho."

"It was on a beautiful summer morning just like this, wasn't it, Uncle Scip," put in Blackburn, eagerly.

"I'm a-comin' to it, honey, I'm a-comin'," replied Uncle Scip. "Yo' pa wuz 'bout thirty-two year ole when Miss Mandy come home from boa'din'-school, an' Miss Mandy, she wuz jes 'bout eighteen, an' ole miss wuz gittin' mighty oneasy, caze she 'fraid yo' pa gwine 'fuse to mah'y *ever*'body. But she allus did have her eye sot on Miss Mandy. But ole miss ain' nuver said nothin' 'bout dat. In cose I knowed yo' pa ain' s'picioned nothin,' an' I wuz mighty keerful, caze I done seen Miss Mandy de day she come; an' Huldy (Huldy wuz Miss Mandy's maid den), she been tellin me heap o' things. Howsomever, I knowed fo' myself, caze I done seen her."

"It was in June, and father was just going to take a horseback ride, and you had Mohawk saddled and waiting at the door," interrupted Blackburn again, with boyish excitement, restless for the climax.

But Uncle Scip was not to be hastened. He proceeded with great deliberation and elegance.

"Yo' pa wuz jes comin' 'long down de steps, holdin' he whip, an' steppin' ez light, an' all on a suddent he looked up an' spied a big coach a-rollin' 'long de drive."

"Uncle Scip," said Blackburn, solemnly, "that reminds me of something father read to me in the Bible to-day, 'And Isaac went out to meditate in the field at eventide: and he lifted up his eyes, and saw, and behold, the camels were coming.'"

"Yas, honey, dat so, hit's right smart lak dat, tubbe sho. Then yo' pa turn he haid right keerless an' say, 'Scip, whose kerridge is that?' he say, jes ez cool ez a cowcumber. I wuz 'tendin' lak I mighty busy, fixin' de bridle an' talkin' to Mohawk, but by an' by I say, 'Look mighty lak Big Dave an' Little Dave over to Marse Alfred's a-settin' on de box.' An then I ain' say no mo', caze I knowed ole miss done sint fo' Miss Mandy dat ve'y day.

"Seem lak dat kerridge nuver would reach de doo'. I done led Mohawk little piece to one side, an' yo' pa he done drawed off he gloves an' come down on to de pavement when Big Dave druv up an' Little Dave he done jump down."

Again the old negro halted and drew himself up with a stately gesture.

"Jes ez Little Dave teched de doo' yo' pa tek a step an' waved he han', an' Little Dave moved back, an' de doo' fell open—an' thar settin' on de back seat of de coach wuz Miss Mandy, all in white, an' smilin', wid pink ribbins tied under her chin, an' a big bo'quet in her han' fo' ole miss.

"Yo' pa he jes stood right still ez a stone, an' he face hit got red, an' he ain' say nothin'. Seem lak he done clean forgit all dem fine manners we brung 'long home, wid us from Yurrup, an' I wuz gittin' 'most 'shamed when I heah Miss Mandy say, jes ez soft an' sweet, 'you don't know me, does you, Mr. Blair?'

"Then yo' pa he jes leaned over an' helt out he han' an' looked her full in de eyes long time. 'When Venus takes us unawahes ——' he say, an' stopped right short. An' Miss Mandy, she burst out laughin' an' jimped out of de coach an' run up de steps into de house whar ole miss and ole marster waitin' fo' her, yo' pa followin' 'long arter an' lookin' same ez he sight been dazzled by de sun."

When Uncle Scip reached this point in his narrative he came to a final halt, the old darky's sense of dramatic effect refusing another word. There were other stories, equally interesting, perhaps, for his memory was good, and through his simple accuracy of detail the past was made to live again with a distinctness that is often lost in the hands of a more polished historian; but this particular story invariably ended here.

Blackburn, having learned this from long experience, sat a few moments in silence, the picture of his beautiful dead mother in her sweet, winsome girlhood making an impression singularly tender and appealing upon his boyish mind.

Presently he rose, and with a quiet "Thank you, Uncle Scip," he moved across the garden. Beside the white rose bush he paused. The shears were lying on the ground where they had fallen from his hand an hour before, and at his feet were the roses, already beginning to wither, which Cicely had spurned with resentful disdain. An angry, tearful little face was before him, and with it there came again that strange new sense of pity which he could not at all understand. Then he reached down and picked up the shears and began carefully to cut a number of the lovely white blooms. He had quite a handful when he turned toward the house.

CHAPTER III

A CONSERVATIVE UNION GENTLEMAN

The room that Blackburn entered a few moments later was low and square. There were four large mahogany bookcases with lozenge panes. On the walls there were several fine engravings pertaining to literary subjects, and there were family portraits and armorial bearings; and on the mantle two tall silver candlesticks beside delicate bits of fine old china from beyond the seas that had been handed down from generation to generation.

Near one of the open windows of this room there sat an elderly looking gentleman in dressing-gown and slippers, slowly turning from time to time the pages of a volume of Addison's "The Spectator"— a lean, tall man with iron-gray hair and beard, deep-set eyes, and a brow that indicated a high degree of intellectuality and spiritual strength. In his face one saw the jurist, the moralist, and even the poet; and as he sat with the folds of his dark dressing-gown hanging loosely about him, his long silvery hair falling upon his neck, there was something both picturesque and potent in his personal aspect. Despite the marks of premature physical infirmity indicated in his wasted form, there was a look of undying strength in his eyes— the strength of deep, earnest conviction and of profound emotion; and there was, moreover, about him a reserve, a loftiness of bearing that compelled for him instinctive reverence even from his foes.

Judge Blackburn Blair had had his foes in plenty in his day — mainly persons of opposite political belief who found it difficult to forgive him his attitude relating to those great issues which properly belonged to the period of the war between the states, but which were being constantly revived during the fifteen or sixteen years that had passed since the conflict reached its close. There were some who were inclined to hold him in a great measure responsible for the stand Kentucky took in that conflict.

A member of that dignified old Whig party which, under various names and through various changes, for more than thirty years ruled in the politics of Kentucky, he was one of those who under the name *Conservative Union* saved the state from Secession, and having saved it, afterwards rescued it from the control of the radical element of the Union party.

A slave holder, the descendant of slave holders, favouring the doctrine of gradual emancipation, with every sympathy enlisted in the Southern cause, and denying the right of Northern congressmen to make laws against the slave property of the South, he yet loved the Union and the Constitution with a patriotic fervour that not every one can understand, and he thus found himself in early middle-age called upon to make one of those great decisions which seem to colour every subsequent event of a lifetime. He chose in favour of conviction, of unselfishness, not pausing to consider what the consequences to his own ambitions such a course would be. It cut short his political career.

It is difficult to accept defeat at the hands of inferior men. What retirement to private life means to a man who knows that he has within himself the powers of great leadership and who has planned for himself a career of public usefulness he knew. But he did not know the place that historians of the future would give to that little band of patriots to which he belonged who saved Kentucky for the Union.

But there were private sorrows awaiting him far deeper than any pain he had suffered from the attacks of those who would not, or could not, understand the principle that had controlled with him — sorrows under which his great heart broke, but which yet left him, though shorn of every personal ambition, shattered in health, and aged before his time, still standing, like a great rock in a desert, secure in that old Presbyterian faith which had been the consolation of his fathers and their strength in many generations.

The first blow had come four years before in the death of his elder son. In the patience with which, after the first storms of anguish had been spent, Judge Blair bowed beneath this shock, there was a revelation of the childlike sweetness and acquiescence toward the Divine that seems to exist in all sound natures —something that braced his beholders while they stood amazed and touched, thrilled with a sense of simple strength and beauty like that which sings, mournful and tender, in the old Greek chorus:

"I had an uncle, old and hoary,
He had one child, his pride and glory.
When on that son death sudden fell,
The old man bore it passing well."

The second blow came two months after the death of his son, in the death of his wife, and it was this wound that, above all others, had never healed.

Younger than he by many years, possessing beauty of that radiant order with which one finds it difficult to associate the thought of death or sorrow, she had always been to him the very essence of the springtime, a being who could never grow old, and one to whom he would ever give all the chivalrous, poetic devotion of his reserved, pure nature.

A portrait of her hung near the old secretary above a little mahogany work-table with claw feet; and it was toward this shrine that Blackburn made his way with the roses. He had placed them in a bowl half-filled with water, and he moved carefully through the room.

It was the portrait of a young and very lovely woman, with warm brown eyes and hair and a face that was pure oval in its fine patrician contour. The hair, satin-smooth, was parted above the low brow and drawn back about the tiny ears in a style that would have been severe for most faces. The head was beautifully poised, the lips slightly parted and wondering, the whole expression of the face being at the same time spirited and thoughtful. A white cape of old lace worn carelessly and with graceful abandon fell about the low bodice and the delicately curved shoulders.

For a long time the boy stood looking into that changeless countenance, his childish longing mocked by the beautiful, silent lips. Presently two great tears welled into his eyes and trickled down his cheeks.

He thought he was quite alone, and he started violently when there was a movement at one of the far windows and Judge Blair rose and walked softly across the room.

The two stood a moment before the portrait in silence. Then an arm was gently thrown about the lad, and father and son looked beseechingly, and with a like timidity, into each other's eyes.

It was an anniversary, and the boy had remembered

CHAPTER IV

TWO ANCIENT ANTAGONISTS

"Cicely, you little minx, go and tell Ben to bring some chairs out here. Cicely ——"

The command came from a little old gentleman in spectacles, with a smooth face and a very loud voice, who had just appeared in the doorway of a large red-brick house covered with Virginia Creeper that stood diagonally across the street from the Blair homestead. The little old gentleman peered through his spectacles in the direction of his neighbor's house. But neither Blackburn nor Cicely seemed to be around.

"Cicely!" he called again impatiently. But there was no answer, only a subdued titter near the corner of the house, which luckily escaped him, as he was in no mood for tricks. "Bless me!" he exclaimed, coming out into the porch and looking anxiously toward a spreading shade tree in the small plot of bluegrass to the left. "Bless me, where's that child gone?"

He gave a vigorous pull at the old-fashioned door bell, and before a servant in response had come more than a step into the long hall, his loud, authoritative voice rang out, "Chairs, Ben, chairs; and go find that young monkey we've got here. The Lord only knows what she'll be up to next. Caught her this morning meddling with my shaving-case, and last night, when I couldn't find my spectacles anywhere,— had to keep up a search for 'em for nearly an hour, and couldn't find 'em high or low,— where do you think they were all the time of my discomfiture? Perched up on the nose of that little Jackanapes — on her nose, Ben — on her *nose*!"

"She wuz jes laughin' fit to kill herself all de time," put in old Ben, apologetically.

"Laughing, was she?" roared Judge Trotter, indignantly, "laughing, indeed! And a pretty subject for hilarity it was, an old man hopping around like a hen on a hot griddle, his spectacles, melancholy witness to his declining years, nowhere to be found, while all the time the lost article in question was quietly reposing upon the nose ——"

He paused abruptly and wheeled, his ear caught by the familiar click of a cane on the sidewalk below. "Chairs, Ben, chairs," he ordered, with a return to dignity, "and mind you don't forget the chess-board."

The large, middle-aged gentleman who ascended the steps a moment later was slightly lame in one leg, but he moved with a certain nervous energy that caused his progress to be little impeded either by his affliction or by his somewhat excessive avoirdupois.

He came quickly up the steps, carrying his broad-brimmed straw hat in one hand, and thereby displaying a heavy shock of reddish hair sprinkled with white, that fell about a brow notably broad and intellectual. His face was beardless, and the gray eyes, shrewd yet kindly, looked forth from a countenance that was rugged and knotty, yet not wholly unpleasing.

"Ah, Dominie, it has been a long time since you honoured us," said the judge, advancing in his best style, and employing a certain pompous mode of speech which he particularly resorted to on all hospitable occasions.

Professor Kennedy took the offered seat. "It is the first opportunity I have had in a week, sir," he replied bluntly, his Scottish accent falling with a certain musical sweetness on the ear.

But Judge Trotter's genial smile had suffered a sudden eclipse.

"Opportunity! my dear sir, did I understand you correctly in regard to the use of that word? Pardon me, but I am growing a little deaf of late."

The professor bowed. "I meant to say simply that it was a matter of opportunity and not of inclination," he said, with a quiet twinkle in his gray eyes. "I've been wanting to get even with you ever since that last game, when the luck was all your way, you remember. Never saw the like of it. But the opportunity," he added, with a kind of pugnacious hold upon the word, "the opportunity has been lacking."

"My dear sir," replied Judge Trotter, with an elaborate wave of the hand, and speaking with great dignity, "allow me to call in question the propriety of your use of that word in this relation. Opportunity? My dear sir, the man who makes his own opportunities never has to wait for them. Lay that down as an axiom, sir, as an axiom. Bring before your mind for a moment the great founders of this beloved old Commonwealth of Kentucky, the garden spot of America, this miniature earthly paradise with its undulating hills and dales, and waving fields of bluegrass. What was it that gave to them their superiority over other men, if it was not the capacity to seize for themselves opportunities which others failed to seize. Take for instance those two grand old military heroes of early times — Governor Isaac Shelby and General George Rogers Clark. In what did their special genius consist? It was this, sir, it was this: when others hesitated and faltered, they hesitated and faltered not. Ah, my dear sir, the opportunity never fails the man, it is the *man* who fails the opportunity."

To these somewhat unflattering and high-sounding periods Professor Kennedy maintained an unruffled calm. If it occurred to him that there would seem to exist no particular connection between his apology for a deferred pleasure and the illustrious examples of promptness in action cited by his host, he made no comment.

He sat waving his great straw hat before his face as a fan, and smiling imperturbably. It was his custom to spend at least one evening out of every week in company with the judge; but during the summer months he generally appeared in the afternoon at about half past five o'clock, when their game of chess could with more comfort be indulged in than at a later hour. After the game the professor always stayed to tea and a special feast was spread, if the usual debate regarding the relative merits of General Andrew Jackson and Henry Clay did not descend to personalties to such a degree that the professor left in a huff, which he sometimes did.

But to-day Professor Kennedy was in his best frame of mind, and not inclined to resent the mention of any notables of the past, however much the conduct of such worthies might seem a reflection upon his own. Presently his eyes wandered away to the beautiful sugar-maple tree in the judge's yard under which two children were sitting reading from a large book beautifully illustrated with coloured prints — Blackburn and Cicely, who had settled their differences, and who were now evidently most peaceably inclined, their friendship being of an order somewhat similar to that of the professor and the judge, liable to occasional rupture, yet wholly indispensable.

"A fine lad — a fine lad!" murmured the professor, approvingly, as his glance rested upon Blackburn, and a gleam of affectionate interest lit up his rugged countenance like the play of sunlight on a rock. "I have taught him these two years, or more, and the Greek and Latin that youngster knows, to say nothing of his knowledge of history and mathematics, would do credit to many an older head. The boy's got grit in him — grit. It is his Scotch Presbyterian blood, sir," concluded the professor, with emphasis.

"Bosh and nonsense," said the judge, who had a genius for contradiction equal to that of old Samuel Johnson himself. "The boy's got as much, if not more, English blood in him, than he has of your boasted Scotch-Irish. I am confident of it, sir."

"He is of a very ancient Scottish house," remarked the professor.

"He is also of an ancient English house," observed the judge.

"That fact, sir," said the professor, "merely furnishes additional evidence to the superiority of Calvinism as a system of religious belief as we find it set forth in the doctrines of the Westminster Confession. The Blairs have always been Presbyterians since the founding of the church."

"His mother on her father's side was a descendant of the old nobility of France, and she herself was an Episcopalian before her marriage. What have you to say to that, sir?" hotly demanded the judge, who was himself a Presbyterian, if anything, but prepared at a moment's notice to take up the cudgels for all other denominations, though caring not a whit, except for the triumph of argument, to establish the supremacy of any — a negative quality which, in this instance, was almost a virtue.

The professor's face suddenly softened. He did not reply at once, and when he did there was a note in his voice seldom heard there. "He has his mother's eyes," he said. "And his mother was the loveliest woman I ever saw, and ever expect to see, on this earth," he added simply, avoiding the judge's glance.

"Nonsense! Look at that," denied the judge, directing attention to an open carriage, just at that moment bowling past, from which a very pretty woman in pink leaned out and bowed charmingly. "She was not an iota better to look at than that young wife of old Matthias Oats you see there."

The professor turned and looked, but with eyes that were dim to the present from long gazing into the past.

"She was the loveliest woman I ever saw, and ever expect to see, on this earth," he repeated dreamily.

He sat smoking his old briar-root pipe, which he

had lit mechanically, in silence for a long time. Presently his eyes traveled again in the direction of the two children, and there was something in the expression of his dour Scotch countenance, as his gaze rested upon the boy, strangely sweet and tender.

Judge Trotter saw the look and his face also changed. He wheeled quickly and looked steadily toward the two childish figures with an expression half-humourous, half-sad. All at once Cicely's young treble rang out in a bubbling overflow of laughter, and her grandfather rose and began to move softly up and down the porch, with head bent, and hands clasped behind him, like one whose ear has caught the distant note of some dear remembered melody. In an old locket which he carried always there was a miniature of the child's grandmother, painted in early youth, with Cicely's eyes and hair, and Cicely's wilful, winsome smile. The face that looked forth from that portrait had grown wrinkled and old, and had then faded from his sight, but there were moments, like this, when it lived again in immortal youth and beauty.

But the professor had slowly gathered himself together, and he was by no means through with the Presbyterians. All at once he began again precisely as if there had been no interruption.

"Take the old names of the past in your state. Where do we find them, generally speaking, but among the Presbyterians? For who is there among you who cannot claim upon some line or other a strain of Scotch-Irish blood, which, like a little leaven, leaveneth the whole lump. My dear sir, if you will turn to the annals of your state ——"

"Your Henry Clay was not a Presbyterian," put in the judge, roused to opposition.

"So much the worse for him — so much the worse for him. Had he been, that old hero of yours, General Jackson, might have had a harder time than he did to defeat him for the presidency."

"There never was a time in his life when General Jackson could not have whipped him with one hand, sir."

"There never was a time when you could not have cut Jackson's mind out of a little corner of Henry Clay's."

And there it was. The red flag had been waved, and with taurine rage the old judge rushed upon his antagonist.

But to-day the professor, who doubtless had a canny thought for the delicious chicken and waffles, which, later on, would most likely grace the judge's table, and which he was in special state to enjoy, was not disposed either to argument or to anecdote, and with an adroitness that was creditable to his native shrewdness, he managed to wave discussion with seemingly no loss of ground, and presently even succeeded in changing the subject altogether. He suggested that their usual game of chess be begun, in recognition of a past defeat, and soon the two cronies were hard at it again, deeply engaged in another warfare, equally strenuous and determined.

A low droning sound came from under the sugar-maple. Blackburn was reading aloud from the great book on his knee. He was rather proud of his reading, perhaps mainly from the fact that his accomplishment shone by contrast, as Cicely could scarcely read at all, being a lazy little thing and inclined to depend upon other people for an enjoyment that she particularly craved but would not work for. Her low chair was drawn close to his side and her piquant little face was fixed upon the pictured page with eager, breathless attention.

It was an old, old tale that Blackburn read, and it was told with a special grace, though very simply, the legend ending with a single stanza from Tennyson.

"Across the hills and far away,
Beyond their utmost purple rim,
And deep into the dying day
The happy princess followed him,"

read the boy, with glowing eyes and cheeks. The story of the brave young prince who makes his way through the strange dark forest, marching valiantly over thc bones of those who have failed and perished, never faltering, never pausing, until he has reached the palace where the Sleeping Beauty waits, took hold of him very strongly. His heart was beating wildly, and his boyish features had assumed the look, grave and earnest, they had worn a few days before as he sat reading in childish wonderment and delight from the old history of Kentucky, and felt himself by some mysterious connection linked with the heroism of the past. He did not know their meaning, nor whence they came, those queer feelings within him; but the blood in him of those who were strong enough to do and dare was rousing him to a strange and startling awakening.

> "Across the hills and far away,
> Beyond their utmost purple rim,"

he repeated vaguely. He slowly turned and fixed his great dark eyes upon the sun just sinking into the west. Earlier there had been a light shower, and now a gorgeous rainbow stretched across the summer sky.

> "And deep into the dying day—"

Suddenly he rose. "Oh, Cicely," he cried, "let's go, let's go!"

Until that moment he had forgotten all about Cicely. Even the lovely princess had played a very minor part in his thoughts, in comparison with the fairy prince whose glorious achievement had thrilled him so. But it occurred to him that it would not be unpleasant to have a little companionship in his wanderings, and on the whole it might be well enough to take Cicely along. He was quite sure that he liked her more, a good deal more, than any boy he knew.

Cicely had begun putting on her bonnet. Having securely tied the strings, she rose and put her plump little hand in his, prepared immediately to depart.

"Blackburn," she asked, "do you think we will find the bag of gold hanging to the end of the rainbow if we start to-night?"

Blackburn turned and looked her blankly in the face. Then he snatched his hand away, brought back again to earth, alas, only too surely by the reminder of the ever obtrusive, vulgar bag of gold.

"Cicely," he said angrily, "there's no such thing as a bag of gold at the end of the rainbow." And then as the child's face fell, and the wilful little mouth began to quiver, he added gently, "Never mind, I'll — I'll get you one, Cicely — some of these days, I'll get you one — never mind." He felt all at once as if he were quite grown up, and old enough and strong enough to do anything; and the trophies of Miltiades were dangling before him.

The two old gentlemen, pausing in their game to watch the scene, turned and looked into each other's face with a quiet smile, and a tear was glistening in the Scotchman's eye. For the moment all differences between them were silenced, lost in the recognition of a common affection stronger than their loyalty to Andrew Jackson or to Henry Clay.

"A fine lad — a fine lad," murmured the professor, winking violently to hide his emotion.

The old judge bowed in stately fashion.

"He is worthy of his noble sires, sir," he responded gravely.

"And a brave little lassie too," added the professor quickly, a merry twinkle suddenly gleaming through the mist in his gray eyes.

There was a moment's silence.

"As sweet a little minx, God bless her, as walks beneath the Kentucky skies," replied the old judge, softly.

CHAPTER V

COMMENCEMENT DAY

Blackburn was in his sixteenth year when he entered college.

It was no surprise either to Judge Blair or to Professor Kennedy that he elected to take the classical course — the boy's bent was most distinct. The oratorical strain in him was not long in hiding; and in the various college debates in which he was wont to spread himself, his intimate acquaintance (thanks to the professor) with the old Greek and Roman mythology, to say nothing of other acquirements in the way of history and general literature, often served him in good stead against the vigorous, but less polished onslaughts of some sturdy young mountaineer who had come down to the Bluegrass for a little "book larnin," and who not infrequently was his opponent in those spirited encounters.

He was graduated shortly after he had passed his nineteenth year, and it seemed but a natural consequence of so much speech-making that he should be the orator of his class.

And at last the great day had actually arrived, and

the past was a dream, and the future — the vast, the untried, the shadowy land of hopes and of mighty efforts—lay outstretched before him and, like a young gladiator stripped for the conflict, he was eager to go to meet his destiny.

The Commencement exercises were to take place at eleven. Blackburn rose early.

Robins were singing in the old elm tree outside his bedroom, and a flood of June sunshine was pouring in through the open windows. His room looked out on the garden, and the spicy smell of roses wet with dew was wafted to him as he dressed.

How glorious, how full and beautiful life seemed to him on that perfect summer morning! How could he doubt or question that time would surely give him all things? Perhaps there is nothing in the whole of existence, not even man's deepest tragedies and sorrows, so profoundly touching as the great, eager, confident heart of youth.

He dressed quickly, but with special care, being possessed of an honest desire to look his best. However, he had not developed any vanity, if there were any latent in him during the last four absorbed, arduous years of study. In reality his mind had been upon his work with a fixedness of purpose that left little room for the manifestation of many of those harmless adolescent traits that one looks for in one of his age. But it was an interesting face that looked back at him from the small oval-shaped mirror over his dressing-table — a face vigorous and gravely handsome, with fine dark eyes and a mouth that was singularly sweet and firm. He was fully six feet in height — a slim young stripling with the eyes of a poet and the brawn of an athlete.

As he tied his cravat he began going over his speech for the last time; and when he came down the steps and entered the library half an hour later his face was still pale with emotion.

Judge Blair was already up and dressed, and sitting calmly reading by an open window; and as he looked up, his practiced eye caught the glow of enthusiasm lingering upon the boyish features. For a moment a quiet smile hovered about the thin lips and then disappeared, giving way to a look of deep sadness, which Blackburn failed to understand.

The young man crossed the room quickly and laid a hand gently on his father's shoulder in morning greeting, standing an instant in silence by the great arm chair in which the judge was sitting.

They were both quiet for a little time — a way with them when moved, and then the father spoke, and there was a slight break in his voice despite its cheerfulness.

"My son," he said simply, "the skies even are

smiling a blessing on you to-day. I think I never saw a finer summer morning."

"Couldn't be better," replied Blackburn, gayly.

Presently Judge Blair rose and moved softly across the room with slippered feet, his long silken dressing-gown falling loosely about him, and accenuating the dignity of his tall figure.

When he returned to his chair he held in his hands the large family Bible from which it was his custom to read aloud a chapter every morning. Blackburn could recall few days of his life in which this act of religious devotion had been omitted; and now upon the threshold of his young manhood he still lent himself to these occasions with the old childlike faith and simplicity of his earlier years.

"Lord, thou hast been our dwelling-place in all generations.

"Before the mountains were brought forth, or ever thou hadst formed the earth and the world, even from everlasting to everlasting, thou art God," read the low, beautifully modulated voice.

In the years that were soon to follow, Blackburn was destined to hear many a voice tuned to expression of the finer emotions of the human heart, but as he sat there in the old library of his home — the portraits of believing forefathers keeping a silent watch above him, and the sunlight of his Commencement Day falling with a lavish splendour all around —with those words, uttered with the deep conviction of one who had outlived every stage of doubt and indecision, there was made an impression upon his mind such as no other person, however gifted, was able ever to produce. It was not the timid faith of the tender and troubled soul crying in the night, but the solemn assurance of one who *knows*, having seen the day-star arise.

"For a thousand years in thy sight are but as yesterday when it is past, and as a watch in the night."

Blackburn felt as if a cool hand were suddenly laid upon his heated brow. And by and by the present, the intense, the absorbing present began to lose its hold and the very vastness of eternity seemed spreading out before him.

"So teach us to number our days, that we may apply our hearts unto wisdom."

How vain and useless seemed so many of man's strivings in the presence of that earnest supplication! Wisdom! Would he find it as he went forward on life's journey? Or would he be like those who through perseverance and unfaltering aim finally succeed even to the winning of the whole world for their meed, only to lose their inward peace? "Just for a handful of silver," or only "a riband to stick in his coat," would he, too, barter away his best, as had so many Kentuckians before him, in the great struggle of political affairs which, from the earliest times, had engrossed the people of his state, and toward which, even now, his young ambition dreamed?

A fine breeze was coming in through the open windows. Out in the garden Uncle Scip was quietly moving to and fro, and from time to time Huldy's voice in imperious command floated in from the rear of the house, where a special preparation was going on in his honour to the delight of two small pickaninnies crawling about the kitchen floor. Surely it was a very pleasant world.

"And let the beauty of the Lord our God be upon us: and establish thou the work of our hands upon us; yea, the work of our hands establish thou it."

Then Judge Blair closed the Book and the two knelt.

When they rose Blackburn's face had lost its strained pallor, and the boyish features had taken on the repose that comes from losing sight of self in the presence of the Eternal Calm.

The State College of Kentucky stands upon a gently rising knoll that overlooks the little city of Lexington—sitting modestly at the feet of learning, so to speak—and a beautiful stretch of bluegrass country beyond. It is a noble site. And if the young men and the young women who daily climb that slope in sight of the whispering willows and the mysterious hollow and the cool little spring to the left of the many buildings, with the dim outlines of towering trees in the distance, and the merry ripple of grasses waving beneath the Kentucky skies, do not feel their long ascent toward Parnassus and the Castalian spring to be a little easier and pleasanter for that climb, then it may be doubted that they will ever attain to a higher plane than the dead level of a merely commonplace existence, and so far as discovering the deeper and sweeter meaning of study, perhaps, to all intents and purposes, it might be just as well for them if they never assayed to climb at all.

He was a clod, indeed, "untroubled by a spark," whose heart, on this particular June morning, did not respond to the tender green about him, as he entered the wide gates that yawned to receive the great concourse moving gayly, beneath a long line of maples, up the college campus.

As early as ten o'clock people began to gather. Young cadets, wearing the uniform of the college a little slovenly, perhaps, being as yet only in the early stages of military training, but to-day walking with heads erect; trim young women in white muslin or pale summer gowns, with arms filled with flowers; the middle-aged and the elderly, mingled in a joyous throng, all animated by a single impulse, and bound for the same place. For the graduating class was large, and a special concern was felt. Furthermore, Blackburn's fame as an orator had already spread a little beyond college circles, and apart from the interest in him, attendant upon his high social place, there was a curiosity to hear him strong enough to bring out many persons of a kind not usually seen at college Commencements.

There was a steady stream of carriages up the drive, and by half past ten o'clock the large chapel was full to overflowing, and the young marshals were moving wildly to and fro in the vain hope of seating the crowd. There was an odour of June roses in the air, and the band was playing, now a lively, now a plaintive strain; and there was over everything — the smiles and the gay greetings and the flowers — a fine evanescent sadness that is difficult to describe, yet so real to everyone who thinks and feels.

The President of the College and the Chairman of the Executive Board and members of the faculty, together with the graduating class, had taken their places on the platform, in the midst of vigorous cheering, when a stately little old gentleman, very neatly and elegantly dressed, and a young girl of fifteen or sixteen appeared in one of the hallways leading into the chapel. The little old gentleman removed his top hat with quite an air, and the crowd moved back immediately, duly impressed, and made way for the two to enter.

The girl was tall and slim and beautiful in her short white muslin gown with two long brown braids falling below her little round hat and reaching to her waist. There was a wreath of pink and white morning-glories on the hat. She carried a great bouquet in one hand, and her blue eyes were sparkling, a certain roguish sweetness lurking beneath the thick lashes.

By some mysterious conjuring, one of the marshals instantly produced chairs and the twain were ushered swiftly and surely through the throng, and seated quite in front of the platform, and just a little to the left of Judge Blair and Professor Kennedy. Blackburn's and Cicely's eyes met.

He leaned forward and bowed, smiling over the heads of the graduates in front of him. There was no self-consciousness in the greeting, and his manner was rather too frank and cordial to suggest a sentimental feeling.

But nevertheless he was glad, glad through and through him, that Cicely had come. He had been afraid that she would not be present. Her school usually did not close so early as the college, and she seldom came from her Louisville home to spend the summer before the middle or the last of June, and this was only the fifth.

However, he had written her an urgent little note, and here she was. He wondered how she had managed it, not knowing that his staunch friend and ally, Judge Trotter, had been desperately appealed to, nor that the determined old gentleman, roused by opposition, had at last been compelled to take a trip to Louisville and in person to make known his command, before the consent of Cicely's parents to the flagrant disregard of the child's studies at a most important time had been finally granted.

Blackburn sat watching her in a kind of wonderment.

How tall and pretty she was — and how much older she had grown in that one short year! It *was* a short year to him, absorbed as he had been. During that time he had thought of her only as the dear little playmate of his childhood, teasing, frolicsome, ready for any fun, and especially for any mischief, and behold, here she was, the same, and yet not the same, with something about her that was strangely, strangely different — although she was not more than a mere slip of a girl still. He couldn't make it out, the mysterious alteration.

After a time he began to be aware of the fact that she had created quite a little stir. He saw how all the young men about him were straining their necks to get a better look at her, and was rather pleased on the whole. However, he decided that there were some among the number that assuredly he would not care to have her meet. That fellow Dilson, for instance, with his coxcomb ways. Then he took himself roundly to task for his sweeping condemnation of Dilson, and moved a trifle uneasily in his chair. At whom was she smiling in such a pleased fashion?

Cicely's rosebud lips were parted, her head was thrown back, and her eyes were dancing. A great palm was in the way, and several persons right in front of him were standing, waiting for extra chairs to be brought in, so that Blackburn had some difficulty in discovering at once who was the tall youth at her side.

How interested she looked! What was the fellow saying to her anyway, to make her laugh like that? The people in front of him sat down and Blackburn leaned forward. It was Dilson. He had forgotten that Cicely already knew him quite well, having often played with him at Blackburn's home when she was a wild little hoiden and they were all children together. It did not now occur to him that he had offered at that time no objection to her acquaintance with Dilson — an acquaintance which, as a matter of fact, was due solely to Blackburn himself. He was conscious of a vague surprise at the strange sudden feeling of resentment toward Cicely's admirer.

All at once, with characteristic decision, Blackburn pulled himself together. The old generosity of nature was asserting itself. He felt as if he should like immediately to offer an apology to Dilson who, in spite of a little harmless foppishness and conceit, recently developed, was on the whole admitted to be a very good fellow. He turned his eyes resolutely away from the winsome, smiling face and the tall blonde young man standing at the child's side, and fixing them steadily on his program, began to go over the opening sentences of his speech. A moment afterward Cicely's presence, and likewise the great fluttering mass of people before him, were forgotten —swept away completely from his thoughts by a soberer contemplation.

Presently the exercises began.

They were rather tedious on the whole. There were a few remarks from the President of the College, and then there was a prayer, and then music, followed by a speech, and then some more music, followed by another speech, and so on, until one wondered whether there could be anything left for anybody to talk about ever any more. Cicely leaned her small head against her grandfather's shoulder and from time to time smothered a yawn. She was not interested in the profound remarks of the young scientists, and she was decidedly bored by the daring flights of the political economists who unblushingly affirmed the belief that if the affairs of government were but entrusted to their hands they would evolve a system superior to anything the country had seen since the days of Washington and Jefferson. After the last one had said everything he had to say (and probably a little more), and had sat down, being applauded to the echo by admiring friends and relatives, and offered great baskets of fruits and flowers, which presently were spread out all around like an oblation to a deity, the band played "My Old Kentucky Home," and then Blackburn rose.

A deafening cheer from the students in attestation of his popularity, followed by a prolonged clapping of hands from the large audience, rent the air as he came forward.

He stood for a moment waiting for the uproar to subside, the handsome young face pale but tranquil. Then a silence that was almost oppressive followed.

For an instant his dark eyes rested upon his father and the professor, and traveled on to the little old gentleman and the slim childish figure to the left. He began quietly, deliberately, the opening words falling from his lips with the distinctness and the simplicity of one who goes directly to his theme untrammelled by either shyness or misgiving. With the first sentence he lost all thought of self.

He had spoken scarcely more than thirty seconds before he had the fixed attention of every person in the room, old and young, through a magnetism and a fervent brilliancy of oratory that held them spellbound. Fans ceased to flutter. All whispering was at an end. The rich, ringing voice grew in compass until it could be distinctly heard far out into the wide hallways, where a large number, crowded together, also listened eagerly. He spoke with earnestness, with singular conviction, displaying a thoughtfulness and a scholarship which would have done honour to that most classic of orators of the state's early days, Thomas F. Marshall himself. Old men who could recall the speeches of Marshall when that gifted man was in his prime looked into each other's face and inwardly marveled. He had completely captured them.

But beyond the polish of his diction and a certain impassioned eloquence which was his as an ancient birthright, and which thrilled his hearers and swept them off their feet in a way dear to the hearts of the Kentuckians, there was something more: the deep and solemn consecration in the presence of his own people of the young life to the higher ideals of existence and to a broad and noble service. No unimportant part in the future history of his state could be his; and as they sat and listened, looking into the young face lit with a singular earnestness and beauty, they saw in him the strength of the great leaders of old, and seeing, crowned him with characteristic impulsiveness, then and there.

When he sat down, he was white and quivering in every nerve, yet he still manifested that steady mastery of himself which he had never for an instant lost throughout; and he scarcely seemed to heed or hear the wild enthusiasm that then broke forth, in an applause loud enough to drown the clash of musical instruments and even "The Star Spangled Banner."

The cheering did not cease until a tall, white-haired old gentleman of a very scholarly and patrician aspect, and with a benign and beautiful expression of countenance, rose to deliver the diplomas. He spoke only a few gentle, well-chosen words, but when his eye rested on young Blackburn Blair he paused.

For an instant the great audience, already keyed to a high excitement, sat breathless; and as the Chairman of the Board of Trustees, referring to a certain June morning more than half a century before when he had stood up as a graduate of Old Transylvania University to receive his diploma, suddenly turned to the young man standing with bowed head reverently before him, there was scarcely an eye in the great assemblage that was not wet with tears, as there fell from his lips, like a benediction, that most touching of all tributes, the tribute of age to youth — the solemn charge of the old soldier whose sword is in its sheath, to the young warrior eager for life's conflicts.

A moment afterwards the crowd was surging out

into the great halls, and for Blackburn there were roses and congratulations, and presently a little hand fluttering a moment in his—and then it was all over, and thus ended his Commencement morning.

BOOK II

CHAPTER I

A WOMAN WHO WOULDN'T GROW OLD

MRS. MATTHIAS OATS, in a sumptuous lounging robe of light blue silk and lace, and with her heavy, copper-coloured hair falling about her, stood before the wood fire in the small library adjoining her bedroom reading, again for the third time, a note of invitation that had come to her half an hour before. She had already sent an acceptance in reply—not, however, without a shadow of misgiving. The note ran:

"My Dear Mrs. Oats:—

There is to be another merrymaking. I am afraid I have invited a rather alarming crowd of young people for next Thursday evening to meet my dear little friend Cicely Overton, who is expected to arrive in Lexington next week, and whom I should probably speak of more respectfully, as it is now nearly ten years since any of us have seen her here. May I venture to call upon you again? You will do me a special kindness if you will come and aid me in receiving my guests. My old bachelor home is always greatly honoured by your fair presence.

Sincerely yours,
ORLANDO WISE."

Mrs. Oats leaned an arm on the mantel, and absently tapped one of her small feet in its delicate blue satin bedroom slipper. She shivered a little in her loose gown.

It had been a beautiful autumn, and the day was particularly mild — one of those bland, but brilliant afternoons which come to Kentucky late in October, when the blue grass is green again as in June, and the skies are burning sapphire above the flaming woodlands. When Mrs. Oats had ordered fire the young negress stared.

"Lawd, Miss Ferginyur, you sho is fixin' to roast yo' se'f dis bright day. Dis ain' no winter, hit's Injun summer. You jes go an' stan' out on de po'ch."

But Mrs. Oats desired warmth, the appearance of comfort — anything to take away the sense of chill creeping over her, which, in reality had nothing at all to do with physical cold. Presently she sank down on the lounge in one corner and tucked the pillows about her, closing her eyes, and still holding the note in her hand.

There was a pleasant glow throughout the small apartment when she raised her head and looked around. There was something cool and critical in her gaze as her eyes rested upon the artistically furnished room with its prevailing orange tone; and she had always felt special satisfaction in this little den, filled with her favourite volumes, and recognized by Mr. Oats as exclusively her own. But this was one of the days on which she vainly sought by means of a contemplation of externals to comfort herself for the loss of better things.

In the soft light about her one would scarcely have thought her to be more than five-and-thirty years of age. In reality, it was her fiftieth birthday, and Mrs. Oats was utterly rebellious. She was of a type that most people have met with, and all men admire; and she was one of those women to whom fate has been cruelly kind in bestowing exceptional beauty, and at the same time withholding beauty's crowning guerdon—love.

There was a large oval mirror in a gilt frame opposite the place where she lay, and Mrs. Oats, turned with a kind of hungry, startled look to her own reflection. No — she was not old and wrinkled, that nightmare had not come upon her yet. Could it be that life was never to be given to her? (Mrs. Oats called it life, that nameless something that she craved.) She had never been able to face the thought that she had reached a time when she must pass out of the glowing sunlight into the cold gray shadows. There was only a hint of the shadows as yet. For if not a young woman, she was still a very beautiful one, with a figure that had not lost its elasticity in spite of being a trifle too stout, and with the freshness not yet gone out of the fine, pearl-like skin — the skin that goes with that peculiar shade of hair that is too lovely to be called red, and that is a glory to the woman who has it.

There was a fine elation in her scrutiny. She knew that she was still the envy of many younger women; and she delighted in being envied, particularly by youth. There was a vague feeling of resentment in her heart toward certain young girls of her acquaintance, to whom she was always especially sweet and gracious. Their radiant happiness seemed to sting — and she was offended by their confidence in their own girlish charm.

In recent years the preservation of her good looks had become a sort of religion with her, perhaps the only religion she had; and in the daily observation of the somewhat arduous pagan rites imposed upon herself, she was far more zealous than the average devotee. Too delicate minded to dream of a possible future widowhood, Mrs. Oats was not herself fully aware of the primal cause of these strenuous and unrelenting onslaughts against the encroachments of age. Assuredly the results thus sought were not for the delectation of Mr. Oats. No one who had ever seen that gentleman believed for a moment that they were for him; and on this point Mrs. Oats never attempted to deceive herself, though she kept up a fine little show before the world.

In her early youth she had married Mr. Oats, a man of considerable fortune, a good deal of native shrewdness, which he used to good advantage as a farmer and financier, and very little education of the order that implies an acquaintance with books or with social enlightenment. He was her inferior in point of birth, and he was her senior by fully five-and-twenty years; and she had married him because she had been left an orphan and dependent, and the situation had become too galling longer to be borne. She had married him in a moment of revolt and desperation, and she had had the rest of her life to repent in, and she was repenting still — particularly whenever her eyes rested upon his huge form and stolid face, with its heavy, plebeian contours.

Presently Mrs. Oats took from under the pillow the note she had thrust there a moment before and again fell to studying it. She was hunting for something which, as yet, she had failed to find. Perhaps it still lurked behind the stiff penmanship and quaint, chivalrous courtesy. In sending her acceptance she had wondered whether it appeared altogether discreet, in a staid old Southern town, and situated as she was, to respond as often as she had of late to these requests. She was an eminently proper person in every way, and thus far she had made no mistakes; yet it rather pleased her to reflect that she might be regarded as still within the territory of potential wrong doing. She was not quite willing to admit that it would have been at all difficult to refuse. But there was something reassuring in the missive itself—something that quieted her anxiety, yet hurt her while it soothed.

All at once she rose, and walking across the room, dropped the note into the fire. She stood watching it burn with a somewhat enigmatical expression chasing itself in an evanescent fashion across her face, and she turned almost guiltily when there was a light tap at the door.

It was only the new maid with a card.

"Miss Ferginyur," broke forth the young negro girl in desperate vindication, and with her dark orbs rolling wildly, "I done tole her you say you ain' at home, an' she say she know you is; an' she say she don' wan' me come 'long tellin' her black lie lak dat no mo'. She say——"

Mrs. Oats lifted a warning finger. "Give me the card, Lucy." "Oh, it's Mrs. Bellows — of course it's Mrs. Bellows. Mrs. Josiah F. Bellows," she read, her eyes scanning the card with a twinkle of amusement. Then she turned quickly. Mrs. Oats never failed to pose a little before her servants, and she was constrained to hide an involuntary disgust.

"That I should actually bring myself to receive Mrs. Bellows in this intimate fashion!" she exclaimed mentally, as there sounded something very like a step on the stair. But with her lips she only said, "Hurry, Lucy — she's coming, bring me some hairpins, and then go and ask her to walk up here. I won't keep her waiting while I dress."

Her hands were at her head and she was just twisting her beautiful hair into place when Mrs. Bellows pushed her way in, stalking past the astonished Lucy with the utmost disdain.

"What do you mean by sending me word again that you are not at home, Virginia Oats, when you know you are?" she demanded, breathless. "It's the third time you've done it lately."

She was a big raw-boned woman of about sixty-five, with faded, light-brown hair much streaked with gray, a huge nose, small, beady brown eyes, and something in her whole expression and contour strangely equine in its suggestion. She wore a black satin gown and wrap elaborately trimmed with jet, a diamond cross at her throat, and a bonnet of hideous design, upon the summit of which there perched a large bird of brilliant green plumage with a bill like a parrot's, and a very unpleasantly inquisitive expression.

Mr. Oats shrank visibly from that dreadful bird. But nevertheless she managed to come forward with her most charming smile, holding out her hand.

"Do pardon me for making you climb the stairs, dear Mrs. Bellows," she said.

Mrs. Bellows came to an abrupt standstill — like a horse that has suddenly been checked. "Well, I'm not in my dotage, am I?" she demanded, sternly. "There's nothing the matter with the stairs that I could see. Why shouldn't I climb 'em? Haven't I been a-climbin' and a-climbin' ever since I was born?"

There was rather more truth in this assertion than Mrs. Bellows had meant to admit. And her climbing had been usually as successful as it was in this instance. She was one of those women who do things by bluster instead of by the gentler art of persuasion; and in the end she invariably conquered by the sheer force of her own strange but vigorous personality. Many years before she had come to Lexington, an entirely unknown person from an obscure part of the state, and established herself in one of the handsome old homes of the town which for the last quarter of a century have been passing out of the hands of their original owners through a steady reversal of fortune.

She had slowly but surely come to the front. Had she settled in New York or London, precisely the same thing would have occurred. It would have been only a question of time. Lexington had been powerless to resist her. Apparently she had unlimited means at her command. She began by entertaining.

No one had called, but that did not deter her in the least. She asked the people she wanted, showing considerable sagacity and worldly wisdom in her discrimination; and she kept on asking them, until she had her way. A good deal in the march of her social struggles had been accomplished through the small children living on her street. It was Mrs. Bellows' custom, whenever she saw any of these little people passing her door, to call them in and proceed immediately to fill their pockets with the nuts and raisins and great juicy oranges always at her command. And finally the well-bred mothers of these same little children, getting wind of all this, had to go and thank her and beg her to desist; and on the next day Mrs. Bellows would invariably return the call.

She was now as distinctly recognized as the court-house clock. No one, save a very limited few who still refused to bow the knee to vulgarity in so bold a form, attempted any longer to make a stand against her; for if one were at all vulnerable Mrs. Bellows had certain sharp little weapons at her hand which most persons preferred to avoid.

Mrs. Oats thought her most amusing. She was rather glad that, on this particular afternoon when she was feeling especially depressed and had given directions that she be denied to every one, Mrs. Bellows had forced her way in. So she started up the tea kettle and ordered cakes to be brought, and prepared for an afternoon of gossip about her neighbors such as she had not had for many a day. She herself was not altogether averse to gossip, provided it were not grossly told. As a young girl living in her uncle's home she had early acquired the habit of pricking up her ears to the floating rumours about her, through a rather pathetic desire to make herself agreeable in her dependent position. And it now happened that Mrs. Bellows was seeking Mrs. Oats for the very reason that Mrs. Oats was enduring Mrs. Bellows.

Mrs. Bellows seated herself in a large leathern chair before the fire, threw back her wrap, and fixed her eyes upon the flickering flames with a disapproval that was almost cold enough to extinguish them.

"Have they come?" she inquired at once bluntly, turning her head slightly in the direction of her hostess.

Mrs. Oats held the sugar tongs suspended.

"Of whom are you speaking, Mrs. Bellows?" she asked wonderingly.

"Overtons," was Mrs. Bellows' laconic reply.

"Oh, the Overtons. They came last night — all but Cicely, who has just returned from abroad, don't you know, and is still in New York with her aunt."

"I reckon that old Judge Trotter's been worse'n a bear with a sore head, getting ready for a whole family plumped down on him, bag and baggage, all on a sudden like that," remarked Mrs. Bellows with a low chuckle.

"The judge has had his home in readiness for more than a month, but it seems they have been delayed. It must be a great pleasure to him to feel that he will now have his daughter and her family with him for the rest of his days."

"And how long do you think that old fire-eater'll be able to get along without a row?"

Mrs. Oats chose to ignore this. "I have often wondered why the Overtons never left Louisville before," she said sweetly, as she handed her guest a cup of tea. "I don't think Colonel Overton has ever been much of a success there."

"Then, mind you, he won't be much of a success here," put in Mrs. Bellows with ready conviction. "If laziness is bred in the bone, it's going to stay in the bone; and what's no-account in Louisville, mark my word, is going to be no-account in Lexington."

Mrs. Oats threw up her hands in horror. "Oh, *dear* Mrs. Bellows," she exclaimed, "I never said he was lazy — I *never* said he was no-account. What ever made you conclude such a thing? I think Colonel Overton is delightful. I am very fond of him; and it is really due to my persuasions that Mr. Oats offered him the cashiership of his bank. He really knows a great deal about banking. It is more in the way of speculation, don't you know, that he has been unfortunate. He was scarcely fitted for anything very daring in that line, but it seems that Mrs. Overton was always urging him on. She is an intensely ambitious woman, and with no knowledge at all of how to live without plenty of money. One always thinks it is somewhat a pity that she is not the man of the family. She, rather than he, should bear the title of Colonel — there is always something so prompt and military about her, don't you think? He is a very gentle sort of man, mild in all his ways."

"Humph, mild is he? Then that's more'n a body can say for that old struttin' gamecock of a father-in-law he's got," said Mrs. Bellows, recalling sundry passes in which she had been decidedly worsted by the haughty old aristocrat, to her lasting resentment.

Mrs. Oats broke into a little low ripple of laughter. "The old judge and I are great friends," she remarked amiably.

"I remember that Harriet Trotter when I first came here to live, with her head always up in the air," said Mrs. Bellows, stirring her tea violently, and making certain awkward little jerks with her elbow that set her jet beads all a-stir.

"It's up in the air still," responded Mrs. Oats, serenely. "She is very proud of her children, I believe, particularly of Cicely. I hear that she expects great things of Cicely. The girl is rather brilliantly educated, and is quite pretty, according to reports. But I don't think she gave promise of anything unusual in the way of looks when I last saw her, years ago. She impressed me as being a little pert looking," concluded Mrs. Oats, with a swift, involuntary glance in the direction of the mirror.

Mrs. Bellows' keen eyes followed the glance. "Well, youth's youth, you know, and every dog has his day." Mrs. Oats didn't ask her what she meant by that.

"Is this Cicely as you call her the one the major's party's given to next Thursday night?" demanded Mrs. Bellows, fiercely, sniffing the air in a way peculiar to her when recalling a slight. "I hear he's asked you to receive again. He's left *me* out."

Mrs. Oats turned quickly and busied herself for an instant with the tea kettle. "Was that only a lucky guess? How could Mrs. Bellows know?" she asked herself anxiously.

"Do let me give you another cup of tea, Mrs. Bellows," she said.

Mrs. Bellows accepted promptly. There was no hope that the call was soon to end. Mrs. Oats knew its object now — that last remark had revealed a good deal.

"Seems as if the major can't get along without you these days. That comes of having a pretty face, I reckon. The major's got a mighty keen eye, for all his Miss Nancy ways. Well, — if the old cat goes away, and so far away as New York — how long's Mr. Oats going to be gone?"

Mrs. Oats' expression never flickered, and she wore a most innocent, and child-like look in her hazel eyes. She fixed her gaze for an instant upon the great bird in Mrs. Bellows' bonnet, with a somewhat abstracted air. "Ugh! the horrible thing," she was saying mentally, "I wonder if it is going to claw."

"Mr. Oats?" she inquired suavely. "I am not sure — I think a week or two, perhaps. Yes — it is awfully good in Major Wise to invite me so many times, and I am always charmed to accept whenever he asks me. I am quite looking forward to next Thursday evening." Inwardly she was boiling, despite the coolness of her tone. One does not have red hair for nothing.

"Humph! what's that old man always giving parties for any way, I'd like to know. Nobody thanks him. Fools make feasts for wise men to eat. And there's no fool like an old fool, any time. Isn't this Overton girl the same one I used to see that young son of Judge Blair's playing with all the time when they were children?"

Mrs. Oats turned a little stiffly. With the change of subject, she could afford a slight alteration of manner.

Besides, she was particularly fond of Blackburn Blair, and she foresaw what was coming. And it was not easy for Mrs. Oats to find fault with any man, especially one who had always been most civil toward her.

"Blackburn and she were great friends as children, I believe," she said.

"Then if she's the one, it's to be hoped she's changed her ways. If ever I saw a wild, hoidenish little miss, it was that child. The boy Blackburn as you call him —"

"Really, Mrs. Bellows, I don't know what else to call him, unless I should say Mr. Blair. Perhaps I should do that in speaking of him to a stranger. He's a very dear friend of mine."

Mrs. Bellows went on wholly imperturbed. She failed to catch a slightly warning note.

"The boy, Blackburn, was not so bad," she observed, proceeding to relate an incident of the two children that had taken place in the now far distant past in which Blackburn shone to a certain advantage, mainly by contrast, in that the boy passing her home had courteously turned aside and opened her gate for her, while Cicely, as usual his companion, on that unforgotten occasion had failed, it seemed, to conduct herself with a like decorum. It appeared that Cicely had not conducted herself with any decorum at all —

hence Mrs. Bellows' lasting disapproval. For that small person, suddenly possessed of a spirit of mischief, on seeing the tall form of Mrs. Bellows approaching, had actually, without so much as a word or nod, hastened to climb up on the stone wall surrounding that lady's dwelling, beginning at once and with great alacrity to hum and dance a sort of improvised fandango accompanied by a considerable fluttering of skirts and wild gesticulation; and all this had taken place right under Mrs. Bellows' very nose, and in open defiance of her amazed and much scandalized gaze. Perhaps this enormity was heightened by the fact that both Blackburn and Cicely had been marked recipients of her favours. Blackburn it is true, in his grave, childish way, had seemed to remember, but Cicely's case was utterly hopeless; and Mrs. Bellows' fixed displeasure toward her had extended even to him. So much for consorting with evil.

During all those years she had not failed to recall this instance of childish depravity, whenever there was the smallest excuse for so doing; but at present her mind was set against Blackburn Blair for a far more specific reason and one a good deal less trivial in its intent. It had its root in an almost frenzied anxiety concerning her own pecuniary interests. Blackburn had not the smallest designs upon her property in any way, but she held him responsible. These interests she believed had been seriously threatened by the course that young Blair, who was rapidly becoming a leader in the politics of his state, having already a considerable following, had taken with regard to certain great national issues which a year before had aroused Kentucky to a most exciting conflict. The result had been a loss to the Democracy of the electoral vote of the state — a thing that had never before happened in Kentucky since the days of the Civil War. However, Mrs. Bellows was triumphant.

"I'm against them Blairs," she announced presently, with one of those lapses into grossly incorrect speech into which she was sometimes betrayed when under an excitement; "not that I ever had much use for 'em at any time," she added fiercely, being naturally opposed to everyone whose birth and place was above her own. From her youth up she had cherished a secret animosity toward all those who had ever belonged to that old aristocratic, slave holding past to which the humble conditions of her own early days offered a striking antithesis. This rancour time had strengthened, rather than abated, and she longed to have her enemies under her feet. "I don't know as I ever had much use for them Blairs. But I'm against 'em now, root and branch, tooth and nail — father and son, kith and kin. That boy ought to be muzzled — going round the country talking all that fool nonsense of his. If I had my way I'd down him — him and all his clan. Just let him show his head for the Legislature another time!

Mrs. Oats' eyes were fixed steadily on the fire.

"Then you are not a Democrat, Mrs. Bellows?" she said.

"I'm an *honest* Democrat," declared Mrs. Bellows, with flashing eyes.

Mrs. Oats was decidedly bored. "After all, why should one tolerate a vulgar old creature like that," she was thinking. She could recall a time when Lexington had been far different. Were there really no longer any bars? Mrs. Bellows was a most alarming exponent.

"Did you hear any of Mr. Blair's speeches during the campaign," asked Mrs. Oats, stifling a yawn. The election was a rather exhausted topic.

Mrs. Bellows put down her tea cup. She shook her head with prompt denial, and the great bird nodded. "I've got something better to do than to spend my time listening to a young fly-up-the-creek like that. Where was Mr. Oats?"

Mrs. Oats laughed and shrugged her plump shoulders. There was something very youthful in the laugh and in the shrug.

"Mr. Oats is a Republican," she answered lightly, "and you know a Republican never changes his politics, any more than a Roman Catholic changes his religion. *I* have always been a Democrat."

She sat tapping one of her daintily shod feet a little restlessly. Then she spoke, hiding the covert meaning of her words by a special suavity, as she leaned a little forward.

"I was under the impression that your strong Abolition views during the war before you came to Lexington to live had made a Republican of you, Mrs. Bellows," she said.

Mrs. Bellows gave a sudden start.

"What did you know about me before I came to Lexington, Virginia Oats?" she demanded, suddenly losing grasp upon herself. In recent years Mrs. Bellows had actually begun to pose a little as a lady of quality. Latterly, to everyone's surprise, she had joined the Lexington Chapter of Daughters of the American Revolution, under the impression that her patent of nobility was thus made sure for all time. No one ever knew how she had managed to accomplish even this much; and it took the old town fully three months to recover from the shock it suffered when she handed in her papers. To be sure it was only a private that she could claim, but no one had ever suspected that Mrs. Bellows owned even a private.

Mrs. Oats' eyes held a peculiar light as she turned her face toward her guest. She was a woman of many resources, and she did not fail to recognize that this was the moment for a decisive stroke. She was far from being a coward herself; and she knew how to deal with cowards when the exigencies of the occasion forced her to abandon for an instant her usual graceful appeal. A sense of indignation was still rankling within her from Mrs. Bellows' malicious coupling of her name with that of the man whom, above all others, she most respected in her heart. Assuredly the woman must be silenced, and silenced finally.

Mrs. Bellows had risen and was standing over her. "What do you know about me before I came to Lexington, Virginia Oats," she repeated fiercely.

Mrs. Oats also rose, and the two women stood staring at each other for an instant. Mrs. Oats was very cool, a half smile played about her lips. There was something soft and feline in the touch she laid upon her companion's shoulder. "I think I may claim to know a good deal, Mrs. Bellows," she remarked sweetly. "As a half-grown girl I once made a visit to your town, a short time after you had left it. Everyone remembered you."

Mrs. Bellows' sallow skin paled. She fixed her beady eyes on Mrs. Oats and watched her narrowly. "You never told me this before," she gasped.

"No? But it was quite a long time ago. It was a very quiet visit, and there was so little to speak of.

I was with an old school friend whose brother had just died. But you know —" Mrs. Oats suddenly paused and seemed to hesitate — "you know how it is in a small place like that. There never is very much to talk about, don't you know. People know everything — the minutest details — even such unimportant matters as how one's neighbor's fortune has been acquired is sometimes a topic. Of course there is never any reason —" again that most becoming little halt and hesitation — "why — why these things should follow, when one has gone to a strange place to live. I had almost forgotten that queer little visit — it was all so long ago. But your mention of the political views of my friend Mr. Blair reminded me of something that I once heard of you."

Mrs. Bellows well knew that that was not what had reminded her. She turned to go. "Well, there's one thing you never heard," she maintained stoutly, struggling to recover herself, but failing signally, "you never heard that I was a hypocrite and a demagogue."

"A hypocrite and a demagogue?" repeated Mrs. Oats, innocently, as if carefully weighing that idea. "No — no, I don't think anyone applied those words to you at that time. I — I was rather under the impression that those are terms of a more recent usage."

She stood a moment looking thoughtfully into the

fire. Her loose silken gown fell lightly about her. She was conscious of its becomingness, and her old airy, almost girlish manner suddenly returned.

"It is easy enough to theorize a little about these matters — even with the dullest of us. Of course *I* don't know anything. But one could scarcely escape taking sides in that contest — no one in Kentucky, at least. People talked of nothing else, don't you know. Did you ever see anything like it? I was forced to become quite a politician. Personally I am entirely with the Blairs, and I thought Blackburn's stand was magnificent."

"Humph! he's got enough of you by the ears — that old professor of his and Judge Trotter; and I hear Major Wise is for sending him to Congress. Well, he'll lead you all a dance, I'll be bound. But the country's safe — for the next three years — anyway." She was still keeping up a brave front; but Mrs. Oats was fully satisfied, she knew that she had nothing more to fear. Mrs. Bellows' back was broken, so to speak. However, it was just as well to make the thing complete.

"I will tell you why I am in sympathy with Mr. Blair," said Mrs. Oats, very mildly. "But first let me help you with your wrap. Ah — there. Is it quite comfortable? Do you know I really think he stands for quite a big idea — the progress and the uplift of the masses, don't you know? Of course the masses are slow to appreciate all that such men as he would like to do for them; and you know very little is to be expected from the newly rich. It has really all turned out just as I expected. People who belong to the lowest grade of society seldom look beyond the moment, and people — don't you know — people who have recently attained — attained wealth, are apt to be inclined to think a good deal more of how to keep it than of the advancement of their fellow creatures in the ranks from which they sprang. It is from persons of high birth like himself that I have always thought one must look for the elevation of humanity in a general way. But there, now, I didn't mean to make a speech. Blackburn would think I was trying to rival him."

Mrs. Bellows turned toward the door. "Newly rich!" she was saying to herself, "newly rich, indeed! How'd old Oats get his money, I'd like to know. I wonder if she actually has the impudence to mean me!"

But she was no longer sniffing the air, she was completely conquered.

"And you won't have another cup of tea?" Mrs. Oats was saying as she followed her guest into the hall. "How good of you to come and take compassion on me this beautiful afternoon when everyone longs to be out! I'm afraid I've fairly roasted you in that warm room."

Mrs. Bellows paused a moment at the head of the stairs.

"Well, you know I always liked you, Virginia Oats, you've got none of them little low tale bearing ways that I despise."

To which Mrs. Oats only responded with that same youthful, sweetly charming smile, which a moment before had sent a cold chill down Mrs. Bellows' spine.

CHAPTER II

THE RECEPTION AT MAJOR WISE'S

Major Orlando Wise lived all alone in a queer old house situated in a blatant quarter of the town that had long been given over to affairs and traffic. The major had been the owner of it for many years, and he had been attracted to it in the beginning by the resemblance it bore in miniature to the beautiful old plantation home of his youth. It was only a very slight resemblance, it is true, but the major was a man of sentiments and able to extract much comfort from little things.

Here he had lived for twenty years or more, a serene and striking figure, with his quiet ways and superb physique, calmly stemming a tide of progress that could never bear him on, and as completely in contrast with all about him as was his antique dwelling with the shops and stalls that surrounded it.

And it was something more than merely a quaint picturesqueness of style, the possession of extraordinary good looks, or the effect of heavy white hair about the well-shaped head in agreeable variance with his dark blue eyes and black moustache, that instantly caught and held the attention at sight of him — something rather difficult to describe, but revealed in a certain fine, chivalrous intention whose very essence bespeaks an inheritance of calm and culture: an era never too hurried to be courteous, never too selfish to be kind.

But what specially interested most persons in regard to him was a certain haunting, fanciful suggestion of a past romance. This seemed ever to cling to him and surround him with a delicate atmosphere of reserve, in spite of increasing years, and the fact that little was known of his past on which to base a love story. Yet why the major was unmarried was a topic that never failed. People talked of it over their tea cups and whispered of it almost under his very nose. The major was serenely unconscious. He had few intimates, even among his lifelong associates, and of these there was only one who ever felt himself privileged to tread upon the sacred soil of his inmost nature.

He and this old friend, Colonel Leonidas Johnstone of the Confederacy, were standing together on the evening of the reception in the major's softly lighted house awaiting the appearance of the major's guests, when the old-fashioned door bell rang loudly in announcement of the first arrival. The colonel, who, at a late hour in the afternoon had been prevailed upon to be present, had just entered the room. His broad, blond-bearded face was flushed from the cold, and he was bending his rotund form toward a great fire of crackling hickory logs and rubbing his hands, exclaiming, "Raw — raw! Who ever would have thought it after such a day as yesterday? Bless me, if it isn't as cold as Christmas!"

Presently a servant's step hurried through the hall.

The major straightened himself like a soldier awaiting orders. The colonel, with a decidedly bored look, at the first hint of an arrival, had turned deserter and fled to the library, where it was his intention to remain the greater part of the evening — at least until supper should be served.

There was a low colloquy in the hall. The major recognized the voice asking, "Then I am the first? And he is there — waiting? Just take these wraps, please; I won't go up stairs," and Mrs. Oats floated in resplendent in a yellow satin gown with bared neck and arms, and with her abundant hair massed high and caught here and there with a jeweled pin.

The major came forward with courtly cordiality.

"Ah, this is very kind of you, my dear friend," he exclaimed, "very kind, indeed."

Mrs. Oats' hand rested for a moment in the major's benignant clasp. Her manner was slightly effusive, but polished, a certain graceful Southern ardour which had been once spontaneous being pinned on, so to speak, with artistic deftness. She moved away toward the mantle with a little light, low laughter.

"Major, have you never learned, even yet," she asked, "that kindness from me is only another name for a very selfish action?"

The major appeared a little confused. An odd smile was still lingering on Mrs. Oats' face, though she was looking with a well-feigned simplicity into his eyes. Her mouth was a trifle large, yet it was the mouth, which had least pretense to classic beauty, that bore the palm of interest over her other features. At times one was not quite sure whether to like or to dislike it heartily. In the main it was most appealing, with winning curves, and strong, beautiful teeth. There was something radiant in her smile. But the major, who was very simple and direct, could not always understand it. However, just now his glance rested upon her with the satisfaction a man feels in beholding a woman whose personality is by no means unpleasing, and whose every word and look is a subtle flattery toward himself.

"I was beginning to indulge the hope that Mr. Oats would be with you," he remarked in his most stately and courteous fashion. "When I wrote I was, of course, under the impression that he expected to remain some time in the East, but Colonel Johnstone has just informed me, he saw him this afternoon on the street."

A slightly perceptible shadow flitted across Mrs. Oats' features, but it vanished quickly. She turned with an exaggerated cheerfulness.

"Yes, he came back to-day. I was not expecting him, and I was quite pleasantly surprised, don't you know." It seems that New York bored him. Isn't that a most remarkable state of things? If he had invited me to go with him, he would not have been bored."

"I am very sure of that," responded the major, gallantly.

"Oh, I mean — I mean —" Mrs. Oats' embarrassment was delightful. "What I meant to say," she hastened to explain, "is that if I had been with him I might have prevailed upon him to go and see things, don't you know, instead of staying all the time about his hotel in the way he usually does. I think he is always hoping that he may come upon a Kentuckian. Nothing that he could find in the whole of New York would be half so entertaining to him."

"Don't you admire his loyal spirit? What could be more entertaining than a Kentuckian? My dear Mrs. Oats, I'm astonished at you!"

The bell was ringing every minute now, and people muffled in wraps and in overcoats were moving quickly through the halls.

Mrs. Oats stood looking pensively into the fire.

When one expected her to smile, she seldom did. Presently she turned and gave a sweeping glance around. There was a particularly festive air to the two rooms, which were low and square, with an archway between. Mrs. Oats had never seen them so beautifully decked for any occasion, and she was conscious of an involuntary pang. Her glance took in everything from the half dozen carved, high-backed chairs placed here and there against the walls, and pushed away as far as possible to gain space, to the palms and ferns of the corners, and the tall mantles banked with buds. Everywhere something pink caught the eye.

'Roses — roses all the way!' she exclaimed. The major followed her glance.

"In honour of my little friend. She always reminded me of roses — pink roses," he said. "To think that I haven't seen the child for nearly eleven years!"

Mrs. Oats moved away. "You have shown most excellent taste — she cannot fail to be pleased, I am sure," she remarked a trifle constrainedly, as several persons entered the room. But the major, wondering a little at the tone, was forced to give himself up at once to his guests.

In a few moments the rooms were crowded to overflowing. It was not possible for the major to invite only a few people. When he began to invite at all, such a generous and affectionate attitude of mind would instantly be awakened within him that the difficulty was ever to stop; and even when sadly weighted by the thought that brick and mortar could not be reckoned, beyond a certain point, as elastic, he would still continue graciously to urge his friends — and not only his friends, but many others whom he barely knew, but who had grown up in the old town in recent years, and whom he therefore regarded as entitled to his hospitality.

Suddenly a band stationed under the stairway struck up gayly. The major's spirits rose. Nothing delighted him so much as to play the part of host. Such amenities as the situation required were in special harmony with his nature; and there was an imperishable youth in him which made him claim instant kinship with all young and happy things.

"Where is the child — why doesn't she come?" he kept asking himself impatiently, while he stood before one after another of the merry throng, each lovely young girl in her pretty finery giving him a sudden start as she entered. But Cicely was late — of course she was late, she must always be just a wee bit behind time as every one knew, who knew her at all.

The major was bowing in the presence of a tall, dark-haired girl in pink, making one of his quaintly chivalrous speeches when the crowd about the doorway parted, and a young woman in a sheer white gown entered and moved swiftly — sweeping the little ruffles of her trailing skirts with easy abandon — to the major's side. There was something proud and distinguished in the graceful carriage. She was a little above the medium height, and she was very lovely in a warm, Hebe-like style that was all curves, and dimples, and soft young flesh delicate as rose leaves. Her neck and arms were bare, and her rippling brown hair, rolled loosely back from the low brow, was piled high and surmounted by a great tortoise shell comb of quaintly beautiful workmanship that gave a suggestion of tender, old-time beauty to the girlish costume. There was a mischievous twinkle in her blue eyes as she came forward. And before the major was at all aware of her, there was a smothered laugh at his elbow, and as he turned two soft arms were thrown impulsively about his neck, and in another instant he was being soundly kissed, regardless of everything and everybody, while a voice whispered, "Oh, you dear — you *dear*! This is the very happiest day in all my life."

"Upon my word!" exclaimed the major, blushing violently, and decidedly abashed. "Bless me!" proceeding to extricate himself at once, and quite unconscious of who it was who had so honoured him.

Still blushing and awkward as a great overgrown boy, his stateliness having completely deserted him, he drew back a step. "Angels and ministers of grace," he suddenly broke forth, meeting the laughing eyes, "if it isn't little Cicely! Bless me — bless me!"

His eyes in wonderment swept the graceful form. Until that moment it had not occurred to him that she would not appear in a short frock and with two long plaits hanging to her waist. As the slim, childish figure vanished and gave away to the rounded womanliness he saw before him, the major was conscious of a fleeting sadness. He missed the little girl of long ago, and he knew that he would miss her always. He studied her face with a gentle solicitude in his gaze, half fearful of what he should find there. But if she had reached a woman's estate, she was yet to know a woman's sorrow, and inwardly the major thanked God for that. But there were possibilities. The major's own great capacity for suffering made him keen to discover in others those secret wells of emotion that lie so far from the surface. Some day her hour would come, intuitively he knew it must; but for the present Cicely's sweet and unclouded beauty appealed to him like the beauty of a flower. His spirits returned.

And yes — he was quite right in selecting pink roses — she was just like that, a pink rose with the morning dew upon it. Great Heavens, where was Blackburn? And what was the boy made of, if seeing her, he could resist her?

The major quickly pulled himself together and began introducing people right and left. In most cases the introduction was entirely superfluous — Cicely remembered everybody, or tactfully appeared to remember, and everyone was charmed, everyone masculine, that is. The girl was just a trifle too pretty, too assured, to please Mrs. Oats in particular. As she stood witnessing the little tableau of a moment before, an unpleasant sense of irritation awoke in her, and it was a feeling that she did not hold entirely alone, though in her case there were perhaps more specific reasons.

As for Blackburn Blair there was some uncertainty as to whether that young man would be present. The major had received a telephone message from Frankfort at two, mentioning important political engagements. Major Wise had been worrying a good deal. Politics? Fudge, fiddlesticks, nonsense! He was considerably put out. One of the cherished dreams of the major's was to bring these two young people together, and it did not suit him to have his plans thus frustrated at the very outset. Had Blackburn actually forgotten the little companion of his childhood as completely as it appeared? He asked himself this question many times during the evening. It was true, he admitted, that the boy was throwing his whole soul into the great political questions of the day. Lovemaking, so far as anyone could see, had played small part in his developing career. The ten or eleven years that had passed since that June Commencement Day, which was the last time he had seen her, had been so full. Next followed the years at Princeton; then a course of study in the law; then the first beginnings of practice of his profession; then a term in the General Assembly of his state; and lastly his awakening to a distinct and startling recognition of the part he was hereafter to play in the affairs of Kentucky — all these things the major knew had come upon the young man with a rapidity and an engrossment of interest that might easily have driven from his mind those distant days when the two had been boy and girl together, just as it seemed hardly to be hoped that he had not also been supplanted in her thoughts. Still the major clung to his dream.

He loved them both with an equal devotion, and there was a fineness in the major's nature which led him to set great store upon the matter of constancy. And the childish affection of these two had been too honest and too pretty in its way to drift into mere indifference. So that if Blackburn had not managed to put in an appearance, it may be doubted whether he would ever again have occupied precisely the same place in the major's thoughts that had heretofore been his.

But Blackburn did put in an appearance at last. It was quite late when he arrived. He came in, tall and handsome in his evening clothes — but grave and quiet as of yore. He had changed a good deal in the past decade. The strippling look had gone. His smooth face showed traces of thought, even of care. But there was an immensity of reserved strength, of purpose in the dark eyes. He stood a moment at the major's side making his excuses.

"Begone, you young dog and find her. She's among the dancers, and she's the queen of them all I can tell you. You're lucky if she'll so much as turn and look at you. Begone!" commanded the major in mock ferocity.

But she was not among the dancers. Blackburn stood a moment in the doorway of the next room and watched the merry couples whirling past. A plain girl nearby turned and engaged him in conversation in the eager, nervous way of the neglected. Seeing her so animated a man across the room presently came up, and Blackburn bowing, moved away.

There was a little crowd in the supper-room. But Cicely was not there. There was only one other place — the library, and Blackburn made his way thither.

She was in the library. And she was sitting in a great chair before the fire, her white-slippered feet resting on a footstool, waving a big feather fan to and fro, and talking to Frederick Dilson. There was a coquettish sparkle in her eyes and her cheeks were flushed. There was no one else in the room, and they were both apparently much absorbed, for neither saw him, and Blackburn was about to move away, when there was a step behind him and the major entered.

He walked straight up to the two, taking no heed of Blackburn.

"Dilson, my boy," he cried, "come and help me. Six more young women on my hands! Isn't that enough to scare an old bachelor out of his wits?"

And then, as Dilson, laughing, but obedient, started off, the major placed a hand on Blackburn's shoulder.

"My dear child, here is an old friend," he said to Cicely, gayly, and turning, he quietly left the room.

CHAPTER III

"THE MIGHT OF ONE FAIR FACE"

There was a twinkle of amusement in Cicely's laughing eyes as they followed the major's retreating form, every line of which evidenced his entire satisfaction in a situation which he felt had been engineered on his part with much diplomatic grace.

The two thus left standing in the middle of the room in a somewhat breathless surprise at the rapidity of proceedings, had a slightly awkward moment. Cicely was the first to speak. She held out her hand with quickly recovered ease, and with the gracious aplomb of the woman of the world coupled with a natural charm of manner. But under all her cordiality there was a very distinct reserve.

"The major seems to take it for granted that you have not forgotten me, Mr. Blair," she observed. "I hope he is quite right. Have you any idea — do you know who it is that is talking to you?"

Mr. Blair! Forgotten her! The young man started perceptibly. He had been studying her face in a complete abandonment. The question brought him to himself.

"I have not forgotten you," he said very quietly at length.

"Ah, that is good of you," she responded, with an attempted lightness that somehow seemed to fail a little under his steady gaze.

Blackburn drew a deep breath. There was something controlled and masterful in his manner from which her femininity seemed to shrink. "Then I am to call you Miss Overton?" he asked, with sudden directness.

Cicely broke into a merry laughter. Ah, that laughter — how it reminded him of other days! At once a small, teasing, winsome face rose before him. And the quick turn of the head — the firm little chin — the delicious ripple of hair back from the low brow — all the same sweet, irresistible, exasperating tricks that his childhood and his boyhood had grown to know so well — everything was there just as it had been, and yet so different!

There was still an eager questioning in his eyes — more eager than he knew. But Cicely, unlike the major, was not going to take anything for granted. Plainly, there must be a new beginning untrammelled by the past. He could see that she was secretly rebelling against the old childish hold.

And he was completely at sea. A moment before, when he had first found her, and before he had seen

Dilson's face, he had felt that his day of days had actually come at last. During those eleven years of waiting he had not called it love, the feeling he had for her. Still he had waited. And always, in the stern restrictions which, in any case, he would have felt bound to put upon himself, there was a helpful impulse toward the right that came to him through his thoughts of her. So that it had been an easier thing to keep his young manhood pure, free from the taint of sins that seems so easily to beset others of his age, that there might be something more worthy to offer her when she came. He was sure that she would come some day.

He had been startled, silenced by her beauty. Until that moment he had not known that he could feel like that. Her loveliness had pierced him through and through. Yet as he sat pale and wondering, he was simply trying to lift the veil of her womanhood in the hope that he might find the being that he long ago knew. But the girl had vanished, and the woman is not easily found who is deliberately in hiding.

Cicely, without replying further, turned suddenly and took a step or two across the room. "Shall we sit here — before this beautiful fire?" she asked, slipping down with a little nestling movement that he well remembered into the great leathern chair which she had abandoned on the major's entrance.

He gravely took the seat at her side, cut to the heart by her coolness. Conscious of the wall that she strove to raise between them, he scarcely knew what to say.

"Perhaps you would prefer to be among the dancers," he finally suggested a little stiffly. "I don't dance myself; but you mustn't let me keep you against your will." He tried hard to compel the hurt tone out of his voice. But she had already seen the pain of his face when she had refused to answer him a moment before. He sat watching her, with his poet's eyes grave and troubled.

Cicely looked up with her old mischievous smile.

"The dancers? Not I. I don't care a fig for dancing. I would far rather talk to you. I wasn't dancing you know when you came in."

"No — I am aware of that."

"Are you quite sure you would have known me if you had not been expecting to see me?" she asked presently, stroking the feathers of her fan with a slow caressing movement. "Ten years — or eleven, is it? — is a long time."

How strange it all was! There she was at last before him, and actually asking him a thing like that! What were women made of anyhow? He confessed to himself his utter inability to answer that question. Cicely, he admitted humbly, was always just a little too deep for him.

"Should you not have known me?" he demanded.

"You? Anywhere."

"Then why do you doubt that I should have known you?"

"Women are different. Besides, you were nineteen — you were quite aged."

"You were fifteen."

"So I was. Do you think me greatly changed?"

"Yes — and no."

"And yet you would have known me?"

"If, instead of the ten years it had been twenty, thirty, forty, even — I should have known you just the same."

"By what token, pray thee?" said Cicely, smiling, and waving her feather fan.

"By your smile," responded Blackburn, calmly, "by your eyes, by your voice, and above all by your most inscrutable ways, which at this moment are making a very unhappy man of me, I assure you. Aren't you the least bit glad to see me after all those years?"

Cicely's long lashes drooped an instant over her eyes. All at once he took heart, seeing the sudden flush that swept over her. Even her neck was pink.

"Don't you remember that I used to call you Cicely? Mr. Blair indeed!" Blackburn was doing bravely. "What a shock that gave me! I felt as if you had suddenly dashed a bucket of cold water over me. Do you think I have any idea of being called Mr. Blair by you — *you?* And don't you think it is a little hard on a fellow to treat him like that when he's been hungry for the sight of you for nearly eleven years?"

"And yet Mr. Dilson was just telling me that it was even uncertain that you would be present this evening in honour of my home-coming. Isn't it a little difficult to think of you as pining for the sight of me — wasting away for eleven long years — you poor frail starving creature, when you were not willing to put forth so small an effort as that?"

"Ah, but that couldn't be helped. I was barely able to make it at all. If I had failed, I should have known that you understood, of course."

Blackburn's face grew instantly thoughtful. In a flash he was back again in Frankfort going over the details of a matter of serious political import.

"Oh, I should have understood," she responded, with a shrug.

She spoke gayly, without the smallest reproach, wholly unlike the woman whose vanity has been disturbed. There was rather an undefined suggestion of relief. Yet there was also a proud little note.

But Blackburn failed to perceive it. He sat looking earnestly into the fire, with brows knit. In reality he was going over again, in his thoughts, the harassing problem relating to the public affairs of his state which had occupied him all day. The faces of a number of scheming office-seekers, whom it had been necessary to talk with while in Frankfort, rose before him. The narrowness of their aim, the insincerity of their attitude toward the great principles of government which they professed to believe in, filled him with an old disgust, in which there was yet mingled a sense of pity for the moral blindness to all that stands for higher citizenship which could thus shut out from men's lives the larger view.

For the time Cicely was forgotten — and she knew it, being made aware of her dethronement by that intuitive discernment which tells a woman, even the dullest, when she must stand aside, and which is at the same time her safeguard and her pain. But his absorption surprised and startled her. Cicely was wise; she let the matter drop.

"Mr. Dilson has been saying some very fine things of you. We were speaking of you just as you came in," she remarked carelessly.

At the sound of her voice he roused himself and looked her full in the eyes.

"Were you?" he cried eagerly. "I thought — I thought —"

"You thought he was making love to me," she said serenely.

Blackburn looked abashed. "Upon my word! you

take it very coolly, I must say," he replied indignantly. He was conscious of a very sudden ferocity of feeling such as he had not known for many a day. The thought of any man's love-making in her case was intolerable — it shot through him with a deadly pang. Apparently it was difficult for him to get the idea well fixed in his mind that he was no longer the special guardian and protector that he had always regarded himself in former times.

"Why shouldn't such things be taken coolly?" she inquired, leaning her head back, and fixing her gaze upon the ceiling. "It's the only way." Presently Cicely brought her eyes down. "But Mr. Dilson was not making love to me. I hasten to exonerate — Mr. Dilson," with a slightly perceptible accent.

He turned quickly toward her. His words came with a sudden impetuosity.

"Cicely, I wrote to you — four years ago, on the day of your graduation at Vassar. The one letter that I ever wrote you! Cicely, why — why did you not answer?"

She grew a little white. All at once she reached out a hand to him and then drew it instantly back. Her face changed.

"Don't!" she said hastily. "Of course you may call me Cicely, and I will call you Blackburn, if you wish—it really seems to be the easier way—but don't."

"I don't understand. Will you explain?" His dark eyes, a moment before so boyishly eager, were somber as they sought to meet her own.

She did not reply at once. Presently she looked up, but without a trace of coquettry, avoiding his glance.

"I will try," she said very simply, her face becoming sweeter as his grew cold. "It is a little difficult. Of course — of course I appreciated your letter. It was so like you — so earnest, and so solemn, and so genuinely kind. I think any girl would have been pleased to receive such a letter on her graduation day; and I was feeling a little sad and tremulous, and regretful of I scarce knew what. Mama was with me." She threw out her hands and let them fall with a despairing little gesture. "Frankly, Blackburn, the reason why I didn't answer your letter was mama commanded me not to answer it. I was far more obedient in those days," she added, with a laugh, which was slightly forced, as her expression grew instantly serious again.

He stared at her in a pained surprise in which there yet mingled considerable alleviation.

"Do you mind telling me her objection?" he asked presently.

Cicely sighed and shook her head. "If you remember my mother at all," she said, with the same constrained laugh, "you know that she is of all things a theorist. One of her pet ideas is that Southern people should be educated in the North — that is in the East — and during the early formative period of their lives spend as much time as possible away from their own home. She is equally convinced that it is to the advantage of the Northerner to become acquainted with the Southern type; and she has no hesitation, in spite of all this, in claiming the superiority of the Southerner in general and of the Kentuckian in particular. Nothing is farther from her thoughts than to make the smallest concession to the North. She has never been reconstructed. But to carry out the theory, she insisted that I should break off all correspondence with my Kentucky friends during those years of study."

"Did she put it to you just in that way?"

"Those were the only grounds stated. Mama never argues. She only acts. In this she resembles Napoleon and Julius Caesar. Oh, but seriously — it did cost her no end of sacrifices to get me through college just at that time, and I really owed her special obedience. You know we are the kind of people that never have any money, and we are always wanting things. Without my poor dear old grandfather there's no telling what would become of us. All this is horribly personal."

She hesitated a moment, and then gave him a quick little glance.

"Blackburn," she said gently, "I did mind it, I did

truly mind not being allowed to answer your letter. I begged for just one little line. But mama was firm. I have never yet been able to take anything like a real stand against her, though I am sometimes bold enough now to make a fight for smaller things. Then I simply gave up in everything, big and little. And when I was through with college, she sent me off with Aunt Catherine. You never saw Aunt Catherine; but at any rate, she played most beautifully into mama's hands. She's the only wealthy one among us. I was whisked away first to Newport and afterwards for a winter in Washington, without so much as a glimpse at anyone at home; and I went meekly as a lamb. But when we went to Europe I cried all night before we started. I just wanted to go home.

"Were you glad to come back when you did come?" he asked anxiously.

"Glad? I was radiant. If you could have seen my dear grandfather's face in the moment when he first caught sight of me! It was something to remember a whole life through. And if I had my way, I'd never go away again — not even so far as Frankfort — so long as I live. But I'm afraid there's no such good fortune in store for me as a quiet life," she added sadly, a swift shadow falling over the piquant face. "My wanderings are not yet at an end."

But she began again before he could answer. "Fortunately, my mother's hands are too full now to give exclusive attention any longer to me. (She used to write me reams — lessons in deportment by the yard, in case Aunt Catherine should forget something.) But Horace is at Princeton, and Gertrude is at Bryn Mawr, and it is necessary to keep them right. Then there are the babies, as we call Alice and Hugh and Ruth. As the eldest, I was a good deal practiced on before the theòries were reduced to a system. I think mama regards me as a failure, thus far, and that is why she let me come home — she was tired of prescribing at such long range. After all her efforts to make of me a cosmopolite, she has only succeeded in making a Kentuckian of the most provincial kind. How I used to talk about Kentucky, in season and out of season, how I longed for it during that interminable stay in Europe!"

"You longed for it? Cicely, you can't know how happy you make me feel!"

She caught herself up at once.

"Oh, but it's not the kind of love for Kentucky that you have, Blackburn — nothing at all like that," she hastened to say.

Blackburn looked blank. "Are there then two kinds?" he asked gropingly.

Cicely nodded. "There are two kinds," she said, with conviction. "There's your kind, and it is like this. You want to do things. You would like to help on, to elevate, to inspire. You want to bring back our old days of departed glory, by a glorious thinking, and a glorious living. You hope to make the present better than the past, and you have the faith to think it could be, in spite of a stiff-necked people that only recently rallied to those enticing leaders, with their molten calf, who cried 'These be thy Gods, O, Israel.' My grandfather has told me. Mr. Dilson has told me. Everyone has told me. I think it is magnificent!"

A sudden flush swept over the young man's face.

"You — you understand?" he cried a little huskily — you do understand? Then all at once he said softly, and as if a great strain had been lifted, "Thank God! It would have been hard — Cicely, it would have been harder than you know if you had not been with me in this thing."

But presently Blackburn's face changed. He rubbed his hand in a preoccupied way across his brow. He was silent a long time, and again she understood.

"Then there is my kind," she said, breaking in upon him with an impatient gesture, "and that is altogether different; and it is so much smaller I am almost ashamed to mention it. I am not possessed of a desire to do anything — anything whatever. I love Kentucky because it is lovely, and because I can't help it — and that is about all there is to it. I love my own dear woods and skies and wonderful waving grasses, and I know that there are no such woods and skies and grasses in all the wide world through; and even if there are, I don't care — no other place on earth cán ever be half so beautiful to me. But all this is as different from your feeling as can be. It is just my way, you see."

"It's a woman's way, and it's a very beautiful way — I've no fault to find with it."

She shook her head.

"It is not altogether a woman's way. Women are willing to make sacrifices for what they love."

"That is a pretty sure test."

"But I told you that my love for Kentucky is not like yours. You are willing to make the sacrifices."

"Aren't you? — such sacrifices as you could make? You can't go around and persuade men to see things as you see them. And you can't very well set yourself up as a target for the ridicule and the enmity of all those persons who may happen to disagree with you. It is true that you aren't fitted to do anything like this. But in my opinion women have a great part to play in the future politics of Kentucky — in the way of influence, I mean. Until recently they have given little thought to these matters, but they came to the front to a rather alarming extent in the last presidential election. In my judgment many of them were sadly misinformed. It was only to be expected that some mistake swould be made. But I, for one, am ready to trust them. Unfortunately, quite a large number had been convinced that they would be financially crippled if the Democratic party succeeded, and they boldly deserted us. Conspicuous among these was our old friend Mrs. Bellows. Cicely, *do* you remember Mrs. Bellows?"

"I would forget. I hear she has become your sworn enemy. Mr. Dilson told me that too."

"What else did Dilson tell you, by the way? It seems that he has constituted himself my biographer."

"Nothing of the kind," replied Cicely, promptly. "We had other things to talk about — you were merely an incidental. But your Mrs. Bellows — horrible old thing! — is an excellent case in point. I should never be willing to bring down on my poor little head the vials of her wrath, not even for Kentucky — if I knew just when I was going to do it."

Blackburn's face grew soberer. "Some day I hope to talk to you more about these things, Cicely," he said very gently. "It is just life to me — what I feel about Kentucky. And I mean by that, of course, Kentucky in relation to the nation."

Cicely's eyes were turned away. "I know," she assented, slowly, at length. "But I should never be able to feel just as you do. My heart is too small for the map of the United States. It seems that it is really not quite large enough for Kentucky. You know they used to call my father a rebel a long time ago — and my grandfather, too. There are no doubt a good many things I can't see just as you see them."

"Oh, but you will, you must — you can't fail to see that there is a great thing to be done, and the only way is for every one to lend a hand. If you love Kentucky — if you live always with just one thing before you —"

Cicely rose abruptly. "Perhaps I don't love it, after all," she broke in with a queer little laugh; "and I am quite sure that I don't live always with just one thing before me. I can think of nothing more tiresome."

He followed her across the room, an expression of pained bewilderment flitting rapidly across his features. His handsome face, with its strong, concentrated forcefulness and youthful impetuosity, was anxious and appealing. At the door she turned and looked him steadily in the eyes.

"You are disappointed in me," she said sadly, and with a sudden humility upon her like that of a little child craving absolution.

He did not answer, and her lip trembled. Blackburn was completely undone.

"You think me sadly changed?" she asked again.

"I think you the most beautiful thing on earth,"

he said quickly, smiling down upon her from his six feet of height.

She flushed hotly. Cicely was a person of many surprises. "Oh, not that — you know I did not mean *that.*"

"Whatever you mean you will forgive me for telling you just this once, won't you? Really I couldn't help it."

But suddenly he caught himself up seeing that she was indeed really hurt.

"I asked you —" it was the old Cicely, the wilful little creature of the past that put the question, though something of a woman's pain quivered in the words — "I asked you to tell me the truth."

He took a step toward her. A quick flame leaped into his eyes.

"Shall I tell you?" he cried. "Shall I?" And then he added slowly, "I see in you the possibilities of everything good and noble that a woman may be. You are my dream come true."

She drew back with a sudden trepidation.

"Blackburn," she cried quickly, a startled look sweeping across her face, "whatever you do — don't think of me — I beseech you not to think of me like that!"

CHAPTER IV

FATHER AND SON

Judge Blair turned his quiet gaze from the cheering fire before him to his son.

"Myra, poor child! was here to-day," he remarked softly and in a tone of regret. "Scipio tells me that she brought the boy to see me. I am pained that neither of us were at home to receive her. She came late, a little before five, I believe. Professor Kennedy dropped in, and I sat with him at the office until dark talking over old days in Kentucky. Poor child — poor child!"

Blackburn looked up with a very gentle light in his eyes.

"I am so sorry about it," he said quickly.

But the gentleness suddenly gave way to something like self-reproach. A quick glow mounted to his temples at the recollection of how most of his spare time had been spent of late. He wondered if his father had taken note of it. He was just a little doubtful of his father's opinion of Cicely. (How lamentable if he should misunderstand her!) And a vague unrest upon that point made it always difficult for him to speak her name. He recalled an accidental meeting on the street one morning a few days after Cicely's arrival; and something, in spite of the old judge's most kind and courtly bearing toward the young girl, seemed to be lacking. But then, Blackburn was hoping for a good deal.

"I am ashamed to think of how long a time I have allowed to pass without seeing her and the little chap," Blackburn supplemented presently. "But Myra always understands."

A smile flitted across Judge Blair's features. He shook his head.

"It is never wise to trust too far to a woman's comprehension in matters of this kind," he observed dryly. "But your cousin Myra, I admit, is superior. Of all your mother's young relatives she has always impressed me as being the most interesting. She is not unlike your mother," he concluded, in a low voice, his eyes wandering away to the beautiful portrait, with the look in them which, from a little boy, Blackburn had learned to know so well.

It was a raw December night. The red damask curtains in the old library were drawn and the lamps lighted, and the firelight gleamed merrily on the great mahogany bookcases with their lozenge panes, and on the tall silver candelabra on the mantle. The two had just dined. And it was the hour that father and son invariably spent together, no matter what pressing later engagement rested upon the younger. Blackburn indeed would have been loth to forego one of these peaceful talks, which opened up such delightful glimpses of the past through his father's accurate recollection, even if he had not long ago realized the value of that deep, abiding friendship, begun in his childhood, which had steadily grown into a tenderer and more intimate relation as the years went by.

The judge had not become much older in appearance in the last decade. His hair and beard were a little whiter, perhaps. His picturesque form appeared a little more bowed, maybe; but the old fire of intelligence still leaped from his eyes. He was of a sturdy and a long-lived race — a race that ever presented a stubborn front to the obstacles in its way; and though he himself had long been frail, with a constitution weakened by excess of suffering, one felt that the mere force of normal feeling in him would keep him alive for many years yet, when others of his age, apparently stronger, but whose lives were less temperate and less earnest, would probably succumb.

Presently Judge Blair spoke again. "The professor and I were discussing that shocking cutting affray that took place out in the edge of the town a few nights ago, and this led up to the frequent homicides that have occurred in the state in times past and present. It brought to my mind the case of the murder of Myra's young husband several years ago. It is a melancholy fact," he added sadly, "that the history of Kentucky still continues to repeat itself in this way."

"I believe that Professor Kennedy has had his thoughts especially turned to subjects of this kind recently," remarked Blackburn, moving back a little from the fire. "He told me that he has been for some time engaged in preparing an article for one of the Eastern magazines on the subject of duelling in the state."

"So he informed me this afternoon. What a record — what a record we have to offer in that line! Few indeed are the old names that can escape."

Blackburn's ardent temperament, schooled to calm and to reflection, found much to ponder over in the subjects they had just touched upon, but that Kentucky would some day emerge from her obloquy, that peace and gentleness would prevail, and that already the great idea of brotherhood was beginning to be grasped by thoughtful people of his state — these things he could not doubt.

But of all the Kentucky tragedies there was one that always came before him with a deeper significance than any of the rest, because it concerned that false and unrelenting public sentiment in his state which questions the courage of the man who will not fight, and demands that he stand ever ready to take the protection of his life and of his honour into his own hands. This tragedy occurred in his boyhood, and the impression it then made upon him was something he knew would never be effaced. Often the recollection of it would wake him, like the grasp of a rude hand, out of sleep. Often he had pondered over it — until heart-weary from the strain, he would turn away from it, only to be confronted with it again, with the same haunting, passionate insistence.

It related to a judge of the Superior Court of Kentucky and an attorney against whose interests the Court had rendered a decision. The judge was known in the state as a man of ability and of exalted character, and the value of his legal opinion and his conscientiousness in the discharge of his duty were unquestioned. But a resentment deep and terrible was aroused in the breast of the attorney, who refused to concur with this general estimation of the judge's character, holding him solely responsible, and alleging that the adverse decision in his case had been rendered on personal grounds. He became an open and implacable enemy, his indignation expressing itself in violent public abuse. One day while the unsuspecting judge sat examining certain legal papers in the attorney's office — where he had been lured under a pretence of friendship — the man, holding a stout hickory cane in his hand, rushed upon him without warning. In a white heat of rage he strode up to the judge and began striking him, first with the cane, and then with a cow-hide. The judge offered no resistance. Unprepared for the attack, and made helpless almost immediately by the savage passion of his assailant, in a few moments he was in a state of utter collapse, his condition being wholly pitiable.

The story spread rapidly throughout the country. Telegrams, letters from all parts of the United States poured into the little Kentucky town, where a man, torn with conflicting emotions, sat bowed beneath the weight of an intolerable humiliation. With all earnestness these messages besought the honourable judge not to do the thing demanded by the people of his state in such a case, but to allow the law to take its course.

Days passed, and still the old natural human instinct, stronger, sterner with a Kentuckian than some can even understand, was resisted.

The judge was a leading member in his church, the superintendent of its Sunday-school. Finally he announced that he would address the citizens of his town in the Court House on an appointed day. He spoke at length. In closing, he announced that he would not attempt to kill the man who had wronged him, and that he would allow the law to take its course. In less than a month from that day, the scholarly Christian judge, who had thus declared himself, put a revolver to his head and blew out his brains, rendered desperate in his great shame — or insane perhaps — by the force of that unwritten law which has come down from a far past to the gentleman of the Southland, and which every Kentuckian must needs obey.

Blackburn made a reference to the case, his face paling. His father sat a moment in deep thought.

"I regard that as the most significant, the most dramatic incident of the kind that has ever come within my knowledge," he said presently. "I have heard persons present on the day that speech was delivered pronounce it the most thoughtful, the most powerful argument based upon the idea that a man should not take the law into his own hands that could be conceived of. Its tragic sequel gives a very mournful meaning to the painful occasion."

Blackburn set his teeth firmly.

"It was a hard test — a hideous test!" he said abruptly. "Few men anywhere, it seems to me, would be equal to what was required in such a case. But in Kentucky," he added, his voice suddenly faltering, as one who urges himself to a particular view, "in Kentucky, the man who could be equal to it would be a saviour to his people."

Judge Blair turned, with a quick, responsive look. And then, as with a sort of prescience of the awful significance with which these words were destined to return to them both, the face of the elder suddenly blanched and his eyes dimmed as his gaze rested upon the white, set countenance of his son.

CHAPTER V

MYRA

As Blackburn came out into the hall a little later a low droning sound broke upon his ear. It was a very familiar sound at that hour, and it proceeded from an ante-room nearby, the door of which was ajar. Through the space two persons could be seen sitting beside a table on which there were a lamp and several battered-looking text-books. The latter had evidently just been thrust aside by the slim, chocolate-coloured youth, who was impatiently fingering the book nearest his hand, and giving a somewhat reluctant attention to the discourse that was being delivered for his benefit by the white-haired negro opposite. Uncle Scip was preaching his nightly sermon. The old man's voice, rich in the pathetic intonations of his race, seemed to fill the room with echoings like the sad murmur of a sea-shell.

"Sonny," he was saying sententiously,"book l'arnin' sho is a mighty good thing, but hit ain' *ever'*thing, an' don' you tek up no sich a noshun dat hit's ever'thing, caze I done tole you hit ain'. Don' you listen to yo' Aunt Huldy an ' de' Publicans. Yo' Aunt Huldy mighty good 'oman, but she's cur'ussome, yo' Aunt Huldy is. Thar's dem newspapers. Dat de trouble wid yo'

Aunt Huldy. I is seen a heap o' trouble come to niggers long o' readin' de news. Ef you wuz to listen to all what dem 'Publicans tells you, you sho would b'lieve thar ain' no white folks in dis town fitten foh de Kingdom 'ceptin' theyse'ves. Now, I 'low you ain' no low down common nigger what drives a mule. You is in trainin' foh a body-servant, an' yo' white folks is quality. But de 'Publicans, dey tells you you is jes de same ez white yo'se'f, an' you must stan' up foh yo' rights 'gainst de folks what is grindin' you down. Sonny," the old negro's voice suddenly sank to a solemn earnestness and persuasion, "sonny, de Lawd done give you a black face, but dat ain' no reason, sho, foh you to give yo'se'f a black heart."

Blackburn slipped quietly into his overcoat. "The old and the new," he reflected smiling, as he moved toward the front door. The sermon continued uninterrupted.

On the steps he paused while he drew on his gloves. The night had grown clearer and stiller. There was scarcely a sigh among the leafless maples. Above the little park opposite a full-orbed moon shone resplendent. Blackburn's spirits rose as he felt the sting of the night air on his cheek. There was a native resistance in him that seemed roused to buoyancy by the cold. He stood looking up into the cloudless sky.

All at once he turned his face toward the old Trotter

mansion diagonally across the street. He had been keeping his eyes resolutely away lest he should be tempted. Now he deliberately crossed in the direction of the house. It wore a particularly festive air. Lights blazed from every window, and several carriages were standing before the door.

As he approached the gate a coupé drove up and a dark, heavily-built man of thirty-five or forty alighted. The man was very handsomely dressed, and in spite of his clumsy build he moved with an alertness wholly unlike the Southern calm of bearing. Blackburn was sure that he had never seen him before, and yet, in the square strong jaw, the blue-black hair and moustache, the controlled look out of the small beady eyes, there was something strangely familiar. The two were face to face as the stranger placed his hand on the gate. For the briefest possible space their eyes met, and in the expression of each there was something like an inquiry and a challenge. To the man's surprise seemingly — for he looked back after ascending the steps — Blackburn passed on.

The hall door opened and closed. Blackburn's face had taken on a look of bewilderment — but scarcely of pain.

At the corner a familiar figure came into view — a tall blonde young man with an open expression of countenance and a flush of pleasant expectation on his careless face. In spite of the cold, his overcoat was thrown jauntily back, and one could see that he was in evening dress. He carried himself with a graceful nonchalance, and he was humming a tune softly to himself. At sight of Blackburn he paused abruptly.

"Hello!" he exclaimed gayly. "Going the wrong way, aren't you?"

"No; I think not," replied Blackburn.

Dilson whistled. "Why see here, how are we going to get on without you?" he demanded. "You're the kind of fellow that always keeps the ball a-rolling, don't you know? I didn't suppose there could be such a thing as a dinner around here without you. What's up — politics again?"

"No. I'm just on my way to pay a call. I didn't know that there was to be a dinner. I haven't the honour to be invited."

Dilson's eyes grew round. "Not invited!" he echoed. "By Jove, what's this?"

Blackburn laughed good-humouredly.

"I am sure I can't tell you," he said simply. "I'm not invited, that is all I know."

Dilson hesitated a moment. He was embarrassed, being inclined to take the matter of invitations rather seriously.

"Oh, I don't really think it amounts to anything," he volunteered kindly, "just a dozen or so — an impromptu affair, I believe. I received a note from Mrs. Overton at about one o'clock to-day, asking me to meet some one from New York. Well, I suspect I'd better hurry along. Good-bye to you, old fellow; wish you were going too."

And again Blackburn passed on.

For a few moments he walked briskly, steadfastly refusing to be disturbed. He had no disposition to magnify a trivial matter into the importance with which young Dilson evidently regarded it. Still he was a good deal surprised. And presently his steps began to lag. His face clouded. He turned into a street that led him away from his previous destination. He wanted to be alone.

What could it mean? He kept asking himself thoughtfully. The occurrence would not be lightly dismissed. The thought of it kept coming back to him and teasing him with the suggestion of a hidden import. With a pang of reminder he found himself seeking a clew in the constraint which, from the first, had from time to time been revealed in Cicely's manner toward him — that sudden withdrawal of herself, against which he had felt he had been able to make but little headway, and which was apt to manifest itself at the most unexpected, the happiest, moments.

He dwelt for a moment upon the girl's impulse and caprice, her instinctive coquettry, thinking of these traits in the gentle, apologetic way with which he was wont to consider them in relation to her, and looking always beyond her surface faults to the true womanhood, the sound loveliness of spirit which he never doubted slumbered in her.

But he could find no explanation in character for the slight. He was at last forced reluctantly to admit that he had received a slight — the circumstances being what they were. He was deeply pained and bewildered.

Still he would not judge her. A certain chivalrous feeling toward her, which, even as a mere boy, had always been strong with him, held everything approaching to a condemnation of her sternly in leash.

For years it had been a daily struggle with him to keep himself well in hand in all matters relating to the emotions, recognizing that, to one of his temperament, the early cultivation of such control is a necessity, if one is ever to accomplish anything in life. But there were moments like this when his temples throbbed, and when the surging of undisciplined feeling in him compelled him to the realization that his self-mastery was still far from complete.

He continued to walk some distance out of his way. When he finally turned and retraced his steps two things were strongly present with him: the fact that she had hurt him, and the conviction that, through life, the power to do this would be hers. But he had fully recovered his usual calm of spirit. He had not fought with himself so long and so valiantly for nought.

With a soothing sense of solace his thoughts turned toward his cousin — in a man's instinctive reaching out for womanly sympathy at a time when his wound has just been dealt him by a woman.

Myra lived on a quiet street not far from his home in a little white house with green shutters, and with a porch in front supported by slender Doric columns over which, in summer, roses clambered, and honeysuckle, and clematis. There was a fanlight over the door on which hung an old-fashioned brass knocker. The house was low, with only a step or two.

The blinds had not been drawn, and as Blackburn came up on the porch, he saw her sitting in a great leathern chair before the fire — a slender, dark-haired young woman in deep black holding a child of three or four in her arms. There was something peculiarly interesting in her appearance — something delicate and intangible, not to be described by curve and contour. The mingled sadness and courage of her features thrilled one through and through. Hers was one of those striking countenances that makes one catch ones breath on first beholding it, and which stands out clear-cut and lonely in any crowd.

The young mother's face as she bent above her boy was tenderly beautiful and touching. Blackburn stood watching her, mindful of her great sorrow, the "eternal womanly" making to him the old, old appeal that it has ever and must ever make to the manhood of the race.

Presently he turned the knob. The door was not bolted, and he softly pushed it open and entered the hall, meaning to have it out with her later on the subject of her reckless disregard of tramps. She was singing in a quiet absorption, and did not hear him.

Blackburn recognized the song as a translation of a quaint little German lullaby, the music of which Wagner introduced into his "Siegfried-Idyll." She was just finishing it as he came in, but in obedience to an imperious command she was forced to begin anew. This time the boy nestled closer, and his eyelides began to droop.

"Sleep, baby, sleep,"

sang Myra, looking down upon the little golden head.

Suddenly the child stirred, loosed himself from his mother's arms, and began to peer curiously over her shoulder.

"*Tousin!*" he broke forth joyously at length, his steady gaze having assured him that there was no mistake. "*Tousin!*" pointing with a moist forefinger in the direction of Blackburn's tall form in the doorway.

Myra turned startled; surprise, however, giving way quickly to welcome in her pathetic dark eyes. Smiling, she put the boy down. He came toward Blackburn in a run.

"Mamma tell about 'ittle lambs; me like *bears!*" he announced stoutly.

"Do you?" responded Blackburn, with all seriousness. "Well, here goes!" and he speedily gathered up the young man, holding him, shrieking with laughter, suspended for an instant in mid-air. "So you like bears, do you? Here's a bear for you, and he's going to eat you up. Fe, fo, fy, fum — I smell the blood of an Englishman!"

The room was filled with the child's glee like the ecstatic warbling of a bird.

"He brought you, Blackburn," said Myra, when the game of mock ferocity had subsided in a temporary lull. He has been talking about you all evening. And I thought it just possible that you might come, so I allowed him to stay down until long after his usual bed-time. You see how he rewards me. He likes *bears!*"

Blackburn sat down by the fire in the chair she drew up for him, still holding the little fellow in his arms.

"It has been a long time since we had a romp together, old man, hasn't it?" he inquired of the boy, not meeting her eyes. And then he added quickly, "Father and I were greatly disappointed this evening when we got home."

Myra smiled — a brave, true smile that seemed to flood the room with sincerity like sunlight. She seldom laughed outright, but in this moment she seemed inclined to do so. She leaned toward him and stretched out her hand.

"You dear boy!" she exclaimed heartily. "You think you have been neglecting me, don't you?"

She was only a year or two his senior, but she treated him as if he were much nearer the age of her little son than of herself. As a matter of fact the deep suffering through which she had passed, while strengthening the maternal feeling which had long existed in her affectionate attitude toward her cousin, had also increased the sense of separateness that every woman feels who has deeply loved and who has accepted her life-story, from the personal point of view, as forever ended.

"I have been neglecting *myself*," responded Blackburn, quickly, finding his watch for the boy.

"Myra," he added impulsively, in a rush of grateful feeling, "how does it happen that you always — *always* understand?"

"But I don't do anything of the kind," she answered, "you musn't praise me too much. Alfred and I have been looking for you every evening, haven't we, darling? We had grown quite impatient."

Blackburn was silent. He sat looking steadily into the fire. Presently there was a step in the hall, and the boy struggled down out of his lap. An old negress in cap and apron stood courtesying in the doorway.

"Here, old fellow, what's up?" he demanded, aiding the child in his frantic efforts to hide behind the sofa.

Myra rose and came across the room. "Come, my little man," she said firmly. "Aunt Kizzie is waiting. Tell cousin good night."

The little fellow came crawling slowly out. Something in those quiet tones seemed to call forth his instant acquiescence.

"How do you manage to make him obey you like that? You're a perfect marvel. I am always expecting mutiny, but it never comes. And the little chap has a good strong will of his own, too," said Blackburn, after the boy, trotting meekly along beside his sable attendant, had disappeared.

Myra threw several handfuls of chips on the wood fire that was fretting and sputtering behind the brass andirons. She refused Blackburn's offer of assistance in the quiet way of a woman who has learned to depend upon herself.

"Perhaps he has discovered that my no, means no, poor little dear," she responded tenderly.

Her eyes rested a moment on a photograph on the mantel — the picture of a young man, with a very high-bred face and an expression of singular purity and power. She turned toward him eagerly, and he could see that she was trembling.

"Blackburn," she asked, "don't you think — can't you see that the baby's resemblance to Alfred is becoming a little more marked?" Her breath came hurriedly in gasps. Her eyes sought his face in a feverish anxiety and impatience.

"I noticed the likeness to-night, more than ever before. I have often noticed it," responded Blackburn softly, all the gentleness of his nature roused by her appeal.

"Ah — I am so glad, so glad! You have no idea how much easier it makes everything in life — how different. I remember the day when I saw the first faint resemblance. He was just eight weeks old. I was playing with him, holding a flower before his face, and his features broke into a smile. For an instant his father was with me. It was the first moment of submission that had come to me during those five terrible months. God never makes our burdens too heavy for us. After that I knew that it would be possible for me to go on. For a long time I have been wanting to speak with you about this, but I was too cowardly. If you had not thought as I did, if the doubt had come, it would have been a hard, hard blow to me. I was unwilling to ask anyone else, and I was afraid to ask you: I knew that you would tell me the truth."

"I have frequently been tempted to mention it, but I always hesitated. I was not sure that you could bear to have me call attention to it. But father and I have often spoken of the strong resemblance. He has at times an expression so like Alfred's that I have been startled. I wish you had spoken with me about this sooner. I might have saved you — something."

"You were his best friend," she said, after a long time, her eyes looking into the fire with the remote sweetness and courage that Blackburn had grown so familiar with in recent years. "With every one else it has always seemed an impossibility to speak his name. But you were his best friend. I can speak of him sometimes — not always — to you. And you have made me happier to-night than you can undersand."

"I think I do understand — a little," he said presently, and in his tone, despite his self-forgetfulness, there was the echo of some inward pain. She turned toward him roused to instant sympathy.

For a moment she studied him thoughtfully though without seeming to do so. She observed that he was a trifle paler and thinner than when she last saw him more than a month before. But she also noted that the look of steadfast purpose in his dark eyes was never more distinct.

She rose and walked over to a little table near the fire.

"May I make you a cup of tea?" she asked.

Blackburn declined.

"You are not as flattering as you should be," she responded cheerfully. "Cicely told me this morning that tea of my making is something that she never expects to have the strength of character to refuse. I had been trying to persuade her to stay to luncheon with me, but she was firm. Nevertheless, I managed to hold on to her for full another fifteen minutes by resorting to an immediate cup of tea. She insisted that she usually detests it. She seemed disturbed."

Blackburn was silent. Myra waited a moment and then went on with a tactful disregard.

"Blackburn, she is very lovely. I thought I never saw her so sweet and genuine as she seemed to-day. She has been many times to see me. But to-day there was something about her that was particularly appealing — an earnestness that the casual acquaintance might not suspect. Her airy little ways are deceiving."

Blackburn looked up from the fire, his eyes glowing with grateful feeling.

"How well you understand her!" he exclaimed involuntarily.

"Oh, there's a great deal in Cicely. I have always known that. My only fear is —"

She hesitated, seeing that he watched her in a kind of breathless suspense.

"Your only fear is —" he repeated eagerly.

"Mrs. Overton," she answered with reluctance.

Blackburn's face grew troubled.

"I have thought of that," he said gravely.

"It is a case of government without consent of the governed," remarked Myra, looking steadily away from him. "Really, I have never seen such influence as Mrs. Overton is able to wield over her children, her entire household — everyone in fact who comes at all within her radius. It is something almost hypnotic."

"Cicely is stronger than you think." The words broke from him with the impetuosity of one who seeks to force conviction.

"She will probably have special need of strength," replied Myra in a tone of sadness which jarred painfully upon him. She saw his disturbance and added lightly:

"She was a good deal put out over a dinner for this evening which her mother had arranged without even consulting her."

His face altered. A light was beginning to dawn upon him.

"Did she happen to mention in whose honour the dinner is given?" he asked.

"In honour of Mr. Michael Broomer, of New York, who arrived last evening."

"Michael Broomer! The name sounds familiar. Where can I have heard it?"

"Do you remember two very illiterate old people, a man and his wife, who used to keep a little candy shop on Main street when you were a child? This is their son. About eighteen years ago the boy went away from here, with only a few dollars in the world. He has now many millions. I read a sketch of him in one of the Eastern papers not long ago. The article described him as a plain man, with little of the education of books, but a person of rare sagacity in business and an immense amount of energy and determination — the usual commonplace expressions for the self-made man. He has traveled a good deal. Cicely met him abroad in an accidental way. I believe he was able to show her aunt and herself some small courtesy.

Blackburn did not seem greatly to enjoy the description of Mr. Michael Broomer. She saw the cloud gather over his features, and what had before been suspicion merely became certainty. Her heart ached for him, but she went on unrelentingly:

"It is evident that Mrs. Overton is disposed to be very civil towards him and to ignore his plainness, the old Broomers, candy shop and all. Fortunately for such a course, the two old people have been dead for many years.

Blackburn's face was very still. He scarcely seemed

to hear her last words. Still, she knew that he had heard them, and that it was best that they should be said. He sat a few moments longer, looking thoughtfully into the fire. Then he rose abruptly.

"Myra," he said, a little unsteadily, his eyes meeting hers in a look that was at the same time a confession and an appeal, "if ever she should be in any serious trouble, if she should need someone like yourself to lean upon for—for strength, will you promise to stand by her?"

She put forth her hands. There was a very true and steadfast light in her eyes. But her face was troubled.

"Through everything I am her friend—and yours," she said.

CHAPTER VI

"THE WORLD'S HONOURS"

"Has it ever occurred to you that you are inclined to be a little indolent?"

Cicely's thick lashes veiled a subtle gleam of humour.

"Mama, what are pink kimonos for?" she asked with well-feigned innocence. "Won't you sit down?" She turned languidly on the lounge drawn up in front of her bedroom fire, laid aside her book, and proceeded to shift the pillows more comfortably. It took some time.

Mrs. Overton sat down in a large, chintz-covered chair opposite. "I am sure I don't know," she responded promptly, "unless it is to encourage lazy people in their idleness. I never had on one of the things in my life. I havn't time to loll. Besides, they are utterly hideous. Why should you wish to convert yourself into a Japanese?"

"I was under the impression that the effect was charming. How unsparing of my vanity!"

Mrs. Overton surveyed her daughter critically, with a thoroughly cool, impartial stare, and as one who has reasons for not overlooking a single point. The girl's gay beauty, with its unexpected hint of seriousness, seemed to rise in a kind of defiance to meet the test. There was something anxious and unrelenting in that prolonged scrutiny with which Cicely was familiar from much repetition and under which she invariably flinched, though the result had always been most flattering to herself. Mrs. Overton leaned back in her chair with half-closed eyelids.

She was a large, well-formed woman, with a very aristocratic bearing, and with an abundance of iron-gray hair rolled back from a low, beautiful brow. She was only a little too stout, being possessed of a will that was sufficiently strong and all-embracing to include even a strict attention to all minor things of life; and she would have scorned to allow herself to become ungraceful. Her features were regular, though scarcely bordering upon the classical, and the expression in her gray eyes was shrewd and a trifle hard. Her manner was very firm and assured; one felt that she had convictions which she lived up to with unfaltering zeal. She wore a steel gray cashmere gown that fitted her to perfection, and she was dressed carefully, with the utmost attention to detail. She had a fine colour which in this moment was heightened by a secret displeasure.

Presently her gaze wandered away absently from Cicely's plump, outstretched figure to Cicely's toggery scattered heedlessly here and there. The room assuredly did not present a very orderly appearance, but there was a careless grace, an individuality in its confusion which served as confirmation of the thought already in Mrs. Overton's mind. There was that in the girlish baubles and paraphernalia and belongings generally that seemed to give a tone of luxuriousness, as something inseparable from their owner.

But the room was very simple in its Southern furnishings. There was a mahogany bedstead in one corner with a canopy draped in dotted swiss; a chest-of-drawers; a cheval-glass; a small dressing-table with an oval mirror; and a low rocking chair, all of old, beautifully carved wood. Several white goat skin rugs were spread about on the polished floor; and there were innumerable photographs and pictures collected during Cicely's foreign travels. However, it was not in any of these things, but rather in some stray bit of colour, an Indian shawl thrown across a chair, a pink slipper peeping out from the folds of the girl's loose gown, or a delicate undergarment, soft and web-like, revealed imperfectly to view, that one caught the dominant note. Mrs. Overton's eyes returned from their survey, and rested with a slightly softened look on the girlish form, with its exquisite curves, its undeniable grace. Beauty surely should have always its proper setting, otherwise — she was thinking — it was like a jewel lost in a dust-heap, or worn on a grimy finger. But she had been a good deal puzzled by Cicely's ways of late. Was she to be confronted with anything so monstrous as resistance to authority? It occurred to her that it would be just as well to set about tightening the reins at once.

"How many calls have you paid this week, Cicely?" she asked severely, keeping well away from the subject that was engrossing her thoughts. "None, I venture to say. It really is most impolitic. Your father and I are much disturbed that you should appear neglectful of any of our old friends who have shown you the courtesy of calling upon you. Have you been to see Mrs. Oats?"

Cicely's shoulders went up in a shrug. "I went, but she was not at home. Besides, she simply detests me," she supplemented ruefully, with an audacious little laugh in which there was nothing of resentment, but a good deal of covert amusement.

Mrs. Overton was not overburdened with a sense of humour.

"You should go again," she replied firmly. "We are under a positive obligation to Mrs. Oats. And what do you mean by saying that she detests you? Surely with all your social experience and knowledge of the world you should be able to steer clear of offence with a woman like Virginia Oats. You know her absurd vanity and weaknesses. Why tread upon her toes?"

"It was not my fault. It was the major's. He

introduced me to her as the Queen of Hearts," remarked Cicely, drolly.

"The major is often very rediculous. A young girl cannot afford to have enemies — one is too many."

"I have two," said Cicely, resignedly.

"Two?"

"Mrs. Oats is one, Mrs. Bellows is two. I really must hie myself to a call on Mrs. Bellows."

"Mrs. Bellows can wait. It will not be the first time," replied Mrs. Overton, dryly.

"But she doesn't like to wait, she told me so, ominously; and you know she came to see us, Mama, in a royal purple velvet, with a train a quarter of a mile long, and with the Tower of Babel on her head. Shall we ignore such elegance?"

"Yes; ignore it — for the present, at least. And don't be given to exaggeration, Cicely: it is never in good form."

Mrs. Overton sat twisting the rings on her fingers. Presently she turned with directness.

"Why did you refuse to see Mr. Broomer when he called a few moments ago?" she asked.

"I sent word that I had an engagement for this afternoon. It was strictly true," replied Cicely, evasively.

Mrs. Overton bit her lips.

"I am much afraid that you are inclined to be a

little indolent," she said, shaking her head. "A young woman in your position should be either a social success or an artistic success. I have always said that your forte is society. I don't mean society in any small provincial way: I mean a brilliant career based upon a kind of scientific understanding of social life, and carried on with deliberation and perfect grace — in short, distinction such as was reached by certain famous women in the old days of the Parisian salons. I regard you as particularly well fitted for Washington life."

Cicely raised herself slightly and looked away. The colour had deepened painfully in her cheeks. She put up her hands quickly, as if oppressed, and drew out the jeweled scarf pin at her throat, letting the loose rose-coloured gown fall away from her neck, which had also grown suddenly pink.

"Mama, I loathe Society — Society with a capital S."

Mrs. Overton stared coldly. Cicely would not meet her eyes.

"I know that I am a bitter disappointment to you," she went on hurriedly. "The training I have had has produced anything but the result you sought. I think there must be something perverse and contradictory in me. It has not fitted me for the career you speak of. Such a life only seems to me all shams and hollowness. Had I never gone away from home I might have reached out ignorantly for these things — most probably they would have beckoned to me, as to most young girls. Now I know; and I — I can hardly think how to express it, but I have come to realize that the simple things of life are the best things, and that to be worldly-minded is to be not only un-Christian, but positively vulgar."

Though she spoke the words calmly, they had evidently cost her an effort, and there was a pitiful shrinking in her eyes. Mrs. Overton's features hardened.

"But what would you do? You have shown no special aptitude for art," keeping a firm grip upon her theory. "Eventually you will get married, of course. Girls of your stamp invariably do. I venture to say that you have had ten lovers where Gertrude will have one. As a matter of fact she is the superior of the two — of all my children in fact. She is more like me. You are like your father; you have inherited his dreamy, chimerical way of looking at life, and it is necessary that you should have someone of a strong will to guide you, else there's no telling what wild, reckless thing you may do. Marriage with most young girls is simply a matter of propinquity. Sentiment, or rather, sentimentality is usually ready; but what is really needed is a little wise forethought on the part of their directors to see that it is turned into the proper channels. There is nothing for you here. You should have a wider field."

"Oh, I don't want any field — I just want a little rest," said Cicely, sadly.

"You don't know what you want. As I have told you before, you have considerable ease and tact. I have seen you manage several difficult situations recently in a manner that was really most creditable. I was quite proud of you. In this your Aunt Catherine agrees with me. She even goes so far as to call you clever. I am not sure. You have too great a tendency toward ridicule. No doubt it is perfectly harmless; but ridicule is never sure ground. The wise woman always avoids making people afraid of her. She is unwilling to risk even a little for the sake of a brilliant *bon mot*; and it is history that human nature eventually hates what it fears — from a mouse to a monarch."

"But I am neither a mouse nor a monarch," put in Cicely, with a grimace, "and nobody was ever afraid of me in my life."

"In that you are wrong. When you begin your silly teasing I have sometimes seen a look of actual terror on Mr. Broomer's features."

"Is it that? I had thought it only an amiable superiority to all such antics. He has always reminded me at these times of nothing so much as a good-natured mastiff solemnly regarding the gambols of a gay and festive kitten."

Mrs. Overton looked straight ahead of her.

"He was just leaving for Virginia this afternoon when he called. He had received a telegram which compelled him to go a day sooner than he had intended."

"So he has gone?" Cicely's tone was somewhat enigmatical.

"I heard his voice out in the hall," continued Mrs. Overton, "and went to speak to him. He seemed very much hurt indeed that you would not see him."

Cicely laughed. "He should not have been. I surely have done my duty by Mr. Broomer for the last three days. I have been seeing him morning, noon, and night."

"I did the best I could to put you in the proper light, and I hope I smoothed things over a little. Still, it was altogether proper that you should have seen him. He is very shy and uncertain. If I had not gone out to speak to him and asked him to come and sit a while with your father and me in the library (Ben had said I was not at home) I am quite sure we would have seen the last of Mr. Broomer. He remarked on leaving that he would be back again in Kentucky in about ten days."

Cicely was silent. Her mother watched her narrowly, noting the way the delicate little tendrils of light brown hair rippled away from the low brow, the firm white throat, and above all the mingled wilfulness and dread on the beautiful face.

"Your father and I are very much pleased with Mr. Broomer," she said abruptly. "There is something strong, powerful even, about him. We were contrasting him with other young men here — young Dilson and Blackburn Blair. We both concluded, at least I did — your father always expresses himself so cautiously,— that in the qualities that bring success he is very much superior to either of those young men. Of course he has not the high-breeding nor the culture of Blackburn Blair, nor the graceful manners of Frederick Dilson, who I must admit has always something very nice and agreeable to say. But in spite of all that, Mr. Broomer has completely won me. He is so steady. He is not likely to be swept off his feet by any wild, fanatical notions such as have recently taken possession of Blackburn."

"If you mean politics, I can tell you that Mr. Broomer is very much interested indeed. He is reported to have spent more than ten thousand dollars in the last presidential election."

"But it was on the right side."

"You mean the Republican side?" asked Cicely, viciously. "That was Mr. Broomer's side in the last election."

"Nothing of the kind. What nonsense are you talking? Mr. Broomer is a Democrat, he told me, as his father was before him.

"Nevertheless, the son voted the Republican ticket. I know that. He has large railroad and coal mining interests and a great deal of money in United States Government bonds."

Mrs. Overton turned a little fiercely.

"What absurd teaching have you been lending yourself to? It would seem that Mr. Blair is not above numbering young women also among his converts. His ideas are just about suited to the intelligence of silly girls who are caught by such sentimental nonsense. I shall take the first opportunity to inform him that you do not stand in need of any instruction from him in these matters."

"You are too late. I am already instructed. Blackburn and I talk politics until you would think I was to be the future governor of Kentucky and it was highly proper that I receive the right training."

Mrs. Overton leaned forward.

"Cicely," she said with much positiveness, "you see a great deal more of that young man than is agreeable to me. I will tell you frankly what I never told you before: neither your father nor I ever liked his father. We have always held him greatly responsible for the fact that Kentucky failed to go with the Confederacy.

Of course he is a very scholarly, elegant old gentleman, with a most plausible manner. Anyone can see that. But he has not good judgment. He is never on the winning side. After the war, if he had sided with the Republicans, every one said that he would have been given a place in the Cabinet or on the Supreme Bench of the United States. Instead of that, in a half-hearted way he united himself with the Democrats, who never forgave him. As ardent Confederates your father and I still resent his course very deeply. I was only a young girl when the war closed, but of course every Southerner's lot was affected by the outcome. Your father lost everything. His father was a very large slaveholder."

"So was Judge Blair, was he not? I can't see anything but unselfishness in his course."

"It is unselfish to show a little practical sense now and then, and to look out for your own interests. If you don't, you may be sure that no one else is going to attend to them for you. It is like father like son in this case, I am beginning to think. Blackburn seems destined to make the same sort of mistakes that Judge Blair has made through life. I can never understand such people. I don't know what to call them, in spite of all their cleverness."

"We call such people patriots, do we not?" inquired Cicely, smiling.

"You may call them what you please, provided I am

not asked to call one of them my son-in-law," said Mrs. Overton, with decision.

Cicely's face suddenly grew roguish. "You would prefer—Mr. Broomer, perhaps?" she asked, with a somewhat provoking assumption of guilelessness.

Mrs. Overton was distinctly irritated. There were moments when Cicely's audacity surprised and disconcerted her. She would have liked better not to show her hand so openly, but she replied promptly and with the utmost coolness: "I should distinctly prefer Mr. Broomer."

"In that case," said Cicely, musingly, "I wonder if I might not have, instead of the ancient lozenge it now delights me to use upon my note paper, a nice little candy shop neatly designed and set forth in bold relief? Don't you think it would be sweetly suggestive? Now with Blackburn everything would be different: one might simply blaze with heraldic insignia."

"In your position you can afford to marry whom you choose."

"But I thought you had very fixed ideas upon the subject of a girl's marrying within her own sphere?" remarked Cicely, mischievously.

"I had. But in recent years I have altered my views somewhat on that point. Your Aunt Catherine writes me that she also has undergone a similar change of sentiment in such matters. Everyone respects the courageous carver of his own fortune, the man who comes up from the people and who hews his way boldly to the front, asking no odds of anyone, and cutting down everything in his way."

"Is he swashbuckler — or one of our mountain feudists? I believe *he* also is somewhat given to carving, though he usually trusts more to his faithful Winchester than to the bowie-knife."

"Don't be silly. Of course in my day women married strictly within their own circle. Class distinctions were very vigourous, and people seldom thought of breaking through. Occasionally the thing did happen even then. But in the time of your grandmother there was no laxity whatever. To guard against all blundering, they usually married relatives, sometimes first cousins even. I have often heard my mother say that when she married your grandfather, who happened not to be related to her in any way, it was thought by her family and connections that she had done a thing that was hardly respectable. It was a particularly narrow view, but quite customary. Now —"

"We have changed all that," put in Cicely, with gay good-humour.

Mrs. Overton was puzzled. She dropped the subject abruptly.

"I left your father down stairs going over some of his accounts," she remarked dismally. "He is nearly distracted. He doesn't see anything but ruin ahead of us, and I'm inclined to agree with him. That loss we had in the Kansas City bank has simply destroyed us. We think we can't possibly give Gertrude another year at Bryn Mawr, and as for the other children they will most likely never see the inside of a college. I am sure that we shall never be able to do for any of them as we have done for you. People usually expend themselves upon the eldest. I don't know why it is that things have got into such a muddle with us, in spite of all my efforts and good management. Your father is always allowing excellent chances to make a fortune slip through his hands. Just the other day there came an opportunity which might have made us entirely comfortable for life, if he had only had the courage to embrace it. But he lacks enterprise, surety, everything in fact that would help him to succeed. He was never anything of a financier."

"Poor Papa!" Cicely stirred uneasily, and the words broke from her with genuine pain and pity. "What a mercy that grandfather is so good to us," she added quickly. The vivacity had completely gone out of her face. The pleading, half-timid look had come back into her eyes.

"Your grandfather is very good of course, but," Mrs. Overton's voice was suddenly lowered, "he is very much straightened — more than he knows. It would be cruel to tell him the exact condition of affairs; he is now so old and so easily upset. Of course the present state of things has come about mainly through us. He made, on his own account, two or three bad investments, it is true. I confess I thought them fine chances at the time, and strongly urged him on. But they went wrong. Still the main trouble has come upon him through us. He thinks me horribly extravagant, but he is usually willing to humour me, believing himself to be a very wealthy man. As a matter of fact he is absurdly far from being wealthy, as wealth goes nowadays. No one in this old Southern town has anything to speak of, and people like us are always in debt or utterly poverty-stricken. I really am at my wits end. When the January bills come pouring in, I don't see how I am to stand it. Without the ceaseless economy that I practice and the forethought we would simply be, like nearly all the rest of the old families here, without a dollar."

Cicely raised herself and looked her mother full in the eyes.

"Mother," she said appealingly, "why should we obtrude vulgar commercialism into our simple Southern life? That is the way everyone talks these days. I hoped that when I came back to Kentucky there would be an end. But it is here like everywhere else. I have never seen a town so changed. The repose, the dignity, the fine patrician independence, that gave to the place its unique charm, seem giving way. This mad rush for money is sickening. It stifles me. As for us, let us try to live more simply, always within our means. I am willing to do without anything — almost everything —"

Mrs. Overton broke into a hard little laugh. "*You?*" she cried. "Look at that pink slipper. Your Aunt Catherine should have inured you to hardships instead of to such luxuries, with your views. As it is the mischief is done. I leave you to find your way out."

She half-rose and then sank back into her chair. Cicely had begun to move about the room. "You don't mind if I dress?" she asked.

The girl's expression was a little difficult to fathom. She seemed scarcely conscious of another's presence. Mrs. Overton sat watching her like a cat with its eye upon a mouse. At length Cicely went to a closet and took down a blue cloth walking-suit. She glanced toward the clock.

"You are going out?" asked Mrs. Overton in surprise.

"Yes, Mama."

"Is there any hurry? You skipped a button there. How well that colour suits you! You must have tried to match your eyes. How does it happen that I have never seen you wear that gown?"

"Aunt Catherine selected it," replied Cicely, from

the depths of the closet. "I have worn it only once or twice. So glad you like it. Ah, there's the bell, and I shall be late of course. I simply can't find my hat."

"Don't you think it would be rather awkward if you should happen to meet Mr. Broomer?" suggested Mrs. Overton. "Though I should like him to see you in that gown."

Cicely turned. "Awkward? Not in the least. Why?"

"You know you refused to see him. There was plenty of time."

"Oh, I shan't bother. Most likely we shall not see him. He will be thinking about his train. He told me he never failed to be on time in his life. Besides, there are several people he will probably wish to see before leaving. We will go straight out Broadway."

Something made Mrs. Overton hesitate a moment. "Isn't it a little late for a walk — nearly five?" she added. "These afternoons are so short. Who is going with you?"

Cicely paused an instant on the threshold, but Mrs. Overton could not quite make out the look in her daughter's eyes. Was it defiance or submission, she asked herself most anxiously. Cicely turned.

"You need not be uneasy," she said; "I shall be with Mr. Blair."

CHAPTER VII

A TOIL OF GRACE

When Cicely entered the library she found Blackburn standing near the fire on the side next the window apparently deeply interested in the examination of something he had taken from the mantel. His back was toward her, and his head was bent in an attitude of such abstraction as to render him completely unmindful of everything save the small object before him. She could not see what it was, and she stood for a moment in a sort of whimsical hesitation, wondering, smiling, but only half-amused at the earnestness revealed in every line of his stalwart figure. She laughed softly, and in the laugh there was an almost reckless spirit of provocation.

He turned quickly, and as he came toward her still holding in his hand the thing that had so absorbed him, the colour flamed into her cheeks. For as the firelight flashed full upon it, she caught sight of a little oval frame containing a photograph of herself that she had forgotten. Her lips parted in a slow smile. She raised her eyes to his, and there was something contradictory, and not to be easily read, in their violet depths. His face was rather pale.

"Cicely, will you give me this picture?" he asked, making his request in a matter-of-fact voice, and going straight to the point without any preamble whatever.

She threw him a merry glance.

"Blackburn, do you want it very much?" she inquired in precisely the same tone.

"I do."

"Let me see which one you have. Grandfather was always demanding a new one. There are as many as if I were a professional beauty. I come upon them everywhere, and they confront me like the ghosts of my misdeeds."

She held out her hand, but he shook his head, laughing. "I can't trust you," he said.

"Oh, I know. It's a little photograph I had taken one summer in Paris. I was longing for home. I have on a white mull gown cut low in the neck, and I am wearing a fichu à la Princesse de Lamballe, and there is a rose in my hair. And in spite of all such frivolities I look as the Princesse may have looked when she knew that her doom was sealed. I don't care for the picture. The look of tragedy does not become my features. Let me have that back, and I will give you another one, maybe — some of these days — ever, ever so much better looking."

But Blackburn was not to be beguiled by such promises.

"Will you give it to me, Cicely?" he asked again, and there was a tremor in his voice that made him seem strangely boyish all at once. "I do want it," he added, as he took a step toward her, "this particular one, more than any other I have ever seen of you. Won't you let me have it?"

Cicely drew on one of her gloves sedately, and her whole attention seemed necessary to complete the process. "You are easily satisfied," she said softly at length, as she bent her head lower over the other hand.

"I am not easily satisfied," he replied quickly.

"Aren't you? I thought you were. Then you could not be contented with half a loaf?"

There was a subtle allurement, a suggestiveness in the words that thrilled him through and through. His gaze was suddenly riveted upon her.

"I could not," he said gravely and with sternly suppressed passion. "I should want the whole loaf — every morsel, every crumb."

"Since you are not a compromiser, I suppose then I am to consider myself very much flattered indeed that you covet that poor little representation of myself. It is an exceedingly modest request — I have half a mind to grant it."

"You will give it to me?"

"Are you quite sure that you want it?"

He was silent.

"I really am in doubt," she remarked lightly, and with a shrug. But as she raised her eyes to his something in his face compelled her to drop her cloak of banter.

"Oh, of course you may have it, Blackburn," she said quickly.

With a simple "thank you" he put the picture in his pocket and followed her as she led the way to the door.

There was a little wind astir and the wintry air was keen. Cicely drew in a deep breath as they went down the steps. At the gate she paused a moment and stretched forth her arms with a gesture of delight. "Oh, I like it — I like it!" she exclaimed. "It surely is some magic drink."

They set forth at a lively pace. Her eyes were sparkling, and the wind was blowing the tendrils of hair about her temples and deepening the wild-rose colour in her cheeks — converting her into a more willing bacchante with every draught of the wine-like air.

He stole a swift glance at her. The change in her was working a transformation also in him. His spirits rose. They walked a block or two in silence.

"There is nothing delights me like a scuffle with the wind," she said presently as they turned into a broad street. "But, 'I was ever a fighter.' Blackburn, do you think I have a strong will?"

She asked the question with a naïvety that caused him to throw back his head and break into a hearty laugh. "I have sometimes thought so — to my sorrow," he replied.

But her face was suddenly quite serious. "And yet there are influences — always influences. How is it possible for any of us to know that we shall prove strong against them? I rather think, though, in my own case, when I give in, it is because there is something in the force that is brought against me that coincides with my own volition. In other words, I am always half-convinced. But let us walk faster."

"We might run," he suggested gayly, refusing to fall in with her altered mood.

"So we might. But it would be a little surprising; and then you know you never would be able to catch me, and that would be rather mortifying for you."

"Catch you! Wouldn't I? You just try me, Atalanta, and see. I rather think I could manage it—and without resorting to the tactics of Hippomenes, either."

She threw him a sidelong glance, and her eyes were dancing again. The nature that is complex is seldom wholly sincere. It is apt to be self-deceived; and yet in that moment she was conscious of a readjustment to life, a sense of wholesomeness of attitude that was a comfortable offset to many things.

"I feel just like a little girl — and a bad little girl at

that," she cried. "Blackburn, do you remember the day we ran off? We went straight out Broadway, and we never stopped until we found a lovely green woods where there were quantities of wild flowers. We were hunting for the Garden of Eden, and we were so annoyed when grandfather came lumbering innocently along in his funny old coach and spied us. Didn't he go for us, though?"

"He surely did. I thought I had never seen an old gentleman with such an alarming command of English explosives in my life."

"But you made him your friend then forever. 'He's a gentleman, sir, every inch of him, and the son of a gentleman', he said, when he carried you back to your father. 'But he needs a thrashing.' It was all my fault, you remember, though you took every bit of the blame. I told you that I knew it — I knew it for a certainty that the Garden of Eden was just outside the town near a most beautiful spot that I had often caught glimpses of from the carriage window; and I believed that even if the angel were still there, barring the way with his flaming sword, he would like us a little, and maybe be sorry for us and let us in, when he knew that we had walked the whole long way, and were so very tired."

"It wasn't altogether sound philosophy," observed Blackburn, with his quiet smile. "Nevertheless, it is apt to be only the footsore and the weary that win their Eden in this life. I am willing to work for mine — and to wait for it. And I shall not mind the dust of the highway, nor the thorn pricks, if only I win it at last." He turned toward her with an unmistakable light in his eyes. "Cicely," he said in a voice that quivered with earnestness but was yet quiet and determined, "we are on our way to it again. Do you think we shall find it? It will depend on you."

She drew back, and looked away. Her steps lagged. She felt his eyes upon her, and her heart was beating desperately. She could not speak. Could it be, she was asking herself, in the sway of a tumultuous rush of feeling, could it be, in spite of all her doubts and fears, there was yet in Love some vital and eternal element, beautiful enough to withstand the thorns and dust of life? Her brain refused to consider. She felt as if suddenly caught up by some tremendous force, resistless as death, yet glorious, that bore her along against her judgment and her will to some sweet haven, where the awakening would be — what?

In Blackburn, it is true, she beheld a lover as ardent and as devoted as the most loyal of her dreams, one who seemed scarce other than her own ideal knight; and although, at times, in his attitude toward the great conflicts that awaited him, she was able to discern a heroism which she could foresee would lift him far beyond the plane of the average political contestant, there was yet that in his complete consecration of himself to his aims that filled her with dismay. She stole a brief glance at him.

"It is getting late," she said presently.

"Must we go back?" he cried ruefully. "We had almost found it."

"Age should teach you more discretion. I enticed you once."

"You entice me now; and time cannot teach me not to follow you. Cicely, you know that if ever I am to find my Eden in this world, you, and you only, will show it to me."

Her chin was buried in her furs, and she was looking straight ahead of her.

"You will be far too busy to indulge in such idle fancies in the coming years," she declared.

"Too busy! Is a man ever too busy to think of — some things?"

But she shook her head. "Some men are not. You — you are like Atlas — you have a good deal on your shoulders."

"But I shouldn't mind having a little more," he responded, with a short laugh.

She dropped her eyes. "Blackburn," she said presently, "do you really hope to do anything for a world gone wrong by the way of politics? It is such a grimy door. How can you endure to pass through it?"

His face altered strangely. "I shall hope to do my little part," he answered simply.

"Oh, but the ignominy, the injustice that will be heaped upon you! And it all seems such a pitiful waste of your powers, the more I think of it."

He turned a startled gaze upon her, but was silent.

"When I think of how many, many may have to go under before the things you believe in can be established —" she began. But he put in quickly:

"The wrong of life — the evil of life can only be wiped out through the medium of sacrifice. It has been so in all ages. There must be always the atonement of blood."

His voice was low and freighted with a profound feeling. It thrilled and awed her to silence.

Night had fallen, and the lights of the town had been turned on. Carriages and persons on foot were hurrying homeward in all directions. The gong of a trolley car sounding in her ears jarred discordantly. She put up her hand wildly. The wind had subsided; and at a whim of hers they were walking slowly out in the center of the street. All at once she pressed nearer to him.

"Blackburn," she whispered breathing quickly, and in a half-frightened tone whose alluring sweetness was to linger with him long after, "have you fully decided? Is there no other way for you but this hard, hard road? I *wish* there were!"

He came to an abrupt standstill. For a moment the two stood facing each other. They had paused under an electric light, and as she raised her eyes to his she drew back at sight of his sternly wretched face. An instant afterward a carriage rolled quickly past, and out of it someone leaned and bowed.

Cicely turned. It was Michael Broomer.

CHAPTER VIII

SWEET BELLS JANGLED OUT OF TUNE

It was the last night of the year and the major was giving a dinner — a dinner of twenty-four, which had set out to be a dinner of only twelve. He was at a loss to explain to himself how it had come about that there were so many; for assuredly it had been his intention to invite no more than eleven. But when he went over the list there was no question that there they all were, three-and-twenty names, as shown by an eager acceptance, to say nothing of the sharp reminder of full a dozen more whom it had hurt him sadly to leave out. As usual his heart had expanded and it was necessary that his table should do likewise.

His home had been beautifully decked for the occasion. Fires blazed from every room, and somewhere, not too near, there was music, and the dining room, lighted with wax candles in sconces and old silver candelabra, was garlanded with holly and mistletoe and laurel; and at each plate there was a little spray of rosemary which the major had placed there with his own hands.

He was in excellent spirits, and something of the peace and the poetry of the time seemed reflected in his fine features, as he sat presiding with great dignity at the head of his festal board.

Mrs. Oats, wearing her most gracious smile and a very becoming light green evening gown, sat on his right, keeping up an easy flow of conversation, and maintaining a tactful supervision. Next her sat Mr. Michael Broomer, who had just returned from Virginia, and who, at Mrs. Overton's demands, had been among the last to receive one of the major's invitations.

Cicely was at the extreme end of the table to the left. The major had arranged the cards with considerable deliberation, and he was rather proud of the result. He saw to it that Blackburn sat next to her, though she went in with Colonel Johnstone, and that Frederick Dilson, like Michael Broomer, was at a good safe distance. He was not at all sure of Cicely's wishes in the matter, but he did not propose to be a party to Blackburn's discomfiture, whatever they might be. And in such a case the major felt that one could always trust him to display the proper finesse. He had whispered to Cicely, as she entered the drawing-room," I am going to give my dear friend Colonel Johnstone over to your tender mercies this evening. Will you put up with a dull old married man?" And that is how he had managed it.

But Cicely had outwitted him. His little scheme

turned out a dismal failure. Dinner was about half over when he discovered his mistake.

The colonel, who he thought could be depended upon to give main attention to the plate before him, to the major's surprise was talking incessantly, while Cicely, with her head thrown back and an expression of vivacious attention in her laughing eyes, was urging him on from anecdote to anecdote, and listening apparently with the keenest relish. Blackburn's handsome face, slightly flushed, was very somber as he sat talking to the chattering young woman at his side. "Bless me!" said the major to himself in consternation, "what's the little witch up to now?"

His eyes wandered anxiously down the glittering table, and rested upon the two with a sharp misgiving. It was obvious that things were going sadly a-glee.

But Cicely appeared in happiest mood. Her gayety scarcely seemed forced, though there was a hint of recklessness that did not escape the major's watchful eye. She was looking particularly well in white and gold, her smooth shoulders showing delicately pink, like the lining of a sea-shell, against the foam-like sheerness of her gown.

Was there not exaggeration in her mirth, he kept asking himself from time to time, or was she really as careless as she seemed? Once she turned and made some remark to Blackburn, and he caught the look, disturbed, wondering, painfully eager in the young man's eyes. The major quickly looked away.

In man's helplessness and denseness he usually turns to woman. The major turned to Mrs. Oats. Perhaps it did not speak very well for his powers of discernment that in all the years of his acquaintance with her he had never found her out. But cleverer men than he have been deceived by women with whom flattery has been studied as an art. The major was not a vain man, but it pleased him to think that Mrs. Oats both admired and understood him. She had been finding conversation for the last five minutes with Mr. Broomer decidedly difficult. She welcomed the major beamingly. Already she had divined his uneasiness, having followed his glance to Cicely's radiant face.

"It looks as if that pleasant little plan of yours were not progressing," she whispered very softly, with a barely perceptible nod in the direction she wished to indicate.

The major shook his head.

"I'm afraid I'm a poor hand as a match-maker," he said sadly. "But what is to be expected of an old bachelor like me?"

Mrs. Oats looked down until her lashes quite swept her cheek.

"Perhaps you don't entirely understand the material

you have to deal with in this case. Young girls are often heartless — and nearly always capricious. It is usually not until one has seen a good deal of life, don't you know, that one begins to have a true realization of the meaning of a great affection. And you ought to be able to understand that in this instance there is a — what shall I call it? — a shallowness? No, that is not quite it — help me to a word —"

"I am sure that she is not shallow," observed the major, loyally, yet disturbed.

"No — no — one would not think of calling her that," she cried sweetly. "How dull of me! But just a wee bit — worldly — don't you think? Or ambitious, perhaps?"

"Ambitious?" repeated the major, thoughtfully, and with aristocratic lack of comprehension; "if she is ambitious, as you think, it would appear that there could not be opportunity for a nobler ambition than apparently is being offered her by my young friend."

Mrs. Oats laughed. "Ah, but the tinsel! Are you also sure that such things do not count for anything with her?" she asked with her usual happy faculty of ignoring the most important circumstance of her own life and the motives that had controlled with her. "It seems to me that we should not expect too much. It is hardly fair, don't you know, to demand that persons should be extraordinary when, after all, they are not at all remarkable in any way. Now I have always said that it would be a great sacrifice on his part if she should ever marry him. He is like you, who are so free from defects of character yourself that you are wholly incapable of discovering the flaws. But if all I hear is true,'' she added under her breath, "her decision is already made."

The major changed the topic. But Mrs. Oats had sown a doubt in his mind — which was precisely what she had meant to do.

At the end of the evening he suffered another pang, which woke a dull sense of pain in his gentle heart, and would not be quieted. It was occasioned by a little tableau that took place on the stairway, which he witnessed from his post in the drawing-room, where he stood bidding farewell to his guests, and making to each the elaborate and elegantly formal speech which seemed to him required in view of the merging of the old year into the new.

Presently he caught sight of Cicely with several others coming down the stairs—Cicely, enwrapped in a long white evening cloak, gay, sparkling, and debonair, followed at a little distance by Michael Broomer. On the young man's strong, kindly features there was something that the major did not like: a look of confidence, if not of actual proprietorship. At the foot of the steps stood Blackburn Blair, tall and still, waiting very quietly. The graceful air of distinction and the unconscious pride of bearing that had come down to him through generations of high-bred men and women, seemed strikingly in evidence, in contrast with the square, homely figure on the stair. His eyes were fixed steadily on the girl's face, with a look that betrayed a complete unconsciousness of any other presence save her own. His manner was very controlled, but there was a hint of deep and well-nigh over-mastering feeling, despite his outward calm. The major saw her shrink and draw back from the power of that long, unrelenting gaze. Then he heard him ask that he be allowed to drive home with her, and saw Michael Broomer turn quickly as if to speak to someone just behind him. There was a pause, a moment's hesitation, an awkwardness almost, and then the group parted and with a laugh that sounded mirthless, yet sadly sweet, to the major's sympathetic ears, Cicely passed on, and out into the night — with Michael Broomer at her side.

CHAPTER IX

MAJOR ORLANDO WISE'S HEART-SECRET

Half an hour later, the major and the colonel were enjoying a quiet talk over their pipes in a little room adjoining the library, the gay guests having departed. A wood fire blazed on the hearth, and on the small, spindle-legged table in the center of the room there was a carved silver stand which held a cutglass decanter of unique design containing about a pint of fine old Kentucky whiskey; near by there was a salver with spoons and glasses which had just been used, a carafe half-filled with water, and bowls of ice and sugar. The two were not drinking men, as one usually understands the phrase, but they were of the old order, and in consequence rather suggestively unlike most of their young acquaintances of the better class, who despite their reputation to the contrary, seldom seem disposed, in ordinary intercourse, to resort to intoxicants of any kind. But with the major and the colonel, the decanter and its accompaniments were still a matter of course, and doubtless would have received due consideration, even if the table on which they stood had not been among the few ancestral relics which, after many vicissitudes of fortune, had finally drifted back into the major's hands — like floating fragments from a wreck.

There was a cloud of smoke, which almost obscured the various objects of the room, but spared the prevailing tone. Antlers, stuffed birds, heads of elk and buffalo, old-time rifles and modern shot-guns, dimly outlined, caught the eye at every turn. For the major was a mighty hunter before the Lord, and it delighted him to have about him the reminders of his pastime. From here, there, and everywhere almost — his own state, the mountains of Virginia and along the James, the prairies of the West and of Texas, from North Carolina, Florida — he had brought his trophies, and his beautiful setter dog, white with lemon markings and a pedigree as long and as distinguished as the major's own, dozed on the rug before them, and dreamed of former triumphs.

Their conversation, after the manner of Kentuckians, had turned upon political matters, wandering away from the discussion of an old but ever-present theme, the war between the states, to their more immediate differences relating to local and national affairs. For the Confederate colonel, by an odd contradiction, had recently become Republican, while the Federal major remained, as ever, the staunchest of Democrats. From Fort Donelson, where their two rival regiments had been engaged, and where the colonel had been taken prisoner, along with some fifteen hundred other Confederates, they had slowly traveled back to the present, without a jolt; and it was only when their talk touched upon current issues that the colonel, who was of a very mercurial disposition, and also inclined to be a little peppery, showed signs of losing his temper. Some reference had been made to young Blackburn Blair and discussion of his pronounced stand.

"I am expecting great things of the boy," remarked the major finally, as he relit his pipe. "He has impressed me as possessing in a marked degree those qualities which lead to a noble statesmanship. He could never develop into the mere politician. He is able to reach toward too large a view; and he's of the stuff that martyrs are made. I believe he'd be capable of sacrificing himself to a principle in a way that would seem almost archaic to our present selfishness."

The colonel slowly shook his head in opposition.

"I confess," he replied irritably, yet a little cautiously, in deference to his friend's opinion, "that at one time I thought of him very much as you do; I was interested in him heartily. But the young man has disappointed me. He seems to have gone off completely of late."

The major smoked a while in silence.

"It is hardly to be hoped," he said presently, "that

such ideas as young Blair has laid hold on are to be grasped immediately and fully. They go further than any mere political creed. They are fundamental, old as nature itself. For their very essence is to be found in that ancient warfare that has been going on through the ages: the Struggle for Life and the Struggle for the Life of Others — the conflict of Individualism with Altruism. Such men as he are prophets, guiding stars, we may call them, to lead their fellows out of the darkness of heathendom to the manger. But it is only wise men and lowly shepherds that recognize at once a heavenly sign."

It was in moments like these that the major revealed himself, and one saw — beneath ways that sometimes bordered upon the eccentric, if not the grotesque — the man, and beheld in him not only the might of conviction and of well-disciplined emotion, but also the student of contemporaneous thought.

Colonel Johnstone's bulky form moved uneasily in his chair. His blonde-bearded face was flushed.

"Theories, mere theories, my dear Lando," he remarked, with a shrug. "These questions are practical, not sentimental."

But the two old friends were not quite in the mood for one of their usual lengthy arguments to-night. Just half an hour before the New Year's bells had rung out, and their thoughts were tinged with a tender melancholy and a sense of nearness to each other which no difference of political view ever could affect.

Gradually their conversation lagged, until both grew silent, finally yielding themselves to a mute companionship which seemed to draw them closer together than any speech. The major sat gazing into the fire with that wistful, far away look in the eyes which bespeaks the peculiar loneliness of a spirit patient, but still unsatisfied. The colonel had often noted the look. Presently he took his pipe from his mouth and fixed his eyes upon his friend.

"Lando," he asked abruptly, "do you ever think of Milly?"

The major did not stir, nor seem to heed the question. He sat looking with the same wistful eyes into the fire, and several moments passed. After a while he rose and knocked the ashes from his pipe. His hand trembled a little and his face had grown white.

"Yes," he replied at length very softly, but without meeting the colonel's eyes — "I think of her — I very often think of her."

As he spoke the words a lingering note of sadness that rarely sounded in his soft Southern speech fell upon the colonel's ear.

I can recall the day we first saw her as distinctly as if it were yesterday," said Colonel Johnstone, after a pause. "It was the summer after our Sophomore year at Princeton, and I was spending a few days with you out at the old place, and we, poor young fools that we were, were arguing day and night about the war, and trying, God knows, to come together, though down in the heart of each of us we knew that the call had already sounded and that we must go our separate ways. Lord — Lord — what a wrench it was!"

The major suddenly put forth his hand and the other grasped it warmly.

"But nothing has ever come between us, old man, even the war could not do that," replied Major Wise, with simple fervour.

The colonel's thoughts were wandering back into many a blood-stained battlefield when all at once he drew himself up with a sigh.

"But we were speaking of Milly," he said.

And again the major was silent. But the colonel's mood was reminiscent.

"I do believe," he declared suddenly, breaking forth with his customary Southern emphasis, "she was the handsomest creature on God's green earth that day! — though she was only the daughter of your father's overseer, and if there was a miserable, worthless, vicious, back-biting brute in the state of Kentucky at that time (and God knows there was plenty of 'em) that fellow Sloan bore the palm. But he was good to Milly, you remember, sending her off to boarding-school, buying fine clothes for her, and trying to make a lady of her. Bless me, she *was* a lady! I defy anyone to say she wasn't as she looked that day."

Major Wise's features contracted a little, and he stirred uneasily.

"You forget," he remarked finally, "that afterwards I knew her — well."

The colonel stared uncertainly. Then he went on, mildly ruminating.

"But you didn't know her then; neither of us, I think, had ever seen her before that day. And Lord Above, who'd ever have expected anything that belonged to that rascal Sloan to look like that! We were sitting out under that old oak in front of the east porch at your father's — remember that old monarch, Lando? — never saw such a tree since I was born — and Milly passed. It was a Sunday morning, and she was on her way to the old Walnut Hill church half a mile away. She was all in white, and there were red poppies on her big straw hat. Somehow they seemed to set off her dark hair and eyes. She had the prettiest eyes I ever saw in a woman's head (begging Nan's pardon), just like a deer's, and I swear she looked a goddess and she walked a queen, as she passed us calmly by. I never saw greater dignity before or since. I remember that we both rose and stood uncovered until she was out of sight, not speaking a word."

He glanced down at his pipe and saw that it had gone out. But he went on.

"Lando," he said a trifle hurriedly, "in all the years I have never forgotten that look, the expression in your eyes. It was just as if a spear had pierced you through and through. But she never flickered. And yet, in thinking it all over, I have sometimes fancied that she too grew a little pale, though she merely inclined her head for the briefest possible space, and passed on. I was sure that she never saw me. It was as if you two out of the whole universe stood suddenly apart, alone with only God and nature."

The fire had burned low, but all at once there came a spasmodic flare from the hickory logs, throwing into bold relief the major's picturesque figure, and revealing his handsome countenance, strangely drawn and seamed.

"Sometimes," continued the colonel, innocently, with his eyes upon the hearth, "when grieving over your loneliness in this still old house of yours, I have all at once been startled by the recollection of your face as it looked that day. And, old fellow, hang me, if there haven't been moments when, but for the impassable social gulf between you, I could have sworn that Milly was the one woman on God's earth you ever could have loved."

The major, whose chair was already in shadow, moved further back into the chimney-corner.

"What got you thinking of — of our young days to-night?" he asked quietly. But even in the uncertain light his face revealed an eagerness that belied the calm of his manner. "Have you — have you heard anything of her?"

The colonel nodded. "Old Sloan's been heard from," he remarked with a chuckle, "captured, I saw, down in North Carolina and tried for murder. Sly old fox! But he's caught up with in his deviltry at last. The villain usually is in the long run, though this particular one has been allowed a pretty wide swath, I'm bound to admit. The inevitable retribution of the moralist was a little delayed in his case, but it got there, all the same — it got there. And I'm free to confess that I'm glad of it. Never have forgiven him the trick he played to cheat me out of that roan saddle-mare I had. Remember that dainty bit of horse-flesh, Lando?"

The major was sitting bolt upright in his chair.

"Was there — was there any mention of — of the daughter?" he asked in a low voice.

"Of Milly?" responded the colonel. "Oh, yes, yes, indeed; there were whole paragraphs in the accounts I read devoted to Milly. She had to come into Court and was compelled to testify against her own parent, and it all must have been rather touching and impressive — everybody moved to tears, even the judge.

Special mention was made of her great dignity of bearing, and of her sad, beautiful face. It was a theme for aspiring young journalists, and some of them made quite a fine story of it. It seems that she married some man down in that part of the country, a mountaineer, I think; and the articles spoke of her two sons."

The major's face had suddenly blanched.

"It came out," continued the colonel, "that she had stuck by the old man through thick and thin and with a tenderness and a loyalty that never were surpassed. Lord, Lord, what is there on this green earth better than a good woman! — unless it is a Kentucky good woman. Well — I must be moving on. Nan'll think we've been making a night of it. Lord Above, what a thing it is to have a wife to go back to! Wish you had one, old fellow," he exclaimed heartily, as the major silently brought in a great coat and a soft felt hat from the hall, "am always wishing it whenever I come here; and to-night — well, as I heard the last of those youngsters' voices dying in the distance, I felt that something surely must be wrong — somewhere — and that by rights this old house of yours ought to be echoing with the laughter of your own happy sons and daughters." He drew out his watch. "Bless me, if it isn't two o'clock!"

The great Custom House clock near by pealed out

the hour, as Colonel Johnstone hurried down the steps.

The night had grown clear and still.

The major stood in the doorway a long time after the clumsy figure of his friend had vanished into the darkness. He noted the fall of the moonlight across his little sward, and the mysterious alchemy which had changed the dull commonplace of the row of ugly brick and frame houses opposite to something benign and almost beautiful. There was a thin covering of snow, and his old elm tree sparkled with icicles. Not a creature was abroad. Not a sound fell upon the wintry air. Everywhere was silence petrified. He was chilled through and through when he finally closed the door and went back to his solitary hearthstone.

As he passed through the dim, garlanded rooms, which a short time before had resounded with the merriment of his guests, and beheld them cold and deserted, filled with melancholy echoings of good cheer, he was conscious of a strange analogy revealed by his own lonely heart, hitherto decked and waiting, whose lights had suddenly gone out.

He sat gazing with hungry eyes into the dying embers, and sadness seemed to envelop his drooping form like a garment. He was strangely altered. An old wound was bleeding afresh, and all unwittingly it had been torn apart; so that never again could the major indulge the hope which for so long had buoyed him up:

the hope of looking once again into the face of the only woman he had ever loved.

He was a poet and a dreamer and beyond this hope his thoughts had never passed to the practical, just as he had never once pictured himself as living without its kind stimulus. In every state of the Union he had sought her, but without avail; and it was only a part of the essential high-breeding of the man that his imagination was able to lift her out of the conditions that held her in a world apart from his own, and to place her on a pedestal before which his homage knelt. But there was that in the colonel's story which removed her from him as death would have been powerless to do.

The light of the first morning of the new year was coming into the windows when he lifted his bowed head and rose from his chair. Something had gone out of his face during those hours that would never come back, but the old patience and gentleness, born of that sense of sympathy with all humanity which had always linked him to his fellows, looked forth again from the kind eyes.

Slowly his thoughts began to travel back to the present out of those misty regions of the past, whose secrets gave him kinship with all true lovers of the world. And presently, like an apparition, the tall form of Blackburn Blair seemed to rise before him with a distinctness that startled him from thought of self. The hurt look on the proud young face, as Blackburn stood at the foot of the stairway, called to him like the cry of a drowning man whom he might save. His heart was beating with a warm new impulse. All at once the major walked across the room and opened his secretary.

Gathering up one of the loose sheets of note paper at hand, he began to write — hurriedly, as if fearful that his resolution might fail him. He was sensitive, and the note cost him an effort.

It was not one of the stiff, characteristic missives that he was wont to send his friends — it came too directly from his heart. There were only a few words, and these were disjointed, and tremblingly penned. Then he slipped the note into an envelope without trusting himself to read it over, and addressed it; and upon these words, along with a great bunch of violets, a a few hours later Cicely's eyes rested:

"My dear Little Girl," he wrote, in fond, familiar fashion, "may an old man send you a thought for the New Year with his blessing? It may seem to you only one of those ancient paradoxes that age is forever handing down to youth. Certainly it is very old; for sad-hearted men and women in all times have been inscribing their names to it, having found out its meaning too late. It is simply this, my child, that though there may be many lovers, love seldom comes to any life but once; and happy are they who can hear the fluttering of the young god's wings in spite of the 'earth-noise' about them—if I may be allowed to borrow a term from my dear friend, Mrs. Browning.

Look on these flowers and let them be to you a symbol of truth and beauty, and believe me,

"Ever as ever,

"Your old friend,

"ORLANDO WISE."

CHAPTER I

A POLITICAL DECISION

THERE was to be an election for governor of the Commonwealth.

The Democratic State Convention, assembled at Louisville, after six days of unprecedented excitement and disorder, had finally declared a nominee, and the name of William Goebel was flashing over the wires.

It was to prove a fateful name to Kentucky — that land of impulse and of passionate strife — a name to summon the bitterest assault and the most ardent defence, the direst foes and the staunchest friends, that ever fell to the lot of anyone in the history of the state: a name to threaten and to conjure with.

Like one of those powerful figures which from time to time rose in the old Roman days, this man of iron will and steady nerve, who asked no quarter and who knew no fear, had slowly made his way up, single-handed, from the humble ranks of life, until, by a display of generalship that was as far-sighted as it was brilliant, he had at last reached a plane of political supremacy which his rivals sought in vain to dispute. There was that in the splendid audacity of the man which was calculated to appeal powerfully to the generous-hearted Kentuckians, proud of their ancient lineage and tradition, yet none the less ready to crown the man of kingly prowess, be his station what it may.

He had resolutely declared himself the friend and the champion of the common people. And in his devotion to their cause he was a kind of self-appointed tribune of the masses — an implacable enemy to corporate power.

He had completely dominated the convention from the first, just as he had for twelve years been the controlling factor in the General Assembly of his state.

Cool, deliberate, sphinx-like in his silence, wholly incapable of oratorical effects, and possessing little of the personal magnetism that usually belongs to the successful politician, he yet ruled men as no other man had ever ruled them in Kentucky; and in his imperious command there was something large and elemental, a kind of antique force that seemed to surround him with the picturesqueness of the remote past.

He had gone into the convention with only about a third of the instructed strength. Undisturbed by hisses, and shrieks, and dark mutterings about him, which threatened every moment to break into open violence, he boldly fought the battle step by step — and won at last in the teeth of the most tremendous odds that ever conspired to bring about a mortal's defeat. That he met evil with evil most people felt constrained to admit.

Among those who opposed him prior to the nomination was Blackburn Blair.

Breakfast was just over. It was a beautiful June morning and the breath of many roses came floating in from the garden. In his deep chair near an open window in the library Judge Blair sat reading a newspaper. His face was very anxious, as his eyes scanned the closely printed sheet.

It was ordinarily a pleasant hour with him when he gave himself up to the peaceful thoughts engendered by the quiet reading of his favorite authors. He was no longer in active practice, and he seldom appeared at his office before ten o'clock. But to-day he had signified his intention of going down a little earlier than usual. In reality he was eager for a conversation with his son upon the subject that was engrossing the thoughts of both. He had had only a few words with Blackburn since the latter's return from Louisville. However, when the young man finally stood in the doorway, it appeared that the judge drew back from the proposed conference.

"You have decided not to go down now?" inquired Blackburn, unsuspectingly.

Judge Blair looked up. "Yes; I believe I will sit

here and read awhile as usual," he said, fumbling among the stack of papers on the table before him. "I thought I should like to look over the platform again but it seems I have mislaid the paper."

Blackburn quickly crossed the room. There was something calm and helpful and reassuring in his manner. But he also seemed disturbed; and there was a look of weariness on his features as of one who had lost sleep.

"Was there any particular point?" he asked. "Here it is." And then he added with a troubled smile, "I am very familiar with that platform."

"Will you read me that portion relating to the election law?" asked Judge Blair, a shade of apprehension betraying itself in the low voice.

Blackburn sat down. "I should like very much to discuss this matter with you," he said, "and we can speak of these things more comfortably here than at the office. Everyone is excited. I should like to go over the ground once clearly with you before I am forced to speak to anyone else."

He read the passage.

"There," observed Judge Blair, tapping with his finger on the arm of his chair, "there is the battle-field on which the great fight will be fought."

Blackburn assented gloomily.

"Already the distant rumbling of artillery on both

sides has been heard," continued the judge, "when it is really allowed to break forth in earnest, I am heart-sick to think of what the consequences may be."

"Mr. Goebel's unrelenting position toward the encroachment of corporate power," remarked Blackburn, thoughtfully, "will surely bring upon him a united and powerful force from one direction — a concentration of brains, and sophistry, and money, and energy not to be easily overcome. Still I agree with you that the great fight will be made right there — that is, on William Goebel, in general, and in particular, on this bill, presented by him in 1898 to the Kentucky senate, which bears his name."

"It gives them ground to contend for," affirmed the judge, judicially. "The Republicans are claiming that this law is in direct conflict with the Bill of Rights, and that under its workings the control of the entire election machinery of the state will be given over into the hands of the Democratic party."

Blackburn was sitting beside a little mahogany work-table near his father's chair, over which hung the portrait of his beautiful mother. His eyes lingered with the portrait for a moment and then wandered away to the garden and rested on a rose bush not far from the window — a white rose bush in full bloom. And suddenly the years rolled away and a little tearful face, wilful, but appealing, blended with the flowers, while a sweet voice cried: "These — I want these — *these!*" The pang of his boyish refusal was a very real thing. It hurt him even now.

His thoughts traveled heavily down the seventeen months that had passed since Cicely's departure.

For nearly a whole year and a half she had been gone!

But presently all the disquietude of that interminable time was lost in anticipated pain. Thus does the future ever give silence to the past.

He believed he could readily foresee where Colonel Overton would be in the coming election. Though his stand had been characteristically quiet, Mrs. Overton had taken care of all that. She had seen to it that his decision was given the proper prominence, though there was little expression on the subject from him. Already there had come from this direction hints of disapproval of the nominee of the Louisville convention.

"The cry of Civil Liberty will prove an excellent catch word," he remarked presently, with a smile, "and the pity is that there was ever given excuse for such a plea. The Goebel law will lose the state thousands of votes — many of them entirely sincere."

The judge turned and fixed his eyes upon his son.

"Have you outlined your plan of action for the next three months?" he asked steadily, but unable to keep a note of anxiety out of his voice. It was evident that it was the revelation he now sought that he most shrank from, though constrained to ask the question. "I know that you did not desire the nomination of William Goebel."

Blackburn did not reply at once. His eyes were lowered. The young face was absorbed in deep thought. Presently he straightened himself, threw back his head, and looked his father very earnestly in the eyes.

"I have outlined it," he said. "I have been wanting to talk the matter over with you."

The judge drew a sudden deep breath, but did not commit himself. He sat waiting, and Blackburn continued:

"I think I realize all the consequences that will follow upon the position I shall take. My opposition to Mr. Goebel is well known. But my opposition is not based upon the grounds that I believe him to be an evil man. I do not believe him to be an evil man. On the contrary I think him a far better man than the average politician, and one not to be compared at all with certain low, purchasable men who are now prepared to open up on him in violent assault. Although I was not in sympathy with certain forces that were at work in the framing of some of his measures, I am free to admit that all of these measures are tending in the right direction; and that they are Democratic in principle. My reasons for opposing him rested upon the fact of the man's own inherent strength — the most masterful, the most stupendous I have ever come in contact with. Like Caesar, he is ambitious — and it may be that like Caesar he is destined to find his Brutus. The spirit that is abroad is a revolutionary spirit, and it may hesitate at nothing."

"Do you recall Milton's definition of fame?" asked Judge Blair, with a quiet smile. His expression had altered.

"He calls it 'That last infirmity of noble mind,' doesn't he, or something like that? Nevertheless I can never give my entire confidence to the man whose supreme effort appears, so far as anyone can see, to be directed toward the gratification of a mainly personal aim, even though that aim include in its self-centered scheme the elevation of the masses. And the power which is not continually held in allegiance to a Higher Direction is a power to be feared. Still it seems to me that in this case the principle is everything. Any objection to the man himself, which may after all be undeserved, should be made subordinate. The small issues should be merged into the larger issues, the election of 1899 into the election of 1900, the state into the nation."

A light lingered on the features of the elder for a moment, and then faded into a look of deep sadness. The sentiments that the young man had just expressed, the avowal of a passionate loyalty to a broad, national idea, that could sweep away, as a smaller view could not, from its far-seeing vision all nearer objects — whence came it, if not as a result of that long teaching that had ever held devotion to the Union to be a sacred duty? Was the son ardent, determined, fixed, like a great rock, in his unswerving principle, about to follow in the father's footsteps, only to meet with the father's fate? The tender heart that had never shrunk from suffering for himself, shrank now from suffering for another. But Blackburn went on:

"Whatever is radical in the measures embodied in the Democratic platform will in time be modified. But I utterly fail to see how a remedy is to be found in abandoning the Democratic party and giving the state over into the hands of the other party. The most that an anti-Goebel ticket could hope to do would be to elect a Republican. But the defeat of the Democratic ticket this autumn would most likely mean the loss of the state in the next presidential election, and in my opinion that calamity should be averted even though some of us be hounded to the death with the cry of 'Goebelite' or 'partisan.'"

There was a long silence. A robin was singing gayly near the window, but neither seemed to heed the rich, liquid note. Their thoughts were grappling with serious things, and eyes and ears were closed to the present. When Blackburn spoke again it was with a slight change of subject.

"Never before," he said, "has the party had presented to it such deep and vital issues as at the present time. The dominant idea of the coming century is to be the fraternal idea, let men refuse to face it as they may; and it is only the outcome of our first distinct conception of a very old idea delivered to mankind some nineteen hundred years ago."

"Sooner or later every man will have to face it, or face a revolution," remarked the judge, dryly. "This idea of unity, I take it, is to be, as you say, the dominant idea of the approaching century. It is somewhat analogous to the idea which jarred France and all civilization at the close of the eighteenth century. Do you recall Wordsworth's verses concerning the inspiration which the French Revolution awoke at its outset? —

> 'Bliss was it in that dawn to be alive,
> But to be young was very heaven!—
> * * * * * * * * *
> Not favored spots alone, but the whole earth,
> The beauty wore of promise.'"

"But the French Revolution failed," added the judge, after a moment's thought, "through unbelief in the Divine."

"Yes," said Blackburn, quickly, "I am sure that men can only become brothers as they recognize that they are made one under the seal and impress of the

Divine Nature; and so it would seem to be reserved for the younger nation — the United States — strong in a sound Christian faith, to establish the old idea of liberty, equality, and fraternity, which was so blindly and passionately essayed a century ago."

"But it is upon the very point upon which apparently Mr. Goebel stands most firmly, that I would take issue with him," he continued. "I am wholly opposed to anything that savours of arraying class against class. His passionate defence of the toiling masses against the oppression of those who through the license of an unjust legislation have been enabled to place themselves in positions of power, is something that must appeal to every man who has a heart in him, and who is not blinded by self-interest. But it is man as man that I am concerned with — the good of the individual that everything in me cries out for. I should surely like to see such laws enacted as would protect the weak against the strong; but I should like equally well to see the strong protected against himself; so that the idea of the oneness of humanity should be attained to, and men, lifted up to that plane of understanding which would enable them to grasp the meaning of justice toward their fellows, should welcome every righteous restriction put upon themselves as an opportunity."

He spoke with intensest fervour, swept on by such a tide of emotion against the Goliath of evil in the land, such a longing for the betterment of his race as swayed the young David in the dawn of his glorious manhood when he went forth to meet the Philistine, rejoicing in his might, and saying: "Thou comest to me with a sword, and with a spear, and with a shield: but I come to thee in the name of the Lord of hosts, the God of the armies of Israel, whom thou hast defied."

His father heard him to the end, and with an outward calm that concealed an inward agitation.

"You have asked me what my course shall be, and I have told you," said Blackburn, rising suddenly, and taking out his watch. "I shall throw myself heart and soul into the coming campaign."

He stood for a moment searching his father's features in great anxiety. He looked pale and wearied, yet steadfast.

Judge Blair leaned back again in his chair, and again he closed his eyes. It was a moment of painful suspense.

Throughout the entire setting forth of the young man's position the clear legal mind of the elder had been alert and busy, watching every step of the way, lest haply some unsoundness of judgment should be revealed — the sophistry and the prejudice of those who see things, not as they are, but as they themselves wish.

But a deep sense of triumph and of thankfulness

stirred the father's heart. The boy had not failed him. He "saw life steadily, and saw it whole."

All at once the old man rose, bracing himself against the table. For a moment the two looked into each other's eyes — the old, confiding, all-comprehending look, and there was something in the manner of the elder like that of one pronouncing a benediction. But he only said:

"I think you have decided wisely, my son."

CHAPTER II

CICELY'S RETURN

One of the heavy oaken doors of the Custom House swung energetically, and Professor Kennedy emerged into the sunlight. He carried a great batch of magazines and papers, and he stood a moment adjusting them more comfortably. He threw a swift glance about him, his gray eyes blinking in the sudden glare.

A considerable number of people were entering and leaving the post office, and moving up and down before the building, so that the street presented a particularly lively air heightened at the instant by the spasmodic gongs of the two rapidly moving trolley cars and the rumble of half a dozen vehicles. Several small boys with newspapers and an Italian fruit vender were also doing their best to add to the general activity. Yes; they were almost a city. The professor, looking on in his quaint, philosophic fashion, admitted it with a shade of regret. It was a favorite remark with him in reference to his first impressions of Lexington, which he had received as a young man some forty years before, that if he chanced in those days to pass on the street so many as two men and a dog within the space of an entire block or two, he had come to believe that something unusual was surely about to occur. The change in the aspect of the place was startling to one of such recollections. The rueful, half-quizzical expression on his scholarly countenance bore witness to his thoughts.

It made him feel old and detached to see so many people with whom he was unacquainted, and who cared not a penny for him. There had been a time when he knew everybody — by sight at least, and when everybody knew him.

All at once, standing out distinct in her fineness from the unfamiliar faces around and reminding him of a rose he had that morning seen in a grocer's window a-bloom among a great heap of beets and cabbages, he spied a graceful figure in a pink linen gown, waiting at the foot of the stone steps, and smiling gayly toward him.

There was a quick start of surprise, a joyful expletive, and the professor moved precipitately, hobbling down the long flight, despite his lameness and great size, with an alacrity which sent Cicely's heart into her throat.

"Ah, my little lady," he exclaimed, "It's a fine sight for these old eyes to see you again after the long time!"

He grasped the girl's outstretched hand. "A fine sight, my little lady, a fine sight," he kept repeating heartily. "But what do you mean by deserting us like this? A whole year and a half! Just think of it. And we were beginning to fear that you had left us for good and all, my dear."

"Would it have been for good, Professor?" demanded Cicely, twirling her pink parasol.

The professor studied her curiously. His face grew thoughtful. She was strangely changed. Whence came the mysterious alteration? he asked himself in vain. She was a little thinner, perhaps; but the fresh, piquant face had lost none of its charm. She was far lovelier. Of that he had no doubt. But there was a look. He had learned to recognize it. And by and by it began to be borne in upon him that her features had taken on the character that only comes with pain. He dropped the playful tone.

"It would not have been for good, little one," he said very gently. "I am sure that it would not have been for good."

He still stood holding her hand, and his rugged Scotch face was both grave and kindly. But presently he added in lighter tone: "The old grandfather and I have had sad times of it since you left us — sad times. There was no one to fill our pipes for us, and to spoil us with coddling, and to tease us with pretty pranks; so that it is no wonder that your heart melted at last at the thought of us."

Cicely looked up quickly and a lingering sweetness shone in her eyes.

"Oh, I had to come back," she said simply. "I knew that you and grandfather would be the happier even if everyone else should have forgotten me."

"No one has forgotten you, my dear," declared the professor, with emphasis.

For a moment her hand fluttered in his like an imprisoned bird and then relaxed, as if soothed by his calm.

"I think my mother at least was not at all glad to see me," she remarked presently with a laugh in which the professor detected a hint of disquietude. "She wanted me to stay longer — very much longer."

"But I felt sure that you would come back; you see I trusted you, my little lady, I trusted you," said the professor, softly, pressing her hand.

She seemed to draw back a little from his seriousness, and the professor was disturbed. There was something baffling in her manner. Various rumours concerning her had floated to him from time to time. They pictured her in a whirl of gayety, very much sought after, very much loved. Such reports were not pleasant news to the professor, with a thought always for Blackburn Blair. "Has she clean forgotten the lad?" he now asked himself, anxiously.

A sudden gleam of humour overspread the girl's

face. "I think I have come just in time," she remarked, with the old mischievous twinkle in her eyes. "Father and grandfather are barely on speaking terms, that is, grandfather just barely speaks to father, to be strictly truthful. I shall have busy times for the next three months trying to harmonize."

"Ah, but there are exciting times ahead for all of us, my dear. The state is terribly roused. Never saw the like of it."

"So I have discovered. I only came last night. Since then I've heard nothing but politics, politics all the time. Even the children are taking sides. I had scarcely got off the train before I saw two little newsboys clawing each other most ferociously. They were all gory and horrid looking. When I asked an old negro standing by what was the occasion of such a display of energy, he remarked blandly, 'Mistis, doan you give yo'se'f no trouble 'bout dem boys. Dey jes lak ever'body else 'round heah now. Dis one,' pointing to the goriest, 'is foh Mr. Goebel, t'other one ain'.'"

"Has your grandfather declared himself?" inquired the professor, anxiously.

The side the old judge would probably take on any question was something concerning which, despite the intimate acquaintance of many years, the professor had never yet ventured to hazard a conjecture. He had not seen him since the convention had declared a nominee; and he confessed to himself the deliberate avoidance of a meeting until his own course had been definitely determined upon. He did not realize to what an extent that course would be influenced by the decision of young Blackburn Blair. However, he had not seen Blackburn. But he had grown to depend strangely upon the younger judgment which he himself had trained.

Cicely smiled with gay, good-humoured archness. "Declared himself!" she echoed ruefully. "I certainly think he has declared himself. The fact is, it has got to be a way with him to declare himself, in season and out of season (usually out) until I am half-minded to believe that he is bewitched and that he should say Goblin instead of Goebel. Papa calls himself an anti-Goebel Democrat, whatever that is, and whenever he does it, grandfather flies into a rage, and gets purple in the face. He told me that he saw in Mr. Goebel's decision of character a resemblance to to General Jackson. I knew then that papa's doom was sealed."

A twinkle shone in the old Scotchman's eye. Far back in his ancestry there was an Irish grandmother. He owed her much. She had bequeathed to him a sense of humour.

"It takes two sticks to make a fire, my dear, don't be alarmed."

"Yes; but when I dared to side with grandfather, just on a venture, and without knowing an earthly thing, mama ordered me from the room."

"Ah," exclaimed the professor, throwing back his head and laughing as he had not done for many a day. "So there are complications. Well, never mind, my dear, never mind. We'll see what we can do, you and I, in the way of throwing oil on the troubled waters."

Cicely bit her lips. She had a rather too vivid recollection of the professor's manner of throwing oil to indulge in hopes from that direction.

She turned away quickly and fixed her eyes on the street. Presently a very showy equipage, drawn by two beautiful Kentucky thoroughbreds, the brilliant sunlight slanting on their polished coats as on a heavy grade of rich golden-brown satin, came into view. Lolling back in the carriage, high and lifted up above the vulgar rabble of the town, there sat a large, raw-boned woman, fearfully and wonderfully dressed, who deigned to look neither to right nor left.

Cicely affected a stare of innocent surprise.

'Who rides by with the royal air?' she demanded of the professor, drolly.

"Your old friend Mrs. Bellows, my dear. Did you know that she has grown literary during your absence? She asked me to teach her Greek."

"Greek! Poor old soul! What ever did possess her? Softening of the brain?"

"No hardening of the heart. Contempt for the masses. A desire to be superior to the low toiling herd who know not Greek. However, she was finally induced to make a compromise in favour of the modern languages. She goes every day for lessons in French. I am told there is much difficulty in keeping order in the class. Ah — she has just caught sight of you, my dear. I believe," he added hurriedly, "if you will excuse me, I will just say good morning. I—I should prefer that she did not see me." And the professor disappeared around the corner with a quickness that would have done credit to a centipede, to say nothing of a man in full possession of only one foot.

Mrs. Bellows' carriage drew up beside the curbing, and Cicely moved forward. "How do you do, Mrs. Bellows," she said, a comical smile still lingering about her rebellious mouth in memory of the professor's rapid exit.

"Humph!" ejaculated Mrs. Bellows, indulging in a prolonged stare. "That's a pretty question, I'll be bound. Let an old woman lay up in bed a whole week with rheumatism and never even come and ask about her, and then just as cool and smilin' as if nothin' had happened and butter wouldn't melt in your mouth."

"Have you been ill, Mrs. Bellows?" inquired Cicely, gravely. "I am very sorry to hear that. But you see I couldn't know anything about it; I only got back last night."

"Thought you come last week."

"Oh, no."

Mrs. Bellows continued her critical survey of Cicely's pretty summer gown and straw hat.

"Well, you've got *chick* and *gout*," she remarked at length approvingly and in tribute to her own recent acquirements.

Cicely was puzzled. It did not occur to her immediately that Mrs. Bellows' intention was to say *chic* and *goût*, and not to make mention either of a young fowl or a painful malady. She dropped her eyes and waited for some inspiration to guide her. All at once the light broke, and she recalled the professor's information regarding Mrs. Bellows' literary strivings. As a beginning it was rather alarming.

"Oh, I beg your pardon, Mrs. Bellows," she hastened to say. "That is such a fine compliment I was not able immediately to take it in. You should have prepared me. I'm not accustomed to having such flattering things said to me."

"Tain't the first time, and you know it. What's the use of pretendin' you don't know you're stylish? Comes from livin' in New York, don't it?"

"Oh, I don't know. There are some very stylish people about here. There are some who would attract attention even in New York," replied Cicely, with her gaze fixed steadily on Mrs. Bellows' gorgeous apparel.

Mrs. Bellows slowly turned her head from side to side and surveyed her elegance like a great ugly bird pluming itself.

"Do you really think so?" she smirked.

"I am quite sure of it," said Cicely, emphatically.

Mrs. Bellows' large bony hands encased in white gloves suddenly grasped a very showy card case which she held up to the girl's view.

"I'm just on my way to call on Virginia Oats," she remarked cheerfully. "I know she don't like it when callers come early in the day like this. Busy prinkin' an' fixin' up, I'll be bound. But she don't never send me away. I won't put up with no such foolishness. She's been sick. Pity 'twan't old Oats. Don't it seem a shame that that old fellow keeps hangin' on? An' there's the major just a-waitin' and a-waitin'. Last time I went to see her she told me a big piece of news. Maybe you've heard it. It's 'bout that young Blackburn Blair."

"I have not heard it, Mrs. Bellows," said Cicely.

"Ain't you heard he's goin' to be married?"

"No; I believe not," replied Cicely, apparently undisturbed.

Mrs. Bellows watched the girl narrowly.

"Thought he was an old friend of yours?"

"So he is."

"Virginia Oats says she knows it's true. It's to his cousin, that young widow whose husband's head was shot off four or five years ago. Talked too much, I reckon."

Cicely was silent.

"I hear he goes to see her all the time, and he don't have much to do with anybody else. Looks like there's something in it. I tell you the rest of you girls will have to get up early in the mornin' if you want to keep track of a pretty young widow like that. Virginia Oats is bad enough, and she ain't very young nor pretty neither, when it comes to that."

Cicely waited.

"She's a beauty," remarked Mrs. Bellows, still watching the girl's face.

Cicely looked up.

"Do you mean Mrs. Mallory? I quite agree with you," she said thoughtfully. "She's the most beautiful woman I think I have ever seen anywhere — the most beautiful and also the noblest."

Mrs. Bellows grunted. Somehow it was being forced upon her that her strength had been outmatched. In fact she was feeling decidedly worsted, and was irritated accordingly. The girl's coolness and generosity were an offense.

"Well, I never did take no stock in them Blairs. I don't see why people don't stop talkin' 'bout 'em, but it looks like you never can hear the last of 'em; an' I never did see nothin' much in her but a pretty face. But I reckon he's got the pick of you, according to everybody else." And with this parting remark Mrs. Bellows sank back into her former elegant nonchalance, turned her face away, and ordered the coachman to drive on.

CHAPTER III

A BLOOM FROM THE WHITE ROSEBUSH

Blackburn moved quickly down the dark hall of his home with his long, sure stride and on out into the odorous summer morning. The expression of weariness his face had worn for a week or more had wholly disappeared, and the alertness had come back to his step, the sparkle to his eye. He was no longer careworn, perplexed with political matters, burdened under a sense of the impending conflict which with cyclonic force was about to sweep over his beloved Commonwealth. In reality he was not thinking of Kentucky or of politics at all. For the time the great public concerns, which had taken such strenuous hold upon him, had surrendered to another interest, passionately private, ardently intense: he was thinking only of Cicely.

Often, into his tenderest and most intimate thoughts of her, the realization of his life work would come, just as reminders of her were seldom entirely absent when pondering upon his future career. So that these two emotions, the deepest, the most vital of his nature, had become so blended and entwined, it would have seemed well-nigh an impossibility to divorce one from the other. But to-day she reigned supreme.

He was almost jubilant; and though his features betrayed a fleeting anxiety, it was an anxiety that fought with hope — and was conquered.

On the steps of the portico he paused and cast a wistful eye to the Canaan of his dreams — the Canaan in his case being merely a red-brick mansion of substantial design standing diagonally across the street. But the old house had been set apart, sanctified, so to speak, by a presence; and for him at least it had suddenly taken on a special significance, like a case that has had returned to it a rare and priceless pearl.

The pearl had been absent for a long time. To be entirely accurate, as accurate as Blackburn himself, the time was no less than seventeen months, two weeks, and five days. He had just heard of Cicely's return.

Her unexpected leaving on the day after the major's New Year's dinner, when her manner had been so baffling to Blackburn's sincerity, had never been explained during the year and a half that had elapsed; and he had not seen her since that night when she had left him standing at the foot of the stairway, and had passed on with Michael Broomer at her side. She had sent a brief note of farewell, which, however, did not reach him until the morning after her departure.

The note simply mentioned that she had been called suddenly to New York to her aunt, who was ill, and who had special claim upon her. It was the note one might have written to a near friend — or to the veriest stranger. Cicely was skilled in such matters.

He had ventured to write only once, and that in reply to her note. It was not a love letter. It asked for nothing; but it was very direct. Cicely did not reply. Yet there was that between them, unspoken, but resistless, that would not let him doubt.

It was only by accident that he had heard a moment before of her return, his informant being Uncle Scip. The old negro's face had fairly beamed as he imparted the joyful intelligence, ending with the remark:

"Dem niggers over thar say dey 'spects thar's gwine be a weddin' soon, an' I jes tells 'em, I 'specs dey is, I 'specs dey is. But *dey* is talkin' 'bout dat black-hyared young man whose pa useter keep de candy sto' down yonder on Main Street not fur fum de Cote House, an' *I* is talkin' 'bout de quality. Ben, he say, he mighty rich, an' he 'specs he be long bime by. I say, 'Go 'long, nigger, doan you come givin' me no talk lak dat. Doan I know he ain' nothin' but poo' white trash? I knows 'em when I sees 'em.'"

Though the dark vision of Michael Broomer thus conjured up kept intruding with painful insistence, in the main Blackburn was conscious of only one thing, one single all-animating, all-glorifying thought: she had come back, the long waiting was at an end. There was something dazzling in the fall of the happy sunlight, something that intoxicated in the flower-scented air, something that made his senses reel in the call of a robin to his mate in the great elm tree nearby. In another moment, maybe, he would be looking into her eyes. How the idea thrilled and startled! Would she "tremble, yet dissemble," shielding herself with instinctive coquettry from what her heart confessed? How long she had been his! Longer was it than she dreamed, or he himself had known? And he had been true to her in every thought and act! He had loved one woman and her only. Few men, he knew well, had such a gift to offer. Could it be that she would disdain it? He would not let himself question her loyalty to him — she was *his*.

A low humming sound came to him, as of someone singing softly in a disjointed bass, like the buzz of a bumble bee. He heard the silken rustle of the maples in the park opposite as in a dream. He came down the steps and moved quickly across the lawn toward the garden. The swish of a scythe fell pleasantly on his ears, for Uncle Scip, disdaining all modern inventions, was busy with his bluegrass in his own way, singing softly at his work. "Cicely — Cicely —" the scythes were saying as Blackburn passed. He paused beside the white rose bush and tenderly, reverently almost, gathered one perfect bud.

Then he glanced at his watch. It was only nine

o'clock, too early for a call. But if only she should be somewhere around! In all events he could leave the rose. He was a poet and he delighted in symbols.

Just as he came across the lawn and was turning past the corner of the house, old Judge Trotter came and stood in his doorway, the queer little figure looking wizened and old in the summer sunlight. But time that had filched so much from the old man had left him in full possession of the loud voice and imperious ways that Blackburn had known since childhood. He was calling to some one in the hall.

"Cicely," he cried, "what are you doing there? Stop your prinking and go into the library and bring me here the life of Andrew Jackson." There was no response and presently the judge turned and disappeared within the house, still loudly demanding the life of General Jackson, and giving vent to his impatience in the words half-fond, half-chiding, "Bless me! Where's the little witch? Cicely — Cicely — don't you hear me? Cicely!"

Blackburn stood perfectly still. His heart was beating wildly, his brain was in a whirl. Some time passed. Not a sound came from the house across the way. He looked to see the old gentleman reappear, but he did not come back. Blackburn walked quickly across the lawn and out of the gate.

The next moment a girlish figure in a white gown

and a large leghorn hat came down the steps of the Trotter homestead. She came slowly, sedately, with her eyes on the ground, and she was out of the gate and on the street before she caught sight of him.

There was a start, a slight hesitation, and then she came steadily toward him, neither hastening nor delaying her steps.

But she had gone no further than the corner before he was at her side.

"Cicely!" he cried impetuously, "Cicely!" And then could say no more as in great suspence he stood searching her face.

But her features gave no sign. A horrible uncertainty began to steal over him. There was something in her manner which he could not understand, a calmness, a self-possession that seemed to create a distance not easily ignored. But it was not the distance of their first meeting of several years before. It was like that, but also very different. However, there was now no mistaking the genuine kindness of her intent.

She did not reply at once, but she was smiling softly, and she held out her hand with the utmost cordiality. Her eyelids were lowered for an instant, and though the lining of her parasol threw a pink glow over her face, he saw that she was paler and thinner than he had ever seen her. Even more than Professor Kennedy he was startled by the change in her, the subdued, chastened light upon her features, which gave a sweetness and a dignity. The longing to possess her utterly, to break down every barrier she would raise between them, urged him on. "Cicely!" he broke forth again, all the pain and the passion and the waiting suddenly concentrated in the mere utterance of her name. And then, with his eyes still riveted upon her face, "You have come back," he said in a low voice.

She met his eyes. "Yes; I have come back," she answered simply and without the faintest tinge of coquetry.

For a moment his heart stood still. His face grew white and set. "Why?" he demanded sternly. "Cicely, you will be fair with me — you will tell me what has brought you back — you will —"

He caught himself up. The colour had faded out of her face also, but suddenly her throat and brow even were pinker than the roses on her hat.

"I will be fair," she said quite seriously.

"Then why? Tell me — now —"

She put forth her hand.

"Is it for me?" she asked, smiling, motioning toward the rose he held.

He looked down at the flower for a moment, and then straight into her eyes. There was a long pause.

She stood twirling her gay parasol. "I don't think

I have ever seen such roses as grow on that bush," she said archly. And then she added gently, "Uncle Scip told me why you would not give them to me once a long, long time ago. Do you remember?"

His face was drawn in its pallor. "I remember. Will you tell me — now? You said you would be fair." His manner was stern and troubled, and the hand that held the flower trembled, as she saw. "Why did you come back?" he insisted.

Suddenly she raised her eyes to his, and there was in them the old surrender and the old appeal which the womanhood of all ages has made in pathetic joy.

"Because I couldn't help it. I had to come. Oh, Blackburn, does it mean so much — so *much* to you?"

She drew back half-startled at the look that leaped into his face.

Wagons and vehicles of every kind were hurrying by. All the noise and the commonplace of the streets were about them. They neither saw nor heard. But presently the ecstatic note of a robin in the old elm caught their ears. A quick glow overspread his features.

Again she put forth her hand, and in silence he placed in it the white flower.

CHAPTER IV

GLORIA AMORIS

His heart was bounding as if trying to leap to her. Speechless, he stood watching her as she fastened the rose at her breast. It took a long time, and she would not meet his eyes; but presently, as by a simultaneous impulse, they both turned and moved toward the house.

The drawing-room was cool and shadowy, and fragrant with great bowls of flowers. Cicely led the way to some chairs in a far corner, and he followed, making, with unerring surety, the circuit of the heavy furniture that stood out white and spectral in its linen coverings. The look on his face, despite his eagerness, was determined and inexorable. It was a supreme moment, and she knew it; and a sudden awe fell upon her, and she put up her hands in a wild little gesture of appeal. He gathered them quickly and firmly into his.

"Please!" she said in a half frightened whisper. "*Please!*"

But he would not heed her pleading. Back of the mighty wave of feeling that drove him on was a resoluteness that had its root in character: a sort of stern sincerity of soul that would bear no trifling with sacred things.

"Cicely, look at me," he commanded.

She turned a troubled glance upon him, and dropped her eyes. His grasp upon her tightened.

"I love you!" he cried, and the words broke from him like a steed escaping the halter, "I *love* you! Oh, do you think," as she struggled to free herself, "do you think you can evade me *now?*"

But she had grown strangely white, and her hands were cold. Her sob-like breathing was piteous. It was evident that she had not meant to resort to subterfuge. He let go of her, staring dumbly.

All at once she looked him straight in the eyes, and his face blanched.

"Blackburn," she gasped, "I — I am afraid."

He stood helpless, and completely confounded. But suddenly his expression changed. An infinite tenderness shone in his eyes.

"Dear, will you tell me," he asked very gently, "of what?"

Her voice was so low he had to bend down his head to catch the words.

"Of Love," she answered slowly — "that terrible, beautiful thing you want to give me, and are asking me for."

For a moment he could not speak, and when he did his voice broke under the tremendous restraint he put upon himself. Everything began to swim before him. The room seemed to stretch far away into illimitable space. A vast stillness, like a veil, enwrapped them, and set them apart. Even Cicely herself was a thing unreal, unearthly in her tremulous, alluring sweetness. Inexpressibly touched, the impulse to snatch her into his arms swayed him almost beyond his control.

"Cicely, do you love me?" he asked very humbly at length.

She did not seem to hear, and she was appallingly still. Her eyes were downcast, and she seemed lost in a profound meditation. Confused sounds floated in from the streets. Dreamy, far off, they seemed as if proceeding from another world. A bee was humming in a honeysuckle near the window. Still he waited. But she would not answer.

Presently with a desperate little movement she turned toward him and raised her eyes to his — and her soul, stripped of its disguises, was kneeling at his feet.

He stretched out his arms with a low cry and drew her to him. "*Mine* — all mine — thank God, my beloved," he whispered incoherently. For an instant he looked into her white, upturned face, intensely appealing in its passionate purity, and something like pity mingled with the fire in his veins; then he bent down his head and kissed her, reverently, and with the ardour of a single, deathless love.

The colour swept like a flame into her face. For a little space she rested unresisting in his arms. Then she tried to push him gently from her. But he held her closely. "Cicely, I have kissed you; will you kiss me — once?" he asked unsteadily.

For a moment she seemed to hesitate. A slight shivering shook her frame; but, with a look that was unspeakably tender and womanly in the completeness of its surrender, she reached up her arms and drew his face down to her, holding it between her palms.

"Now — I give you all!" she said.

She drew back from him, crimson, smiling, but with a note of sadness in her voice and something like tears in her eyes. She moved away toward the window, and stood silent for a time, absently fingering the blinds.

"Blackburn, I never meant to come back to you," she said presently, after they had sat down.

But he was far too happy to be disturbed. Seeing her, in all her loveliness, before him, and his at last, he was not in the mood to distress himself by the contemplation of a catastrophe that had not occurred.

"When I left here a year and a half ago," she continued, "it was with the fixed intention of never coming back again. The letter from Aunt Catherine came the morning after the dinner at Major Wise's. I had just waked. Blackburn, do you remember that dinner?"

"I have good reason to remember it," he responded grimly.

But she went on. "The maid had just brought me a great bunch of violets and a note from the major — the dear! — when the postman came with a letter. It also was brought up to me, and it was from Aunt Catherine. From week to week she had been writing, begging me to return to her. This letter was a positive command. She wrote that she was ill, and really needed me, reminding me somewhat delicately, it is true, of my obligation to her, but still reminding me. It seemed to me that the hand of destiny had penned that precise and elegant mandate. I did not give myself an instant to contend, to consider. I sprang out of bed and wrote a telegram. I said that I would leave for New York that night. I did leave that night; and when the train pulled out of Lexington I told myself that I was looking upon the place for the last time. I —"

"But why — Cicely — why —" he put in, wondering, and beginning to be troubled in spite of himself.

She turned to him with sudden heat. "Do you think it was not like tearing my heart out of me to say good-bye to my father and my dear old grandfather like that?"

"Was there no one else?" he asked, with a look of pain in his eyes.

"Let me go on. I had my doubts about the seriousness of this illness. Aunt Catherine only had the blues, I felt sure. She is quite subject to these moods of depression, and thinks it is rather cheering at such times to have me around. I knew what the visit to her would mean — only a return to that heartless and wearisome life of the world, with its endless round that I had learned to detest."

"Why need you have gone back to it?" he insisted. "There could be no possible claim that should have subjected you to an existence like that against your will."

Her voice suddenly sank.

"I had begun to doubt that I was born for better things," she said, as the colour slowly faded out of her cheeks.

"*You!*" he cried — You, with your dreams and your aspirations and your flutterings of soul! Cicely, how *could* you have ever thought that such a life was meant for you?"

"I had learnt to play my little part in that. I did not feel equal to any other. Oh, Blackburn," she broke forth all at once, "can't you see — can't you see that with all my might I was resisting — I was resisting *you?*"

"Why?" he demanded stubbornly and somewhat sternly.

She turned her face toward him, quickly altered, and beautiful with the light that shone upon it.

"Because I knew your strength — and 'we needs must love the highest when we see it.'"

"You loved me, and yet were willing to desert me like that?"

"I loved you — with all my heart and soul and brain; and that is why I was able to take myself out of your life."

"Did you believe that you did that merely by going away?"

"In time I thought you would forget. All men do."

"And you? Did you also mean to forget?"

"I tried. God only knows how hard I tried during these last seventeen horrible months. They were horrible months. I never seemed able for an instant to forget your face as it looked during the moment that you stood there at the foot of the major's stairs. Day and night it haunted me, until I felt as if I were actually going mad. Then there came a time when I no longer tried to forget."

He waited. "And then?"

Presently she went on again.

"I told myself that I would keep my dream of you always undimmed — a glorious, perfect thing that could not die; that I should not live to see it fade away into the cold gray commonplace of married life. In my whole existence I have never seen an instance of what has seemed to me to be a truly ideal marriage — not one. How could we hope that marriage between us would not gradually become what it is with many others, when it is not something worse: a comfortable and highly satisfactory arrangement, or at most a pleasant friendship? I knew I could not live and watch your love, day by day, grow cold. I sometimes think I am not made of the material that other women are made of. I am strong to endure some things. If I knew that life for me in the future would mean the loss of everything that stands for luxury or comfort; if it meant hardship and trial and poverty, or even want, I think I should be strong enough to bear all these things. It was not that. And there were moments when I felt that I would gladly go with you into a desert, and when the bare thought of sharing your life came to me like a trumpet call to a sleeping soldier."

"And yet," he said — "and yet —"

"I tried not to hear the call," she interrupted quickly — to close my heart and my ears to it." She shook her head, and a smile that was sadly sweet chased itself across her features. "It only grew louder. Until at last every little whisper of the spring — every bird that sang from a tree top, every leaf that stirred, every flower that looked up from the sod, was in league against me. I simply had to come back. Blackburn, haven't I frightened you a little with my fears?"

He threw back his head and broke into a laugh — a low, triumphant laughter.

"Not a bit. I am willing to take all chances. I know that a love that is real is only the stronger for each day of upward striving and attainment. If there be two to strive and to attain, in the closest, the most intimate of human relations, then the result is all the surer. Dear, if I did not know that my love for you will be even greater than it is to-day, after you have been my wife for many years, I should put it from me as a thing unworthy of you and of myself."

She was silent, and her face was pensive and a little grave despite the glow upon it.

Presently the old clock at the head of the stairway rang out the hour of ten, the loud stroke reverberating through the still house like a challenge.

She turned to him with her old roguish smile.

"Since I am to be your wife, don't you think you had better go and earn our bread and butter?"

But Blackburn refused to stir.

"Don't you remember," she urged, "that you promised me once, a long time ago, you would get me a bag of gold? I was crying for the one at the end of the rainbow."

He rose. "I shall keep my word," he replied steadily. "It may not be a very large bag of gold, and it, therefore, will not be weighty enough to impede our progress; but it will be quite sufficient for our needs, as we go forward on life's journey, and I will surely get you one."

She had moved across the room, and was taking her hat from a table where she had thrown it when they came in. She turned.

"I will walk part of the way with you," she said, "I was going down to the post office when I met you."

"Cicely, will you?" he cried eagerly. "But you can go the whole way," he added greedily, "just as easily as not." And then, as she came toward him, radiant, smiling, he paused. *"Cicely! Cicely!"* he exclaimed under his breath.

For a moment the two stood looking deep into each other's soul, awed and speechless in the presence of the eternal mystery.

"I will go the whole way," she said, after a moment. And together they went forth into the golden summer sunshine.

CHAPTER V

THE HEART OF SUMMER

It was six weeks later and near the close of one of those ardent days of the waning summer when the very heart of nature seems to stand revealed — a living, throbbing, trembling thing, stirred to a passionate avowal by the sad hint of change borne on some passing breeze.

Cicely leaned her shapely form in its taut riding habit against the stone wall surrounding the historic spring, and shaded her eyes from the westering sun.

'A picketed station on fair Elkhorn
Surrounded by groves of the milk-white thorn!'

she quoted gayly. "Blackburn, can't you see it? Certainly that is fair Elkhorn over there to the right, and with the aid of a little imagination the picketed station can be supplied."

Blackburn followed with his own the direction of her eyes gazing dreamily toward the gently rising knoll whereon once had been the rude fort of Bryan Station—famous for an ever memorable siege in the pioneer history of the state. Then he stood a moment in silence, watching her animated face, flushed from the five mile ride, in a vast content. "He looked at her, as a lover can," but his happiness was of a deep and voiceless kind; some subtle consciousness of a special spiritual nearness held him mute. Since that day of days, when doubtfully, yet surely, as he believed, she had given herself to him, and when his very soul stripped of its profound reserve had been bared to hers, there had been times of lavish, glowing speech, of abandonment, of declaration; but now something in the tender effulgence of the August afternoon, and in the promise of fulfilment that spoke on every hand, filled him with a kind of calm that was but another expression of an inarticulate joy. Never had she seemed to him so sweetly gentle and appealing. Her beauty thrilled him through and through. It was a part of the indefinable, eternal beauty.

From time to time a chorus of laughter, a word or two, or a call from the distance would fall upon their ears, for a merry party had gathered and were now scattered through the grounds in the neighborhood of the spring, sitting in groups under the great trees or wandering along the shady banks of the tiny stream which goes glinting in and out of the bluegrass meadows like a silver thread set in some rich green fabric.

"A hundred and seventeen years ago!" exclaimed Cicely, "and what a degenerate it makes me feel! When I come here I always feel as if I am on holy ground and ought to take off my shoes."

"A degenerate?" echoed Blackburn, quickly. "I should think it would be just the reverse of that, and a sort of inspiration to you. It was the women of Bryan Station, you know," he added significantly, with one of his sudden, illuminating smiles, "whose splendid act of heroism made it possible for the men to resist the siege. I can't think of a wilder, sweeter story, or one more in character with the womanhood of the state, than the story of the women of Bryan's Station. And it touches on the eternal verities: womanly sacrifice, shown in their willingness to go to the spring for water within gunshot of hundreds of Indian warriors, womanly tenderness, shown in their desire to supply a purely human need."

Cicely turned away quickly with averted eyes.

"And here is their monument," she said in odd constraint, "to tell the world of the good deed done, and above all of how they made it possible to resist the siege in the year of our Lord 1782."

"It is a fine, solid bit of masonry," responded Blackburn, also turning and scanning the wall with his quiet, measuring gaze. "It will be here, I venture to say, for many a year to come — long after our present disturbances have passed away. In the meantime it stands as a kind of silent protest against the selfishness of our day."

He was quiet a moment and then he sought her eyes.

"Cicely, do you know about to-morrow?" he asked in a low voice.

Her face changed, and her eyelids were suddenly lowered.

"Yes," she said, "I know; I saw the notice in the newspapers."

"The campaign has fairly opened now. I shall have to be away a large part of the time. I have agreed to make speeches in a number of counties far and near. Still, I had not expected to go before the first of next week. That is why I have not mentioned it."

There was a long pause.

She stole a swift glance from under her downcast lids. He was looking far away into the distance. His face was eager, masterful, and determined, and there was about him a kind of restrained restlessness as of one impatient for the fray. He seemed wholly forgetful of the present — forgetful even of her.

Cicely slowly opened her eyes and stood watching him as one stunned. She was breathing quickly and she had all at once grown very white. In a sort of desperation she pressed nearer to him.

"Must you — *must* you go?" she whispered, with trembling lips.

He pulled himself together with a quick start; and then as he saw her all pale and spiritless, the proud head lowered, the sweet face drawn with pain, a low cry half of joy and half of pity broke from him. One little cold ungloved hand hung limply at her side, and he crushed it in his warm, strong clasp.

The colour flamed into her face, the light into her eyes.

In a twinkling she was herself again — like a rose with the dew upon it — radiant, alluring, smiling at him through her tears. Neither spoke. He could hear her quick breathing, troubled, desperate despite her gay assurance. The deep concentration of her gaze held him mute and spellbound; and presently his own face paled a little under her piteous, womanly appeal, and he realized that it was to be a hard fight — the fight between love and duty, between her strength and his strength.

"Must you go?" she repeated softly.

He did not answer. A sudden cloud had overspread the summer sky. A jay called harshly from the thicket across the road, and he heard Frederick Dilson's clear tenor voice ring out from some distant point beyond the bend of the little creek. A fine, thin breeze had arisen and was stirring the delicate tendrils of light brown hair about her temples. Her lips were parted, eager.

Presently she drew her hand away. "Never mind," she said sadly, "never mind." She put up her hand to her face and shaded her eyes again, though the sun was shining only faintly. "Let us go up there and sit down on the hillside, and wait for the others to come. It is nearly time for tea, they'll all be back soon, I should think. I'm a little tired."

He followed her without a word. Some carriage seats and cushions had been spread out under the trees, and Cicely sank down with a gesture of weariness near a great hamper filled with glass and china.

"Now I can imagine myself a genuine pioneer woman, for I think, even more than the spring, this must have been a favorite spot. Did you ever see a nobler view? How often they must have come here and watched the sun, as we are doing now, dip into the great unknown West."

He turned to her with a sudden pleading in his eyes. "It is so much to me, so much more than I can ever tell you, that you care for the old stories," he said in a low voice. "I don't see how it would have been possible for me to love a woman to whom they meant nothing."

She laughed a little mockingly. "Does my hold then rest upon anything so slender? They might have meant little to me, or nothing at all. In either case I think you would have loved me all the same."

He did not answer.

"Wouldn't you?" she asked at length, studying his clear-cut profile, the curve of the strong chin.

He met her eyes. "As long as you are you I shall have no choice left me," he said at length, simply. "But you could scarcely be yourself and at the same time be indifferent to the things you now care so much for."

"I might change in regard to a great many things — among them these. I might forget. I might *want* to forget."

"You couldn't. Some things are implanted in us too deeply, their roots have sunk too far down into the inmost nature; so that to attempt to tear them up is either to meet with utter failure, or to mar our plot with great ugly holes that are usually pitfalls for our friends or a cause of stumbling for ourselves."

Cicely sat gazing straight ahead in an attitude touchingly familiar to him since their childhood: her elbow on her knee, her firm little chin resting in her hand, her eyes filled with a plaintive unrest. Could it be, she was asking herself very humbly, that she was capable of descending to the low plane of being jealous of his work — his great life plan of such splendid sweep and import? If the quality of jealousy existed in her at all, as yet it had not made itself known to her. She recalled with the pride of a proud woman the entire absence of such feeling in her at those times when she had heard his name mentioned with that of his beautiful young cousin, Myra Mallory. She had been pained it is true, but not from an unworthy cause — rather for the reason that the veil of a deep and sacred sorrow had been torn aside by rudely profane hands.

But there had come a startling recognition of forces in her own nature hitherto unsuspected — resolute, resistless, terrible. She drew back cold and trembling on the brink of an incoming tide of feeling. A pitiful sense of the aloneness of the spirit, that vast inner life of each which neither could pass over into, filled her with dismay.

And she could not know that his enthusiasms were himself, that to love him in any fine and elevating way was to love his work, which was beginning to grow hateful to her. She could think only of the separateness of their lives while he went to meet his destiny, and when she must be apart from him, though by his side. She regretted, as she had never before regretted it, that she had not long ago thrown herself heartily into the cultivation of some art or special branch of study, believing that through the medium of such resource she would have been able in that future which still she scarcely dared to face, to find refuge from herself and dignity of spirit.

"I can understand that I might grow to hate many of the things I now care for," she said presently in a strange voice.

He stared at her uncertainly.

"I don't think I know just what you mean," he said after a time slowly and very gently.

She laughed a trifle nervously. "I think it means simply that there are two ways of being patriotic, as I once told you sometime ago — your way and my way. It is useless to pretend that the two ways are the same."

He was still staring at her blankly.

"But I thought —" he began.

"You thought because I was able to discern the element of picturesqueness and to thrill a little, in a sentimental way, under a past heroism that I might also be able to rise to a spirit of present sacrifice, such sacrifice as appeals to you. I'm afraid it is no use. I can't. Blackburn, I simply can't feel about Kentucky and the nation as you do," she said sadly and brokenly.

"And I'm beginning to loathe the very name of politics," she went on hurriedly, before he could speak. "Under the present conditions it all seems so degrading. How can I know that you will come out of it all unscathed?" she cried, deceiving herself as women are ever wont to do in such moments, shifting the dread. "If I were an ambitious woman, personally ambitious, I mean, I should feel different. But I am not ambitious. Some women would have dreams of Washington and a brilliant social career. For myself these things make no appeal. As for you, if they should wish to make you governor by acclamation, or send you to the United States Senate in the most flattering way you could imagine, it would not add the least thing to you in my eyes. I think I should be only sad to think henceforth our parts would have to be played on the larger stage, instead of here — here, always, in this sleepy old town away from the fret and the 'earth noise.' I have seen too much of the world ever to care for it again."

"But surely — surely, you cannot think that I am asking you to care for such things!" he exclaimed, perplexed and pained.

"You are asking me to love a man who expects, his whole life through, to be devoted to something that will inevitably force us both out into the world. Do not blame me if sometimes my thoughts travel ahead with unspeakable fears. You will never know, I can never tell you, of all I have passed through, with myself and with others, before I gave myself up to you as I have done. You are so strong. It is an ancient strength, and of a kind that holds a woman like a captive bird, fluttering to escape. But it has all been so beautiful; we have been so deeply happy; all the loves of the old, old world have seemed to be alive again and singing in our hearts. And I, during the long bright summer days, I have lulled myself to forget the pain of the past, to hush the anxiety of the future. But I have known always, always, that this moment would have to come. To-morrow is the first step into that long loneliness that is before me. Oh, Blackburn, the absorption, the separateness of a politician's life!"

"But I cannot see it at all like that," he broke forth, touched to the very heart's center by her piteous appeal, yet, manlike, unable to grasp her womanly pain — the pain that has stirred so many hearts like hers when roused to a fearful joy.

She shook her head sadly. "If only you could be satisfied to be just what your father is. His calm, aristocratic aloofness has always pleased me so."

"My father? But my father has always been very earnestly interested in everything that concerns the welfare of his state and of the nation. He lived a most active political life at one time. It was only after the state had turned against him, and when it no longer desired the service of such men as he, that he returned to private life."

Suddenly his face grew white. "Cicely, how can I make you understand?" he asked sorrowfully. "I thought — I hoped that you felt as I do about it all. I have been so happy in the belief that in this thing, too, we were one."

She bowed her head and he watched her for a moment in silence. It was a decisive moment for each. For him it meant a well-nigh overmastering temptation.

His hand on the turf beside her was tightly clinched; the muscles about his neck and brow showed like cords beneath the flesh. All at once her beauty seemed to become something mocking and beguiling. He drew back in a kind of terror from the feelings that swayed him, the strange witchery of the tenderly wistful face, the allurement of the lovely form, the gleam in the violet eyes. The woods seemed to swim before him. The future grew dim, uncertain. He could no longer think clearly. He was trembling in every nerve. Then he rose and stood leaning against the bole of the great tree whose branches sheltered them from the last rays of the dying sun. He dared not trust himself to look at her again; and after awhile he began to walk backward and forward for a few yards in front of her, his hands thrust into his pockets, his brows knit in thought.

Presently he dropped down by her side. He had grown calm, but there was a look of deep suffering in his eyes. "Cicely," he said eagerly, "I shall have to be away from you a great deal for the next two months. Am I going feeling that you are not in sympathy with me?"

She looked up quickly. "Not that — oh, not that," she cried helplessly, the tears starting into her eyes.

"You know it is just life to me, this work I feel myself bound to do. It is as if I heard the very voice of God calling me to it. I need not tell you what I feel."

She did not answer. And again the great yearning for her swept like fire through his veins, and his heart was wrung with pity for the dumb anguish of her eyes.

The gay voices and the laughter were coming nearer. In another moment they would be in view. He bent down his head quickly toward her, and his heart was beating wildly.

"Dear," he said low under his breath, "won't you try to understand, won't you try? I have to go. But I shall not go alone. Day and night you will be with me. I shall see you, hear your voice, look into your very eyes just as I am doing now, even when miles and miles away from you. Am I to go feeling that you regret the stand I've taken, and is it that that is troubling you?"

"It isn't that. If I were a man I should give my vote just as you will give yours."

"And yet you want me to be silent? Cicely, tell me, tell me what you want?" he cried, wholly baffled by her words.

There was a moment's hesitation, and then she turned to him pale and with parted lips, as she stretched out both her hands.

"I want—*you*—*you*—*you*," she whispered as he

drew her quickly to him; and nothing else in all the whole wide world!"

It was a gay crowd that came hurrying up the hill and finally took possession, hungrily demanding the contents of the well-filled baskets that awaited them.

Mrs. Oats sweetly and surely took command, assuming a leadership over all the other married women present which no one seemed inclined to dispute, and presiding over the toothsome spread with a tactful ease that was essentially hers. There was something in the mere idea of superiority, even in minor matters, which appealed to her strongly. To be recognized as above the average was something always worth striving for; and she was capable of a concentration of intent which the ordinary certainly know little of. So that in her desire to awaken consideration for herself, she was often led to the performance of tasks wholly without interest for her, just as she had long ago learned the value of an outward expression to cover an inward lack.

From time to time she bent a scrutinizing glance on young Dilson, who had been aiding her; and it was toward the end of the feast that a vague comprehension of his state of mind gave to her tones that special softness and intimacy which she usually reserved for those on whom she sought to make a distinct impression. Hitherto her acquaintance with him had been rather slight. She would have been glad then and there to convert him into a pleasant friend—one who should yield to her the admiring and respectful fealty which a young man may give to a married woman many years his senior who has appealed to his imagination and stimulated his thought. She saw that he was disturbed. But are not friends, like hearts, caught on the rebound?

She was bending over a freezer of chocolate cream, careful of her lilac gingham gown and the grace of her posture, while she manipulated the large iron spoon with which he had just laughingly presented her, when it suddenly occurred to her that all along she had been merely wasting her strength. The mortifying conviction was beginning to take hold of her that his animation which, during the earlier part of the afternoon, had been the life of the party, was now entirely forced, and that he was at present standing at her side and receiving from her hand saucers of frozen cream far less from a desire to be helpful to her, than for the reason that he was vainly trying to shut out from his thoughts a painful recollection: the sight of Blackburn and Cicely sitting together on the hillside half an hour before when he with the rest had returned from the tramp.

She too, as she came up with Major Wise, had caught the look lingering on Blackburn's strong, poetic face, which the quick eyes of his rival had read too surely. Cicely, with her woman's wit and her sure defences against prying eyes had deceived her for a moment—but for a moment only. The elder woman's heart had been stung to a secret rebellion, a bitter repining for her own lost youth and joy.

As she stood studying the girl all rosy and smiling, proudly guarding her happy secret, the graceful form erect with an added grace, the blue eyes sweetly kind, as reflecting some inner light that would seek to warm and comfort everything within its range, Mrs. Oats had been conscious of a sense of unreasoning irritation; and she had known that sharp pang of envious feeling that seemed always to come to her in the presence of the heyday of life and love.

Presently she turned to Frederick Dilson. "The last?" she cried. I thought there were still several more. Those two over there, have you cared for them?"

The young man looked in the direction she indicated. He saw two figures outlined in the distance—Cicely and the major, sitting a little apart from the rest, and talking very earnestly.

"Everyone has been cared for," he said.

Mrs. Oats noted the quickly averted eyes. "Then

you have only to get that basket of grapes over there and our task is done," she announced, throwing out her arms with a gesture of relief and a ripple of laughter.

But his thoughts were two far away to observe the hollow ring in her voice, and she knew it.

He had no sooner left her than the animation upon her features gave way. She turned and walked quickly toward the waiting carriages. She wanted to be alone; and she was not willing that anyone should look on her as she was at that moment, dreary, dejected, her countenance unbecomingly darkened instead of wreathed in the usual radiant, captivating smiles. The indifference of Frederick Dilson toward her was forgotten, it is true; but it had served as the last straw to weight her down.

Something in the young joy she had witnessed had roused her to an old and desperate longing, hitherto scarce confessed. It made her almost reckless. A humiliating realization was upon her, and she knew that she had crossed that fatal border line where a woman tells herself that the feeling that sways her has assumed the concrete, the definite. She was not wise enough to know the effect upon character of such admission in a case like hers—she could not grasp the ethical; but she was capable of a shivering horror at the thought of anything that should seem like defiance of that conventional code she strove to live up to. Yet her eyes looked deep into the distant past; and through all the years she saw only a single face—the face of Major Wise.

She was moving along unobserved back of the gay company, with her soft, cat-like tread, when pride altered her impulse to avoid to that of a deliberate seeking. All at once she turned and retraced her steps.

Cicely was speaking in a low voice as she came up, and Mrs. Oats caught the words: "I wanted you to be the first to know, even before my own father and mother. I knew that you would be glad—so glad."

Mrs. Oats turned aside. The quiet tones thrilled her with their sweet and passionate reserve. To be loved as that girl was loved, what would she not have given for one hour of happiness like that! And how cheap and tawdry seemed the baubles for which she had bartered her ideals! Cicely rose, held out both her hands, and the major bowed low above them with a fervent "God bless you, my child, you have made this old world young for me again! It is like a glimpse of the lady of ones dreams to look into your eyes."

He stood and watched the graceful form as it moved away from him, and Mrs. Oats waited. He was about to move toward three or four young people to his left when she came up rapidly, a little breathless, but smiling, and perfectly at her ease.

"Is it eight yet?" she asked. "No? How deliciously dismal the chorus of those frogs down there. I like it because I know that in a few moments I shall be far away from it. It makes me feel so strange and creepy to be in the country at this hour, there are so many lonesome sounds, don't you know?"

She sank back into the seat Cicely had just vacated, and the major, hesitating a moment, took the one at her side. A faint, cool wind was sighing in the tree tops. It was the moment between dusk and darkness. About them was the remains of what had once been a majestic forest, and one of the most beautiful tracts of land that human eye has ever rested on stretched out to their view. Sitting under the last of those mighty oaks and elms of the early settlers, one can know, even now, a faint throb of the enchantment that seemed ever to stir the pioneer heart; and one has only to close his eyes to see the primeval woodland, dark, mysterious, terrible, where lurked bear and wolf and cougar, and the still more cruel savage, and to hear the ancient forest as of old calling, calling, calling, like a stern, but tender mother summoning her child.

The major's face was dreamy, peaceful, patient, the face of one who had weathered all life's storms. But his thoughts were traveling backward, and to another summer evening more than forty years before. All the tenderness of his nature had been aroused by the girlish confidence that had just been poured into his ears. His eyes followed the tall form of Blackburn Blair as he moved across the lawn to Cicely, where she stood with several others, talking carelessly with the rest—but waiting, waiting always for him.

Mrs. Oats too watched the meeting in silence. Suddenly she looked up into the major's face. Something in her expression made him catch his breath. Neither spoke.

Then the major nerved himself to a stern duty.

"Once," he said very gently, "just once in my long life I knew the happiness that those two young ones there are feeling at this moment. It was more than forty years ago—more than forty years ago."

Mrs. Oats was looking straight ahead. There was not the quiver of an eyelash, not the movement of a muscle. Her face was like marble.

Presently the major spoke again. "She was the one woman I have ever loved." And then he added quickly, with fine chivalrous feeling, "or that ever loved me."

And still Mrs. Oats stared dully into the twilight with her white set face. She did not speak nor stir. It was the first moment in all her artificial existence in which she had ever been really beautiful. But she did not know it. She had grown old.

CHAPTER VI

IN WHICH BLACKBURN IS ARRAIGNED

"Blackburn, you know I have never wanted Cicely to marry you."

"I am well aware of that, Mrs. Overton," responded Blackburn, promptly. "It is a matter of regret to us both that we have not your and the colonel's approval. Nevertheless — "

His tone had become firm. He paused abruptly and looked with quiet courtesy toward the thin, elderly gentleman sitting calmly and with an air of detachment near an open window in old Judge Trotter's library.

"Nevertheless?" repeated Mrs. Overton, a little coldly.

"She has decided."

"What children you both are!" she exclaimed, with a laugh and a shrug. "No doubt she has decided. But what do such decisions amount to in nine cases out of ten? I confess that I am still not entirely without hope. Cicely is very uncertain. Just when you think you are surest about her, is the time she is most apt to fail you. She gave me a positive shock when she told me of her engagement to you. I had thought she was entirely reconciled to other plans her Aunt Catherine and I had for her. She has a way of keeping things to herself that is almost irritating; and she was always inclined to be a little wayward. I think I can say truly that Cicely is the only one of my children that I have never quite been able to manage, or to understand. In the main, I have had my own way with her, it is true. But it has been a struggle from the first. As a little child she would sometimes throw herself down and cry for hours before she would give in and do the thing I demanded; and even after I had gained my point, I usually recognized that she was only half-conquered, if so much as that. I suppose she hasn't that firm little chin for nothing; and I of all people, of course, would naturally be most inclined to be patient with her. She gets her will-power entirely from me."

"I have always suspected her of being a little deep," remarked Blackburn, smiling cheerfully, and generously ignoring Mrs. Overton's calm assumption of superiority over her patient spouse.

"But she was always sweet," continued Mrs. Overton, dispassionately, "only headstrong and rather difficult. The way she has clung to you in spite of my opposition is only another instance of a characteristic obstinacy."

"Pardon me if I would suggest another word," said Blackburn, soberly.

"Oh, it's a very good word, Blackburn — we needn't change it, I think. If you and she persist in this — in this most unwise determination, I venture to say that the day will come when you will agree with me in thinking that much in Cicely that looks like strength of character and feeling is only stubborness, after all."

"I am willing to take my chances on that."

"But there may be consequences, a risk to her happiness as well as yours. You are as positive and as wilful as she is. You are not at all suited to each other. Pardon me, Blackburn, but it is only to be expected that her father and I, foreseeing the probable, I may say the almost certain, results of a marriage between you two, should desire to avert it by every means in our power. I have never tried to conceal from you that we were doing our best."

Colonel Overton stirred uneasily. He was a tall, careworn, frail-looking man, with a sharp-pointed face and an expression that was at the same time deprecating and kindly. Both his moustache and hair were entirely white, but the impression of age that one received at first glance, gave way somewhat on closer scrutiny. He still bore himself with the air of a soldier, but there was evidence of physical weakness in his excessive thinness and in his taut, sallow skin, like parchment against the shock of crisp, curling hair, which he wore rather long and brushed loosely back from his really fine brow. There was something winning in his delicate, old-fashioned courtesy, his unmistakable high-breeding and apparent sweetness of attitude toward all the world; so that one pitied rather than condemned the suggestion of a lack of moral strength which seemed to force itself almost instantly upon the attention.

"Don't you think, my dear," he said in his soft Southern voice, leaving his place by the window and taking a nearer chair, "don't you think you slightly overstate the case? In the main, I believe, I feel sure, that I have only seconded your wishes."

"We were entirely agreed," replied Mrs. Overton, positively. "You think, you have always thought, just as I have thought, and still think, on the subject of this marriage. At least you have so expressed yourself to me."

The colonel assayed a little joke.

"It is always a wise man who is able to know when a woman has made up her mind," he observed, with a slightly embarrassed laugh and a sly wink out of the corner of one eye. But presently he turned more seriously to Blackburn.

"My boy," he said a little anxiously, and in affectionate appeal, "you must not think, you cannot think that we have, either of us, anything against you personally. Such a thing could scarcely be possible in your case. On the contrary, you have our highest respect, as you must know—our very highest respect. Furthermore, there are many reasons why your union with our daughter would seem a consummation becoming and desirable in every way. Our families have been friendly, yes, intimate, for generations. If there have been differences—ahem—differences in certain vitally important matters in times past, I have ever maintained for your father, the Honourable Blackburn Blair, that regard and esteem which he has seemed to me so richly to deserve. I trust that it will never be said of me that I failed to recognize the integrity of any man who possessed it, merely because the Confederacy, which I loved as I did my life, was denied by him. I like your pedigree. You come of fine old Kentucky and Virginia stock. You have been reared in that atmosphere of culture and refinement which best fits a man for a tender chivalry toward the—the—ah—weaker sex—and which is the birthright and special distinction of the high-born Southern gentleman. I am told that your morals are excellent; and finally, my dear boy, you have ability, which, though at present somewhat misdirected, if you will pardon me for saying so, is worthy of those illustrious sires, many of whom are a heritage in which any man would feel a worthy pride. Let me point you to your ancestors in the pages of history. Where will you find—"

The colonel was about to enter upon a somewhat lengthy enumeration of Blackburn's progenitors when Mrs. Overton threw up her hands irritably.

"For heaven's sake spare us the list—spare us," she exclaimed. "That is one of the troubles, so far as Blackburn and Cicely are concerned, they'd have together more ancestors than they'd know what to do with."

"I don't think they'd have occasion to do anything with them, my dear," observed the colonel, pacifically, stroking his moustache.

"The main question, Blackburn, to be considered," said Mrs. Overton, staring straight ahead of her, and returning to her point with renewed zeal, "is simply this: Cicely is unfitted to be your wife. Had I ever intended that she should spend her life in this quiet corner of the world, I should not have sent her to her Aunt Catherine, and in this way accustomed her to pomps and vanities, so to speak, which it is out of the question she should have here."

"She cares nothing for the pomps and vanities," declared Blackburn, stoutly. "Their loss will mean nothing to her, I am sure."

Mrs. Overton studied him thoughtfully. "How little you know her!" she exclaimed at length. "All women care more or less for these things, most of them, more. Even when we are praying to be delivered from pride and all vain glory we are not unmindful of our own or our neighbor's hat."

"Cicely shall have so many hats that they shall cease to interest or disturb her."

"The hat was merely a figure of speech, Blackburn," remarked Mrs. Overton, severely. "You know perfectly well what I mean. You cannot think that there will be any brilliancy or excitement in the life you offer. But it is only natural, after the training she has had, that these things should be as essential to her as the air she breathes. When she tells you to the contrary, she is merely deceiving herself and you. You might as well transplant a hot-house flower and expect it to thrive in frozen soil, as to ask her to be contented outside of her proper atmosphere. She is one of those rare women who show from their cradles that they are born for a great social career. She should be the wife of an important diplomat—or at the worst a man of fortune."

"To all of this I can only say to you what I said a moment ago," said Blackburn, very calmly. "She has decided."

Mrs. Overton was verging upon impatience. "Her Aunt Catherine tells me she has refused some excellent offers. There was a Russian, a man of high birth and considerable wealth. It is true he was much too old for her; but it was just the same in the case of younger men. I think she honestly tried to forget you, knowing how I felt. For the first marriage in a family is always so important. It seems to decide the future status of all the rest. I have tried to make her feel that true unselfishness would lead her to look beyond her own girlish whims and fancies; and Cicely more than any of the the others, for I have talked to her more on this subject, is acquainted with her father's present financial condition. It isn't every girl who would have the opportunity of doing as much for her family, if she would only listen to reason. But for the first time in my life my authority has been openly defied. It seems useless to say anything further to her. Of course her father and I cannot do anything if she persists. We shall not be guilty of the bad taste of anything unpleasant in a public way. Our only hope now is that you yourself will see the matter in the right light. Blackburn, will nothing make you give her up?"

She turned to him with a tragic gesture of her black gauze fan. Blackburn threw back his head and laughed boyishly.

"Nothing, Mrs. Overton, I assure you, nothing whatever," he said at length, and without the smallest evidence of offence. On the contrary, there was in his manner a composure and a good-humored pleasantry which to Mrs. Overton was intensely exasperating.

He had been listening to her most attentively, with a dispassionate courtesy that was wholly impersonal. His face was calm, as of one who has himself well in hand. He looked a man every inch of him in his remoteness, and in his complete superiority to the situation.

It was nine o'clock of a warm summer evening. Cicely had gone out, he knew, but he was expecting her every moment to return. He found himself waiting with the eager confidence of a sure lover for her light foot-fall and the delicious rustle of her garments. Mrs. Overton's high colour had deepened. She was beautifully gowned in a costume of black silk and lace and she presented the sleek, well-groomed air of a woman who has been accustomed always to give particular attention to every detail of her appearance, inspired, however, more by a spirit of thoroughness than of vanity.

"Now that you have taken the unfortunate political stand you have, I am more than ever troubled over this affair," she remarked, wearily, at length.

Blackburn looked up quickly. "I am very glad, Mrs. Overton," he said, "that you have mentioned my political stand. You may not be greatly interested in hearing what I have to say on the subject, but there are certain matters relating to the present crisis in the state's public affairs that I should like very much to talk over with the colonel, if he will hear me."

"There is only one thing I care to hear about," she declared, with a shrug of the shoulders and ignoring the colonel as completely as if he were not included, "and that is how you can possibly endure to have persons speak of you as a 'Goebelite.' I should think it would be most unpleasant."

The colonel tapped his foot a trifle nervously.

"My dear," he implored in his mild voice, laughing amiably and wholly unconscious of the fact that he was falling into a customary expression, "don't you think you slightly overstate the case? You would not object to being called a 'Goebelite' if, like Blackburn, you were for Mr. Goebel, would you?"

His guest showed no disposition to defend himself and Colonel Overton continued.

"Blackburn," he said, "I have been very much disturbed to see you injuring your prospects as you are doing by supporting a man like William Goebel." The colonel's tone had grown paternal. "Even if the attack that has been made upon the man is in a measure unjust, it seems to me that it would have been advisable for one so young as yourself to go a little more slowly in a matter in which very serious consequences may be involved. Your own future will doubtless be much affected by the pronounced stand you have taken. I am told that though you have added somewhat to your reputation as an orator by certain speeches you have made, the anti-Goebel press of the State and elsewhere are heaping upon you an abuse that it would have been prudent to avoid. It is well known that for some time you have been looked upon as a probable candidate in the next race for representative in Congress from this district. But the feeling against any man who endorses that Louisville convention and the dictator who dominated it to the point of fraudulently obtaining the nomination, is intense—I may say violently intense."

Blackburn shook his head. "Pardon me, Colonel, if I pass over your reference to my prospects; they are not in the present question. As regards the enmity toward Mr. Goebel and the abuse that has been heaped upon him, everyone knows it is primarily to be traced to his strenuous and unrelenting stand against the encroachments of corporate power. But what I wish especially to bring before you in explanation of my own position is simply this: the importance of this election in relation to the national matter. Much will depend upon Kentucky's action at this time, for if Kentucky—"

Mrs. Overton rose. The conversation bored her.

"How like a Kentuckian, Blackburn, to think that

the fate of the nation depends upon us!" she said, with a laugh. "I marvel at your enthusiasm. If you had been through all that we have in times past you would feel as we do, that when the South lost the Confederacy, it lost everything. It is impossible to be greatly interested in these new issues. Still, if I were a man I should find it utterly impossible to give my vote to any man who had killed, as your Mr. Goebel did in recent years, a brave Confederate soldier. That alone would be sufficient for me, even if there were not other excellent reasons for not supporting him."

After she had left the room the two sat a while without speaking. As a mere form the colonel presently suggested mint julep and cigars. He knew that Blackburn took neither, but he would have felt himself sadly lacking had he failed to propose both.

"I believe this is the first opportunity, Colonel," said the young man at length, "I have had of explaining to you fully just what the idea of Democracy has come to mean to me in its broader and deeper sense. It is not a sentiment. It is a very distinct reality. The thunderings of Sinai were not more sure. It is to be the dominant note of the coming century; and it is something strong and resistless as the ocean, or a mighty, on-rushing wind, inevitable as death. It is the cumulative idea of freedom which has been slowly growing through the centuries, so that now for the first time in the history of humanity man is beginning to grasp the fine principle of brotherhood and to rouse himself to the realization of all that that may mean. Everywhere we see evidences of this new spirit at work: in religion, where a broader catholicity is breaking down non-essentials in creed and dogma and the claim of superiority on the part of one denomination over another; in literature, where the temporary rebound to the romantic in fiction which is finding its setting in the vital emotion of Revolutionary or other historic times—cheap and sensational as the product too often is—is mainly a revolt against the realistic greed and commercialism of prevailing conditions; in social life, in the body politic, everywhere we see evidences of some mighty force at work among us that is to reorganize the world. For a long time its rumbling was only indistinct. It is daily growing louder. Even the dullest now are not deaf to it. Many are wilfully closing their ears to it. But all hear it. It is because back of it is a miracle which stands as an eternal symbolism to the ages—the miracle of the Incarnation. Let no man claim that in any true sense he has laid hold of the Christ idea who has not grasped the thought of service, the sinking of the individual interest in the interest of the many."

He spoke earnestly, with the tendency to lapse unconsciously into the oratorical which was strong with him, as with most Kentuckians, when under the pressure of excitement. His young face was eager, daring, hopeful. His dark eyes were lit with a sacred fire that the colonel knew not of. But even he was roused. He looked troubled and ill at ease.

"My dear boy," he said a trifle nervously, "I greatly fear that these new theories you have imbibed may prove an intoxicating draught that will lead you into error. It seems a pity that your bright future should be destroyed by the delusive demagogism of the moment. Who knows but that this whole idea will melt like a bubble in the course of the next year or two?"

"Truth once started on its way never turns back. If it exist vitally in the heart of one man, and one only, its progress will be sure."

"Well, I must say that it sounds to me, it sounds to me like quackery of the very worst kind. I have never thought you lacking in practical sense. These matters before us now are eminently practical. A thing may be right in theory and wrong in practice. In politics this is often the case. With the old doctrines of the Democratic party, I am, as you know, strongly in sympathy. I was always an ardent free trader, and as little inclined as a man could be toward affiliation on any point with the views of Northern statesmen. I am a true son of the South, sir, and that I shall be to the end; but when the party attempts to force me to accept what I regard as unsound and as positively vicious, then there is nothing left for me but to withdraw my support."

"You admit," said Blackburn, "that in its cardinal doctrine of a protective tariff the Republican party sounds the keynote of selfishness. I think you will admit also that you are opposed to the present pernicious influence of wealth in political affairs, and that you do not wish to see our government given over to the money power; and I am sure also that you are heartily opposed to the ever-increasing, unrighteous combinations of capital which are destroying the many for the sake of the few, which are directly tending toward a complete centralization of power, and which, if allowed to go unrebuked, would turn civilization backward to the days of the Middle Ages. In all these points, Colonel, we are agreed, are we not?"

Colonel Overton shifted his position.

"I am opposd to the evils of trusts, Blackburn," he said tapping his foot. "I suppose all right thinking men unite on that. It was Thomas Jefferson who said that 'monopolies are sacrifices of the many to the few.' But I confess that, without the aid of a constitutional amendment, I question the power of any federal anti-trust legislation to meet the case. Much that is said upon this subject by Democrats seems to me to be chimerical and insincere. Legislation has always shown itself powerless to remedy evils."

The colonel looked disturbed. His brow had suddenly become puckered, and one long, lean forefinger tapped his lips absently. "Well — well," he added presently, as if shaking off unpleasant thoughts, "these questions are not to be disposed of in a single jump. I am not inclined to take an altogether gloomy view of what has been done thus far. The truth is, I am not in any sense a pessimist over the future of this country."

"Nor am I!" cried Blackburn, heartily. "The country is still so young. I cannot believe that we have reached that stage in our development when, following the usual course of nations, we shall begin to decline. On the contrary, in my opinion, we are entering upon the grandest period we have yet known in our national life. For it is to be the commencement of the reign of the spiritual as opposed to the merely material. In spite of the merciless greed all round us, the seeming triumph of evil on every hand, I yet believe that we are on the verge of a moral and a religious awakening such as the world has never seen. A sure deliverance is on its way in the good that lives in good men's hearts. It is a divine thing. It cannot be overthrown. For my part, everything in me cries out for a share in this work; and I marvel that any man can lull himself to forgetfulness of his suffering fellows by thinking only of his own more fortunate condition. And so, sir, you ask me to wait, to temporize, to be silent, and I can only say to myself as did Mordecai to Queen Esther: 'If thou altogether holdest thy peace at this time, then shall there enlargement and deliverance arise to the Jews from another place; but thou and thy father's house shall be destroyed."

Colonel Overton rose and began to move softly up and down the room, his hands clasped behind him.

"It is not surprising," he observed at length, with as near an approach to ill-temper as would be possible with him, "that your father's son and I should differ in matters political. To me this state issue now before us is the supreme issue, and to go off on other matters is merely visionary and illogical."

"It is only to be expected, Colonel, that my father's son should place the nation above the state," responded Blackburn, with a quiet smile.

The colonel returned to his chair. "Feeling as you do, Blackburn," he said a little coldly, "I can see that no other course is open to you than the one you have taken. I can only regret this — both for your own and my daughter's sake. To go back to the state matter and to William Goebel —"

"Pardon me, Colonel; but so far as William Goebel

is concerned, it will take another generation fully to understand him, just as in the case of General Jackson, the man —"

There was a hurried, feeble step in the hall, the nervous click of a cane, and old Judge Trotter suddenly appeared in the doorway. He held a large volume in one hand. His expression was stormy. He had been dozing in an adjoining room, but he had all at once caught mention of his beloved hero Andrew Jackson, and instantly he was awake and ready for an onslaught as fierce and bloody as the wars of the Creeks and the Seminoles. In some way it seemed to be borne in upon him that the colonel, because of his oppositton to Blackburn's views, had dared to profane the sacred name by using it as an argument in his own defence. He was in a rage.

"Listen to this," he demanded hotly, fixing his eyes sternly upon his son-in-law, and rapidly turning the pages of his book, "Listen to this!" And straightway he began to read, with a deep rolling of sentences supposed to be particularly Jacksonian, the message of 1832:

"Distinctions in society will always exist under every just government. Equality of talents, of education, or wealth cannot be produced by human institutions. In the full enjoyment of the gifts of heaven, economy, and virtue, every man is equally entitled to protection by law. But when laws undertake to add to these natural and just advantages artificial distinctions, to grant titles, gratuities, and exclusive privileges, to make the rich richer and the potent more powerful, the humble members of society, the farmers, mechanics, and labourers, who have neither the time nor the means of securing like favours to themselves, have the right to complain of the injustice of their government. There are no necessary evils in government. Its evils exist only in its abuses. If it would confine itself to equal protection, and, as heaven does its rains, shower its favours alike on the high and the low, the rich and the poor, it would be an unqualified blessing.' "

The judge closed the book with a triumphant bang, and turning without a word, he marched majestically from the room.

His entrance had been so cyclonic, and his quotation was so amusingly apt that neither the colonel nor Blackburn dared looked into each other's eyes for fear they should both break forth into laughter. It would have been a dangerous thing surely for the colonel to do; and it may be questioned if such levity would have been tolerated from even Blackburn himself.

Still struggling with himself the young man rose. "You see, Colonel, he closes the argument," he remarked, with one of his brilliant smiles, "there is nothing left for me to say."

He stood a moment waiting boyishly after he had held out his hand.

"I can't tell you how I regret that you cannot see it all as I do, Colonel," he said at length with simple fervour. "There are — there are many reasons why I should wish to please you if I could — one above all others. I feel that in robbing you of — of your daughter I incur a debt that I can never hope to pay; and I wish to thank you for even the small measure of approval you can give me. Good-night."

CHAPTER VII

IN THE MOONLIGHT

As he went down the steps there was a soft white fluttering and Cicely came toward him up the walk, swinging her light gauze scarf. She came slowly, with an eager, half-amused questioning in her eyes and a low sweet laughter on her lips. There was a subtle allurement in the lagging step and in the gesture of the bare, beautiful arms, for a moment outstretched and then hanging heavily at her side, which told that she was weary waiting. The mystery and the enchantment of moonlight were all about her; and with her Hebe face, her soft breathing like the faint sighing of the night wind in the tree tops, her star-like eyes, she was to Blackburn a thing unreal, almost too wondrous to be believed in.

A startled exclamation broke from him—the low quick cry of joy that so strangely resembles the cry of pain. He took a hurried step toward her, and all at once paused.

She was late in returning, and he had abandoned the hope of seeing her, so that when he suddenly came upon her in her ethereal draperies he stood looking at her in the dumb surprise — wistful, empassioned, yet not quite sure — of one who in a dream dimly beholds a longed-for face.

"I have been waiting here for you," she said, with quickly lowered eyelids, overcome by an unaccustomed shyness, as in silence he took both of her hands in his, and his deep gaze sank into her own. She drew back a little from his ultra-seriousness, and moved toward the gate.

"Was it so dreadful, Blackburn? What did they say to you?" she asked presently, with ineffectual archness. "I think it must be a very valiant knight I have."

But his eyes were still riveted on her face — as if they were striving to pierce the beautiful outer covering and would look upon her soul.

"Cicely, can anything, *anything* ever separate us now?" he cried impetously, brushing aside as irrelevant everything but the one thing which in that moment seemed supreme to him.

Cicely leaned her white arms on the iron gate. The small brown head was lowered. There was a soft trembling of the lace about the ivory shoulders. He had at times a masterful way with him that, womanlike, she both adored and shrank from. She seemed struggling with a kind of secret pride.

"You have won me — absolutely," she said at length in a low voice without meeting his eyes. "Why do you doubt?"

"Then look at me!"

She slowly lifted her face to his. "As ever you will have your way. Now — are you satisfied?"

"Satisfied! I shall never be until you are mine, all mine — every bit of you. Cicely, I wonder if I shall ever be able to make you know what you are to me?"

Her look was very sweet and truthful as his hand closed over hers. But she seemed vaguely troubled.

"Perhaps I can know a little by what you are to me," she answered simply. "But now that you have me, has it never occurred to you that something may be lost — that there may be a penalty for your rashness?"

"A penalty?"

She tapped lightly with her left hand on the iron railing, and the ring that he had given her made fitful scintillation as she marked the rhythm of the lines she quoted. There was a sadness in the low voice that went to his heart.

'Who wins his love shall lose her,
Who loses her shall gain,
For still the spirit woos her,
A soul without a stain;
And memory still pursues her
With longings not in vain!'

"But it is false — altogether false," put in Blackburn, with decision.

She only laughed and shook her head and went on to the end.

'He loses her who gains her,
  Who watches day by day
The dust of time that stains her,
  The griefs that leave her gray,
The flesh that still enchains her
  Whose grace hath passed away!

'Oh, happier he who gains not
  The love some seem to gain;
The joy that custom stains not
  Shall still with him remain,
The loveliness that wanes not,
  The love that ne'er can wane.

'In dreams she grows not older
  The land of dreams among,
Though all the world wax colder,
  Though all the songs be sung,
In dreams doth he behold her
  Still fair and kind and young.'

He stood leaning against the gate at her side, listening with the quiet concentration with which he was wont to give attention.

"It is wholly unsound," he said presently in his sure, determined way. "The love that dies in possession is unworthy of the name.

There was in his voice a ring of confidence that thrilled her through and through. She pressed nearer to him.

"But I fear it, Blackburn, I fear it, the change, the horrible changes that might come. A love grown careless, cold — "

He looked at her in wondering surprise.

"Does it seem a thing possible to you that we should grow to love each other less because together we had climbed over some of life's rough places?" he asked gravely.

"It is not a woman's way, but sometimes it is a man's way. I can't forget that."

His brow cleared.

"I am not troubled by such foolish fancies. My fears are altogether real. Cicely, if anything should be said to you of me intended to make you think less well of me, will you close your ears?"

"I will close my ears."

"Then no one — no one shall come between us now?"

She did not answer.

His heart suddenly stood still. "Cicely!" he drew nearer to her in alarm, stung by her silence. "Cicely — tell me! *No one?*

"No one — nothing but yourself."

He drew a long deep breath.

"Oh, Blackburn, if only I could be sure," she cried.

"Sure of what?"

"Of what I shall be to you in the long, long years when so many other things will be calling to you."

He looked at her strangely. He was unable to understand her mood. In the great unselfish love he bore her there was a simplicity and a directness that refused to grapple with anything so intangible. But he saw that her pain was real. A great wave of tenderness and pity swept over him and a sudden passionate longing to silence all her womanly fears shook him to the very heart's center.

His eyes rested a moment hungrily upon her. The street was still. He reached out his arms to her, and his strong will encircled her like a flame.

"Well, *I* am sure!" he said positively, and bent down his head and kissed her.

CHAPTER VIII

JOY'S GRAPE

'September days are dreamy days,'

sang Cicely absently in a low voice to herself as she moved about her room. She had just come in from a morning walk, and she was radiant with life and hope and joy. The early mail had brought a letter from Blackburn bearing the postmark of a little town in the southern part of the state, where he had gone to make a speech. Ah, that everlasting speechmaking! But the letter had thrilled her through and through with its unrestrained passion and pride of possession, and still more by its deep undercurrent of emotions that he seemed powerless to translate. She moved softly, decorously, and with downcast lids, as if her eyes still held the secret of a vision; and she was lost in revery as she laid aside her hat and untied the scarf at her throat.

'September days are dreamy days,
  September hills are blue;
September ways are quiet ways,
September days are dreamy days,
The distant hills are blue with haze
  That sunbeams sparkle through.
September days are dreamy days,
  September hills are blue.'

She got quickly out of her white linen and into a loose gown of muslin and lace, and then took up the little song again standing before her mirror:

'September is a lady fair
  Whose smile is somewhat sad,'

she sang, searching for a comb among the confusion of articles on her dressing-table.

'The first gray strands are in her hair,
September is a lady fair,
Who has a sweet and gentle air—
  But not the youth she had!
September is a lady fair,
  Whose smile—'"

All at once she paused, letting her hair ripple to her waist, and broke into a laugh — as if suddenly becoming conscious of herself and of the song. She stood for an instant blankly staring her reflection in the eyes, and with a rather startled and inquiring expression. Then she reached forth her arms to it with an affectionate gesture and a little glad cry of satisfaction that had in it less of vanity than of finer feeling. She was still young and beautiful, thank God! — and for him.

She turned away with a swift impulse and crossed the room to her desk. It was one of those vivid moments, intense and quiveringly alive, which frequently possessed her, when Blackburn seemed actually to stand before her — not his usual self, as she was accustomed to the sight of him, but a being godlike in his proportions and clothed with a peculiar majesty and beauty. He did not speak, but his eyes looked deep into her eyes, and his arms held her close and tenderly, despite their iron clasp.

A wave of crimson swept through her, dyeing cheek and neck and brow. Her breath came quick and uneven between her parted lips. The longing to pour out her soul to him in one of those spontaneous and glowing messages which she had been sending him during his absence from her urged her to expression. Some loose sheets of letter paper lay scattered about the desk, and she caught up one of these dipping her pen into a more vital fluid as well as into ink. She wrote:

"My dearest, the first month of the autumn!—and yet I am just entering upon my spring. I cannot persuade myself that it isn't May, for a thousand little song-birds are singing in my heart, and I feel—if I may compare myself to anyone so lovely—as I think the Sleeping Beauty must have felt when the Prince knelt down and kissed her out of her long sleep—I mean the moment when she first opened her eyes. I have just opened my eyes; and though things are still a little confused with me, and I cannot fully get my bearings yet, I am so intensely conscious of *You*, so thrilled in every nerve and fibre of my being that it seems a matter of little moment that I am no longer able to think calmly or clearly. But one thing at least I know for a certainty (and this too is less a matter of thought than of feeling) that all my past has simply been a dreaming and a waiting—a dreaming and a waiting for you. My life has just begun. And there has never been anyone else who has robbed you of even a little! I wonder how many women who have loved can say as much as that? Yet I am sure that every woman who has deeply loved a man would wish to say it if she could.

"To-day the earth was glorious, with scarcely a hint of coming frosts. Can it be that the leaves are actually going to wither and fall—and soon? I heard an old farmer on the street to-day, speaking to another of something that would occur, I don't remember what, about the time of the 'fall rains.' *Will* it rain? Must it! I hurried past, hearing already in my ears the dismal, sobbing sound. But the sky was blue and glittering like a jewel, and the air was most deliciously balmy and cool; and I was comforted, for it was truly a beautiful world, and I gave myself up to its allurements in a sort of frenzied delight—the more so, perhaps, because of the reminder that it was just a little too beautiful to last. I was restless and set out for a long walk; and for a while I wandered about in a purposeless fashion, like a hamadryad, unfamiliar with city streets (as surely a hamadryad should be); then instinct led me to the woods—and to you. I found you, for you are never very far away from me these days, my beloved, although there are miles and miles between us. I was quite out in the country, and as I had taken the car for part of the way, the town way, I was not a bit tired. I sat down on an old mossgrown rock near the roadside, and all around everything was still. Then it was that I looked up and saw you, in a sudden burst of sunlight, coming toward me, quickly, and with shining eyes. Dearest, I am never sure which are the most real moments—those in which I see you with my bodily eyes, or with the eyes of my soul.

"And do you know, I am not altogether sorry now—I was at first, but not now—that we must be separated from each other for a little while? Thank God, it is only for a little while, and I think it may prove a good thing for us both. We were getting just a wee bit beside ourselves, and our eyes were becoming dazzled, at least mine were; so that it is well enough to try to view things a little by the light of common day. But dear, your letters! Who of all the pretty maids that have known you would believe that you could make such an ideal lover—who but me?—if you will pardon the vanity of that. I have always suspected your possibilities in that line—and feared them. To-day, after reading your letter over

—oh, so many times—I was reminded of something that some one said of you once—on the principle of suggestion by contrast, I suppose. Do you remember that coquettish little girl from New Orleans who visited here some months after I first came home? You took her in at the major's New Year's dinner, and in spite of the example that she set you, you were about as flirtatious as a church steeple. Afterwards, when I went to get my wraps, I heard someone ask her for an opinion of you. 'Oh, but he is charming,' she said with her funny little lisp, 'but don't you think he is a trifle stiff and cold?' (That was magnanimity personified.) Stiff and cold!—*you?* I should like to know what she would have had to say of the letter that came to me this morning. Dear, I wonder for how long you will be sending me such burning words? I wonder.

> 'Think you, if Laura had been Petrarch's wife,
> He would have written sonnets all his life?'

"But I wont. I really will not. Blackburn, I am trying my very best to put away all doubts—trying to be peacefully happy in the thought that I have ended the struggle at last. Do you know how I think of you sometimes? You are not always my lover. Once in a while—rarely, but often enough to leave an impression upon my mind that lingers with me—once in a great while then, do you know what you are? You are *just a little boy*, and I—I am sitting near you, while you work or play, watching you with your mother's loving eyes, and her deeply happy smile. How she loved you! Somehow I seem to understand.

"You write: 'Until Saturday I shall have no rest day or night. Then—!' And my heart echoes *then!* In the meantime it is filled to overflowing with one lovely, reviving, all-animating thought, and I would pour it forth upon you like the contents of an alabaster box. It is this, dear, and if you will bend down your head I will whisper it. I love you, 'O thou soul of my soul,' I *love* you!

"CICELY."

Blackburn was in Louisville when the letter reached him. It came into his hands shortly after he had entered the Galt House with several persons who had accompanied him to his hotel in order to talk over certain important political plans. It lacked just two hours of the time when he was to make another speech. He was feeling tired and a good deal disturbed at the turn matters were taking, and it was a relief when after a wearisome discussion, he was finally able to disengage himself. He went to his room and opened the letter with an avidity that would have brought a look of surprise to the faces of the old politicians he had just left, had they seen it. But he was no longer the wise young statesman cool, capable, discerning, whose skill was so much more than a match for theirs that their astuteness was apt to stand a little crestfallen in the presence of his sounder and loftier judgment. He was a lover now, every inch of him, and he gave himself up to the reading of the letter with a look in his eyes that none but Cicely had ever seen there, unmindful that he was fatigued, forgetful that he was dinnerless, and that the hands of his watch were moving steadily toward seven.

In a little more than an hour afterward he stood up before an immense audience of excited Kentuckians and spoke as if inspired.

CHAPTER IX

A COLLISION IN THE COURTHOUSE

With the coming of October the political excitement in Kentucky showed still more alarming signs of increase. All along it had outdone the fiercest heat of summer; and Nature's cool hand seemed powerless to still the fever in men's blood. The two parties stood confronting each other like hostle armies in array, or like two savage beasts about to spring. It was a novel situation for the Democracy of the state, which had been in power, with the interruption of a single Republican administration, since the close of the Civil War.

Old farmers, battle-scarred, hearing again the echoes of forty years before, as they jogged along the sweet country roads, would cast their eyes upon the peaceful landscape about them, and recall another autumn when the same quiet scene had mocked the tumult in their breasts. In Lexington groups of men about the Courthouse and the hotels and on the street corners, were seen at all hours of he day engaged in earnest, anxious conversation. Women also were profoundly interested; and the various questioning growing out of the matter of the future governorship of Kentucky was something that even the most trivial felt herself called upon to decide as seriously as if she were actually to have a part in the impending conflict. Perhaps she did have a part, albeit an inactive one.

Among those, and there were many, who expressed themselves with special acerbity toward the course taken by young Blackburn Blair, was a lawyer at the Lexington bar, of the name of Tippleton.

He was a rough-featured, heavily-built man of about forty, with light-coloured hair and moustache, very keen gray eyes, and a kind of boorish supercilious bluster, sometimes mistaken for forcefulness, which won for him friends in certain quarters, despite a natural irascibility of temper.

The Hon. H. Clay Tippleton, as he was always most carefully designated by the anti-Goebel press of the state, had formerly been a Democrat of the type that scruples at nothing that will promote the advancement of himself and of his party. Such men are seldom rare in any party. Their usefulness is apt to be duly recognized. His coming over into the ranks of the opposition was heralded far and wide as a signal triumph. It was announced in flaming headlines and set forth as a "death blow" to the Democracy. The newspapers opposed to William Goebel rang with florid praise of this "pure, high-minded Kentuckian" whose pride of integrity scorned to give support to a party that had sunk so low as to attempt, by means of "an odious election law," to infringe upon the sacred rights of franchise, and to impose upon "a free, liberty-loving people a reckless buccaneer" who, if elected, would surely bring "the grand old Commonwealth," with its noble past and tradition, to the lowest depths of infamy and shame.

Regarding the awful iniquities predicted of the despised William Goebel something was left to the imagination, the mere mention of the names of the two men in such juxtaposition being deemed sufficient.

Thus the character of the Hon. H. Clay Tippleton was made white and spotless as that of the new born babe. So that he himself, though feeling at first somewhat awkward under such flattering description, was beginning to forget that little matter with the railroad and a certain famous trust which had so effectively converted him to the anti-Goebel faction, and which, to some, might not seem in full accord with all the pleasant things that had been said.

His enmity toward Blackburn Blair dated back to the time when the latter had defeated him in a warmly contested nomination for representative from the city of Lexington in the Kentucky General Assembly. The surprise and rage he had then felt, coupled with the natural dislike of the ruffian toward the gentleman, had long slumbered in secret resentment. It was beginning to flame out now into open wrath—which so many were prepared to describe as a righteous indignation.

In newspaper articles, in public speeches, in social intercourse—wherever opportunity gave the smallest excuse for such a thing, he was ready with adroit denunciation and subtle innuendo. His keenest weapon was ridicule. Sometimes he used it well; and the method he resorted to was not unlike that employed by Tobiah the Ammonite of old when he sought to disconcert the godly Jews who were striving to rebuild the walls of Jerusalem.

As for Blackburn he went calmly on his way, sometimes grave and troubled, often with a laugh on his lips, and always with the zeal of a Nehemiah in his heart.

Disapproval of his stand, whether publicly or privately expressed, seemed powerless to change or to disturb him. He was like a rock in his unyielding fixedness of conviction.

But a climax to all this personal abuse on the part of his ci-devant political rival was reached one morning in the court room.

The trial was on of a young man who had killed another in a drunken brawl in a saloon. There had been a kind of hand to hand scrimmage in which it appeared some four or five had taken part, and the result of it all was that pistols had been drawn, and one man had been killed. A good deal of interest was manifested in the case on account of the youth of the persons implicated.

Tippleton had been secured as one of the counsel for the defence, and Blackburn Blair had been called in by the prosecution.

It was the third day of the trial, and one of those still, brilliant October mornings when the Kentucky skies are like glittering sapphire and the bluegrass, green again as in May with its marvelous second growth, spreads out before the eye in emerald loveliness. The thought of prison walls seemed a melancholy antithesis.

The lawyers engaged in the case were just assembling as Blackburn entered the courtroom. He was looking particularly well, despite the trying campaign, and his smooth face, with its clear olive tone, showed an almost boyish freshness.

Near the doorway he met Tippleton, who was standing talking with several politicians of his own stamp and persuasion. Blackburn bowed generally and passed on, unsuspecting of the fact that the suppressed laugh that followed from the group was called forth by a low joke at his expense — the result of an elephantine attempt at facetiousness on the part of the man who hated him so cordially.

It had not occurred to him in the brief consideration he had given to it, that there was anything personal in Tippleton's undisguised enmity. But already the friends of Blackburn Blair were beginning to fear an open rupture, knowing the insolence of one man and the pride of the other. It was even thought that Tippleton might attempt to provoke a difficulty right there in the courtroom. Such things had been known to happen in that Court before.

However, a certain confidence was felt by those interested in the younger man, in Blackburn's innate dignity of bearing, and in his well-known views on all subjects relating to the matter of self-control. It was these views, upheld by a strenuous living, that in a way seemed to set him apart, and to give to his character an almost clerical remoteness. Nevertheless, there was a vague anticipation that something unusual might be expected to occur, and when the case was reopened a considerable number of visitors had assembled, drawn thither by various promptings—curiosity in the main.

The usual preliminaries had been disposed of, and the trial was proceeding rather tamely, and the large crowd present was beginning to yawn when a certain witness was put on the stand. The man, who happened to be a well-known character about town, seemed likely to call forth some amusement by his comical appearance. The crowd woke up.

He was a queer white-haired individual of about sixty, with a sly, but good-humoured twinkle in his eyes, very shaggy as to the beard, very red as to the nose, and with a huge paunch that gave to his gait something slow and impressive, and put one in mind of Santa Claus. However, he had a few moments before been likened to a still more memorable personage by one of his admiring associates. "I jes tell yer, boys," the man had remarked with a circular wave of the hand in front of his own person, "I jes tell yer about that 'ere Sam Winks. He's one o' them great, big, fine-lookin' fellehs that kinder makes yer feel small — a sorter Pontius Pilate of a felleh!"

Blackburn was to conduct the cross-examination. With his first interrogation to the witness an angry scowl came over the face of Tippleton, who sat with his head down and his eyes fixed steadily on the questioner.

The examination was compelled to proceed slowly on account of frequent interruptions from Tippleton claiming that the questions asked were impertinent, having no bearing upon the case at bar. Again and again he was ready with objections. Blackburn was sustained by the Court.

Finally, at the close of a somewhat exciting argument as to the competency of a certain question the objection was again overruled, and Tippleton became silent. But his face had grown livid. By this time it was evident to every one present, except the cross-examiner himself, that the man had all along simply been trying to pick a quarrel at any cost.

Suddenly Blackburn sprang the question:

"Were you under the influence of liquor?"

The witness straightened himself haughtily.

"I was not, sir," he declared, looking about him with an air of outraged dignity. The crowd tittered.

"Had you taken anything of an intoxicating nature to drink?"

The witness looked slightly disconcerted. He hesitated a moment, cast his eyes down upon his crumpled shirt-front bespattered with tobacco juice, and glanced helplessly toward Tippleton. Then he made a grand stand.

"Oh I — I believe I *had* taken a drink — like any other Kentucky gentleman," he admitted, with a swagger that well-nigh upset the equanimity of both judge and jury.

"Had you taken *two* drinks — like any other Kentucky gentleman?" asked Blackburn, with a smile. A ripple of amusement went through the crowd.

Instantly Tippleton was on his feet, the rage of a madman depicted in his countenance.

"Does the gentleman mean to say that no Kentucky gentleman ever takes a drink?" he demanded in fierce derision.

Blackburn turned quickly and flashed back good-humouredly:

"Does the gentleman propose to make a personal application? But I did not say that," he added coolly.

"You implied it, sir."

"I did not imply it."

"You did."

"I did not," said Blackburn, rising.

"You're a liar!" roared Tippleton, shaking his fist and making a dash forward.

The courtroom was in an uproar. All at once bedlam seemed to break loose. The judge, pale and indignant, sat sternly demanding order. But no one gave the smallest heed. Supposing that pistol shots would follow immediately, some one in the rear of the room yelled, "This is the time for disappearing," and made a wild rush for the door. The crowd followed pell-mell. Benches were overturned, chairs were knocked down, and for a moment the majesty of the law gave way to a by no means unusual, but, to express it mildly, somewhat undignified confusion.

Blackburn stood white and motionless, his features sternly set. Simultaneously with Tippleton's last words, lawyers had closed in between the two. One of the counsel for the defence had taken Tippleton more directly in hand, and was explaining hurriedly that the matter had been misunderstood. The crowd paused, hesitated, and, slightly aggrieved and disappointed, began to return.

All at once Tippleton's bull-dog features relaxed. He shook himself loose from his adviser, and came forward with a great show of magnanimity. He apologized most humbly to the Court and to Blackburn, and said that he *had* misunderstood. The examination proceeded.

The incident, which was one of those lightning occurrences which are over and adjusted almost before one has time to catch his breath, was apparently closed for the present. Almost immediately things quieted down.

But few that had witnessed the passage between the two men believed for an instant that the matter would end there. They were Kentuckians.

CHAPTER X

THE TEST OF COURAGE

"An' is it ar-rmed ye are, Mr. Blair?"

Blackburn paused near an electric light, suddenly conscious that the steps that had been steadily gaining upon him since he had left his home had been following him deliberately. An uncouth figure emerged out of the shadow. Blackburn eyed him closely.

"Mike, you old idiot, you, I thought you told me positively that you had sworn off until after the election!" he exclaimed at length, a half-humourous expression flitting across the young face despite his chiding.

His glance rested upon an odd-looking individual in a shabby gray suit and old slouch hat, who gave one a conflicting impression, first of youth and then of age: a thin, wiry little creature with a round, knotty countenance — at present very much in need of a shave — relieved by a twinkle of Hibernian shrewdness in the deep-set eyes. The man was one of Blackburn's staunchest political adherents, and he brought to his zeal in behalf of the young statesman a sort of dog-like devotion unsurpassed save by his skill in manipulating certain clandestine maneuvers which were constantly going on in a well-known corner grocery of the town. Regarding the corner grocery and its emanations he was a complete reprobate. Regarding his loyalty to Blackburn Blair he was as faithful an esquire as ever followed a knight.

He had been walking rapidly, but with a shambling, somewhat secretive gait, which, however, appeared to be less an index of immediate purpose than of a natural indirectness of character, for he spoke up boldly when once he had reached Blackburn's side.

"An' is it ar-rmed ye are?" he repeated with a note of persuasion in the cracked voice, seeing that Blackburn seemed not disposed to answer him.

They were within a few yards of the entrance of the hotel whither Blackburn was bound by appointment to meet an acquaintance whom he was expecting from Louisville. He glanced up at the structure impatiently and drew out his watch.

"See here, now, Mike, it is nearly nine, and I must hurry along. What's all this? Out with it, Conolly." A second glance had revealed to him that the man had not been drinking.

Mr. Conolly was standing with half-closed eyelids.

"Whin a gintleman has inemies, Mr. Blair," he remarked, with an insinuating jerk of the thumb in the direction of the hotel, "it's a good thing f'r him to begin lookin' round to see which iv his fire ar-rms is in bist condition, it is."

Blackburn followed the gesture. "Are my enemies lodged in that particular abode?" he asked with a laugh. "I'm afraid it would take a good deal larger place than the Phœnix to hold them all, Mike."

"My wur-rud f'r it, but 't ain't but wan inemy what's ready to shoot, so th' on'y thing f'r ye is joost to load up and begin th' shootin' ye-erself, Mr. Blair."

"Oh, I don't believe anyone has murderous designs against me, Mike; at all events I think we'll take the chances on that. I suppose you have reference to that occurrence in the Courthouse this morning."

"It's what iv'rybody has riference to. An' is it ar-rmed ye are?"

"Armed? You know I never go armed. I don't propose to have any trouble with Tippleton. He's a peppery sort of felllow, but I conclude it's all over with him by this time. He let himself go for a moment this morning, but you know he apologized for it."

Mike nodded knowingly. "But it's throuble ye'll be havin' with him, all the same. It's a cow'rd, he is, the low crathur, an' th' first sight iv ye'll be enough."

"Oh, I hardly think that. I suppose I'm the man to do the resenting, but I don't feel resentful. The fellow isn't worth it. I'm in high spirits to-night,

Mike, and it's a glorious victory that's before us. Just you keep sober, and it will be a grand day you'll see in November."

He turned away with a cheerful nod of the head and walked quickly toward the large white building which, having risen in commonplace newness out of the ashes of a past picturesqueness, stands upon the site of the historic Postlethwaite's Tavern of a hundred years ago.

There was the usual crowd of loafers about the hotel, moving through the corridors, or sitting with chairs tilted back in the brilliantly lighted office eagerly devouring the latest news of the campaign as set forth in the evening newspapers. And there was a steady stream in the direction of the bar-room, out of which from time to time complacent looking individuals would emerge, pausing frequenty to enter into noisy, disputatious conversation with others who had just come in upon the one theme that was engrossing everybody's thoughts: the immediate political situation of the state.

There were several groups engaged in discussions of this kind when Blackburn entered the lobby. Among these, some distance off to the right, there was one composed of six or eight persons of which Tippleton seemed to be the central figure, his dominating self-consequence naturally forcing the rest into the attitude of listeners and himself into the importance of speaker.

He appeared to be holding forth with special eloquence, judging by the expression upon the faces of his auditors, who broke now and then into coarse, derisive laughter accompanied by shrewd winks at one another in evident token of their approval.

As the stentorian voice which had been a potent factor in the man's acquirement of a popular reputation in the way of a ringing stump speaker began again, Blackburn caught the mention of his own name uttered with a sneering accent. In the next moment it was revealed to him that the Hon. H. Clay Tippleton was relating the adventure of the morning according to his own version of the affair, and by an elaborate juggle of rhetoric making himself out a hero "without fear and without reproach" — to employ an expression frequently on his lips — while his antagonist, one Blackburn Blair, was described as a "Goebelite," a creature almost too mean and despicable to be mentioned in the presence of those pure, high-minded spirits he saw before him, who with him were labouring so zealously to save the "grand old Commonwealth" from impending doom. Of these pious deliverers Tippleton had no hesitation in claiming that he was the chief. As a matter of fact he seldom had hesitation in claiming anything which he regarded as advantageous to himself, and if persons were disposed to trust to him they were led to believe that there had not, in the last fifteen or twenty years, occurred an act of wisdom in the Democratic history of his state which was not to be traced directly and solely to him.

The man young Blair was seeking was a slight acquaintance, a lawyer from Louisville, whom he had seen but once or twice in a most casual way many years before, and of whose appearance he retained only an indistinct recollection. However, as he glanced about him he thought he recognized this person among the men surrounding Tippleton. He turned and walked toward the group, his gaze fixed upon the tall, red-haired man who, with slightly averted face, was sitting next the oracle.

His entrance had been unobserved, and he was within a few yards of them when one of the number looked up and saw him. The man started violently. Others stirred. Instantly a kind of electric shock seemed to go through the company, and every man present wore as abashed an aspect as if he had been caught in the act of stealing. Tippleton, noting the change of expression on the features of his auditors and being somewhat annoyed at the interruption, wheeled suddenly in his chair and saw Blackburn approaching.

For a moment the florid face of the bully went pale. He caught in his breath quickly and one hand grasped the round of his chair in a sort of convulsive tremor. Great drops of perspiration stood out on his forehead, and his teeth were clenched.

But Blackburn came steadily forward, looking intently toward the red-haired man on Tippleton's right. All at once the man turned his face more directly toward him, and Blackburn saw that he was not the person he sought. He paused, and Tippleton, misconstruing his hesitation, rose precipitately, thrusting the chair in which he had been sitting in front of him. A low angry growl like that of a savage beast roused from its lair broke from his lips.

"Damn you!" he muttered, recovering from his momentary loss of spirit, "don't you look at me like that! Damn you!"

Blackburn fixed a piercing gaze upon the enraged countenance of the man before him. "I don't propose to have any trouble with you, sir," he said in low, distinct tones. Then turning to the rest, "Pardon me, but I thought I saw Mr. Mannering of Louisville here among you. I am expecting him. I find that I have made a mistake."

The coolness and dignity of the words threw Tippleton into a frenzy. He grasped the chair in front of him and flinging it violently against the wall shattered it.

"You God damned coward!" he hissed advancing, "I'll see if there's any fight in you, you snivelin' parson, you lyin' hypocrite, you —"

There was a sudden scraping and overturning of chairs. The office had all at once waked up to the situation. A Kentuckian may not be called a coward and a liar and a hypocrite with impunity. The excitement was intense, and in the pandemonium that followed a far more realistic scene than that of the morning seemed about to be enacted. Two men grabbed Tippleton and tried to hold him. In the same instant a revolver was thrust into Blackburn's hands by Mike Conolly with the words, "Now see that ye lit him have it, Mr. Blair." The crowd gasped and fell back.

Tippleton shook himself loose, but saw that he was too late. He reached desperately to his hip pocket, but the weapon caught. A ghastly pallor overspread his countenance. There was a second's horrible suspense in which every one listened for the report from Blackburn's pistol.

It did not follow. He stood white as a statue, sternly waving the revolver from him. There was a low whisper of surprise like the swift rush of wind. An instant before he had had his adversary in his power. By his own act he was now at the mercy of a poltroon and a bully. The crowd stood awed and mystified. Vaguely it was being borne in upon them that back of all this marvelous self-mastery there was a deliberate purpose unknown to their philosophy. Every eye was riveted on the straight form and the proud young face still with passion. Every pulse leaped at sight of a generosity that seemed to them simply quixotic or foolhardy, but which, nevertheless, to the impulsive-hearted Kentuckians was the splendid act of a hero.

Tippleton was slow in getting possession of his pistol on account of a recent lameness in his right wrist. Suddenly a gleaming nickel weapon flashed in the electric light. He raised it.

But something stayed his hand. "Put up that revolver!" the rich voice of Blackburn Blair rang out with compelling power. "You know that I don't intend to kill you."

The gaze bent upon Tippleton seemed to subdue him as by an almost hypnotic influence. His hand fell to his side. He half turned away. Trembling with rage and shame he stood glowering under this second conquering and humiliation. To his keen discernment it was evident to him as to everyone else present that he had lost and Blackburn had thus far won by the encounter. Unable to endure the thought, he leaped toward Blackburn with an oath.

"So you won't fight, you coward?" he snarled, brandishing the pistol like a man crazed. "Then take that!"

The slap in the face that followed seemed louder than the pistol shot which in the moment echoed in the lobby through Tippleton's clumsy, left-handed manipulation of the weapon he held. An awful hush fell upon the crowd. Instantly Mike Conolly was ready as Tippleton stepped back. In a flash Blackburn seized the pistol — hesitated — dashed it from him.

Then without a word he turned and went forth into the night.

He was far out in the open country when he came to himself a little and looked around. The night was cool and still, and the moon was shining softly. His gaze was bewildered like that of one stunned and incredulous. His step was uncertain. Two belated travelers, fortified within by a generous supply of Kentucky whiskey, mistaking him for a kindred spirit, looked back familiarly from their vehicle as they passed the tall, staggering figure on the roadside, and smiled and waved in drunken appreciation of his plight.

Like one crazed Blackburn Blair had strode through the streets of the old town, looking neither to the right nor to the left, seeing nothing, hearing nothing, conscious only of the hideous murderous impulse in his heart, the consuming fire in his veins. A great terror of himself had been upon him. It held him, with but slight abatement, still. He could only walk on, and on, and on. His face, livid, lined and seamed as if years had passed over it, bore the marks of devastating passion. His eyes were bloodshot, his lips dry and parched. His breath came in painful gasps. Three times he had slackened his pace, paused, and turned as though he would retrace his steps, impelled by that savage instinct for blood and vengeance which, once aroused in a man, drives out the civilization of centuries and makes him a part of the barbarism of the past. In those moments the hereditary pride of generations of high-spirited men before him who had never brooked an insult, the sense of outrage and insupportable humiliation which every gentleman feels under the sting of personal assault, and above all the deadly, implacable resentment of the Kentuckian against such a wrong, seemed urging him, with stern insistent command, to the commission of that very crime which he had supposed to be an impossibility for himself, and which he had always deplored as a fatal stigma on his state.

It had been with him a solemnly recurrent theme, acquainted as he had been since the days of his earliest recollection with one after another of those grim death tragedies that have made the name of Kentucky a byword and a reproach. It had taken tremendous hold upon him; and in the careless attitude of his people toward the destruction of human life, his thoughtful mind foresaw the sanction of that general spirit of lawlessness destined sooner than he knew to find culmination in an act of infamy which was to bring the eyes of the civilized world upon them.

From time to time as he sped onward in the darkness there had flashed into his mind snatches from various speeches he had made in public and in private on this point. They seemed to mock him now. *Resistance to evil destroys the passion for evil* — yes, he believed that still. But he could not think. An iron band seemed bound about his brow. His temples throbbed violently. A hundred little demons danced before his eyes and whispered in his ears the jeers and slights that would be his. To look into men's faces and know that all, or nearly all, even the kindest, would hereafter think of him as one whose courage had failed — that there must always be doubt of him! His young manhood cried out in passionate rebellion against the thought.

A few hours before and the future had stretched out all-glorious. Now it was only a barren waste. His career of usefulness, of political leadership among his constituents, he knew, was at an end. Never again could he hope to have weight among them. For though, in the abstract, one might speak of self-control, of temperance, of the sanctity of law and of life, among Kentuckians there was but one course for the man in his place. He must take the law into his own hands. He must kill, or attempt to kill the man who had thus insulted and wronged him — or go through life with the brand of coward upon him. There was no other way.

He could not hope to be understood save by a few— and even these — perhaps — A great wave of distracting emotion shook him as he pictured the pain of these friends, their embarrassment in the futile effort to put him right before the world. Old Judge Trotter's fiery vindication, the calm logic of Professor Kennedy, the gentle persuasion of Major Wise! — the thought of it all cut him to the heart. Upon anyone nearer than these his mind dared not dwell. Cicely, his father, Myra — to think of them was maddening. His eyes rested upon the grassy slopes about him and the peaceful autumn fields. Too soon had the harvest of his young life been gathered. Long before he had come to full maturity of his powers he was cut down.

He was passing a woodland several miles from the town, and still grappling with despair, he plunged into its shadowy depths and flung himself, face downward upon the turf at the foot of an ancient oak. All around was stillness intensified. The moonlight fell soft and beautiful as a silvery veil in the open spaces between the trees. There was a soothing note in the light wind that just faintly stirred the crimson and gold overhead. The very heart of nature seemed to beat softly, touched by his suffering. The cool pressure of her hand against his hot brow was a caress. He sat up and looked into her eyes, and found them gentle as a mother's. Far as he could see stretched the fertile fields and luxuriant pasture lands of his beloved state. His gaze lost itself in a dim outline of towering trees showing a dull gray in the moonlight. Overhead vastness, illimitable, inscrutable! A hush fell upon his soul.

He was alone with God and his own thoughts. The moments sank into hours. Once he took out his watch and struck a match. It was three o'clock. Across the road a horse neighed. In a sort of dull, semi-consciousness he knew that his limbs were cramped and cold. But still he sat there, staring with vacant, wretched eyes, while he wrestled with the strange destiny upon him.

He was beginning to realize that it was to be a sacrifice, and as he prayed that the bitter cup might pass from him, suddenly there flashed upon him the realization that his whole life had been but a preparation, a reaching toward this, the supreme moment of his existence in the divine plan.

Vague pictures of the past and of the future floated before him. One took on a startling significance. It was a scene in the old library of his home. The lamps were lighted. The curtains were drawn. His father and he were sitting before a cheerful fire talking over the countless duels and murders and homicides in Kentucky. All at once his own words came back to him, uttered in reference to the case of the judge who refused to kill his assailant, and who, goaded to desperation under stress of the public sentiment of his state, finally took his own life. "It was a hard test—a hideous test," he had called it. "Few men anywhere," he had commented, "would be equal to it. But in Kentucky—in Kentucky the man who could be equal to it would be a saviour to his people."

The words pierced him like a sword thrust. Again he threw himself forward and lay with his face to the earth. The prayer of a pure and earnest soul mingled with the sigh of the forest.

Day was breaking when he rose. But his face was calm. The long hours of anguish, of struggle, of resistance were passed. His features seemed glorified by some marvelous inner light. His step was sure and firm. He made his way back to the town—and to the life before him. He had passed through his Gethsemane.

CHAPTER XI

MYRA'S MINISTRATION

Rumours of the affair spread rapidly through the town and with the wildest exaggeration. Myra Mallory was one of the first to receive an account of it, her informant being Mrs. Bellows. Just half an hour after the occurrence that "estimable woman" — to employ a phrase once used to his cost in description of her by a well-intentioned but misguided young journalist who had mistaken her aims — drove up to the door of Blackburn's cousin and sent in a card, following upon it almost immediately, with spreading train and waving plumes.

"Well, I reckon you've heard the news!" she exclaimed drawing herself up with a halt in the middle of the hall. She was breathless, and her violet satin waist, tightly stretched over her huge form, heaved spasmodically. There was an expression half-cunning upon the long, bony countenance, with its unpleasant equine suggestion, despite her show of friendliness.

Myra was standing before the fire in her little sitting-room, tall and slim in her black gown, and somewhat difficult. She came forward slowly, still holding

Mrs. Bellows' card, and her white, beautiful face, clear-cut as a cameo, betrayed a faint surprise. She held out her hand with that delicate combination of reserve and cordiality which few women are capable of in its perfection, and which enables those who possess it to maintain an attitude of thorough kindliness without the smallest loss of personal remoteness. But such a manner was apt to be lost on Mrs. Bellows. In her present frame of mind she regarded it as an affront. She sniffed the air dangerously.

"Humph! look like you ain't very glad to see me!" she remarked, with a short, embarrassed laugh, and a shrug of the shoulders. "That's what comes of meddlin', I suppose. You get no thanks; an' I've always said that if people would just mind their own business in this world, we'd all be the better off. But I was just passin' the house, and it did seem kinder stingy not to drop in an' tell you. I was callin' in the hotel when it happened."

Myra offered a chair. "What has happened, Mrs. Bellows?" she asked. "You know I live so quietly, I hear very little of much that takes place in the town."

Mrs. Bellows studied the still, high-bred features rather curiously, conscious of a secret longing to disturb their serenity.

"It's about that cousin of yours — young Blackburn Blair. There's been trouble down at the hotel, and that big, red-faced Tippleton just wiped up the earth with him, a few minutes ago. Thought the boy was game, whatever he was, but he didn't show much fight to-night. Talkin' people like them Blairs is mighty apt to come to grief. It's a mercy he didn't get his brains blown out — what little he has. I'm told that Clay Tippleton cursed him right and left and told him what he thought about him, and then just marched straight up to him and hit him a loud smack in the mouth. They say you could hear it far off as the Courthouse. Comes of being a 'Goebelite.' Serves him right, I reckon. That Blackburn Blair was stirrin' up a hornet's nest in this state. But this ends him up in politics. He won't do much more fool talkin' now. You can't show the white feather 'round here. We come of fightin' stock."

Myra was sitting with folded hands, looking steadily into the fire. Her face had lost none of its calm, but her lips were firmly closed. To Mrs. Bellows she was an enigma. She asked no question. She appeared to be thinking very intently, and as if she were almost forgetful that she was not alone.

Mrs. Bellows stirred impatiently. "Maybe you knew it already" she suggested, with a shade of disappointment. She was becoming somewhat crestfallen over the manner in which her intelligence was received. "It's all over town. You'd think them Blairs owned the earth. The way this place goes on over a lot of old broken-down aristocrats, that ain't worth thinkin' about two minutes and a half, is something I never could understand. Who told you?"

Myra looked up. "You are my only informant, Mrs. Bellows," she said.

Several seconds passed. Mrs. Bellows was discomfited. The situation was becoming intense. A sleepy call from above broke the unpleasant stillness. Myra rose.

"I am sorry that I cannot ask you to stay longer," she remarked gravely, "but it is late, and my little boy seems restless."

Mrs. Bellows moved toward the door with offended dignity.

"I know it's late, well as you do," she observed shortly, that's why I come. Anybody can carry the news in the daytime. I'm on my way now to that Overton girl to tell her. Wonder how that high-steppin' mother of hers 'll feel about her daughter marryin' a coward. I hear it's all settled, an' the time's fixed. Thought you was the one he was after?"

Myra led the way into the hall. "Good-night, Mrs. Bellows," she replied steadily, looking her visitor for an instant full in the face. Mrs. Bellows flinched a little under the proud gaze, and fumbled uneasily with her feather boa. Just before unlatching the hall door Myra hesitated.

"I don't know that I am privileged to ask a favour of you, Mrs. Bellows," she said in a low voice which slightly revealed her effort at self-control, "but I should regard it as a special kindness if you will say nothing of this matter to Mrs. Overton and her daughter."

There was a suppressed anxiety in the appeal which made Mrs. Bellows prick up her ears, and strengthened her in her determination.

"Do you think I'm a-goin' to let that poor child lay up there all night knowin' nothin' maybe of what's happened, when just a little trouble from me, and there's the whole story? There never was a lazy bone in my body, an' I feel like a colt in a ten acre field to-night, after all them warm September days. I always did say that October was the month for me. Sam, drive to old Judge Trotter's."

Myra stood a moment in the doorway after the carriage of her unwelcome guest had disappeared, looking up and down the street with troubled eyes. The cool night air was a relief. Her heart throbbed with sympathetic pain. Inaccurate as she knew the story must be that had just been told to her, she yet could not persuade herself that it was wholly untrue. As she stood there, grieved, uncertain, the darkness of that hour when they brought her young husband home to her dead from an assassin's hand, seemed to close in about her. And mingled with all the dumb agony of that time was the recollection of Blackburn's goodness, his great gentleness and thoughtfulness toward her, his deep sorrowing for his friend. A longing to be helpful to him in this his supreme moment made her eager, restless. Her sincere affection and respect for him could not harbour any doubt, but she felt that she must know the facts, late though it was. The pride that she felt in him was the pride that a sister feels toward a dearly loved brother for whom she has dreamed noble things; and the bond that united them in closest friendship was something beyond the tie of blood, for it had its root in the single, steadfast, deathless love that each gave to another.

The trees had not shed their leaves, and though the moon was shining the street was partly in shadow. A step came toward her under the maples. As it drew nearer a familiar figure came into veiw. It was Frederick Dilson. She went quickly down the steps. He started when he saw her.

"Won't you come in just a moment?" she asked.

The young man entered the house without a word. As he paused under the light in the hall she saw that his kindly face was flushed and much disturbed.

"You — you have heard?" she was trembling as she put the question.

He bowed his head. They looked at each other in silence.

"Mrs. Bellows has been here," she said at length. "But tell me the thing just as it occurred. I want to know everything."

He told her the story as it was told to him by one who had been an eye witness — but briefly, without comment or periphrase. His voice was husky.

Suddenly the young man threw back his head and straightened himself. A light flashed threateningly from his eyes.

"It's a beastly state of things, Mrs. Mallory," he said firmly, "and it can only end one way. A gentleman cannot live under such shame and insult. I have not seen him yet. Blair is more to me than a brother. I can only counsel him to act as I myself would act if I were situated as he is. He must kill that villain. You and I and half a dozen others, perhaps, know his utter fearlessness. But it is not possible that he will not be misjudged. The town is all agog to-night over the affair, and it is being telegraphed far and wide. It is particularly unfortunate just at this time, for his enemies have been simply waiting for some kind of break. Blair's political stand and social place of course give the main importance. But, in view of the fact that Tippleton is a pronounced anti-Goebel man, and in with many of the wire-pullers of the state, the opposition will play the thing for all it is worth. I take it it will be worth a good deal. Though that is merely a minor consequence. To be cursed, struck in the face by that low, dastardly hound —!"

He broke off all at once, his lips white and trembling. "God, what is the man made of that can endure a thing like that!"

Myra had been moving softly up and down the floor. Her straight brows were contracted in deep thought. Her hands were tightly clasped at her breast and her head was bowed. She paused. A soft radiance looked forth from her dark eyes.

"What is he made of?" she asked in a voice that thrilled and vibrated through the little house like the strings of a musical instrument. "Of the material that heroes and martyrs are made — the men who are willing to suffer and to die, if need be, for a principle such as few are able to rise to, or even dimly to understand."

He looked at her in a kind of wonderment.

"Would you urge him," she cried in a fine scorn of his misconception, "would you urge him, when he has reached the height he has, to descend to the low plane you other men live on—you who no more scruple to take the life of a human being than of a dog? What hope is there ever to be for Kentucky while men think and speak as you do? What is it that leads to the countless acts of violence that are continually occurring among us, if it be not just some such false ideal of courage as is yours? Courage? It is not courage. It is cowardice — fear of public sentiment, that you cringe before. It is like a giant in our midst, or some hideous heathen deity. Its victims are many. But he only is brave among you who is strong enough to defy it. Can't you, won't you understand?"

He shook his head grimly. "I can see but one course for him," he insisted through his set teeth. "But I can be silent, if you ask that, knowing what he is to me. I think you do."

There was an old-fashioned settee in the hall of white carved wood and he had taken the seat beside her. But a sudden restlessness seemed to overcome him and he sprang up.

"This thing has gone harder with me than you can know, Mrs. Mallory," he said, a new dignity looking forth from the handsome blonde face which heretofore had seemed to her somewhat lacking in manliness of expression. "It has hurt me not only on his account, but on account of—someone else who will have to suffer because of it — someone for whom I would give my life to save from pain."

He did not meet her eyes, and his voice broke boyishly.

She put forth both her hands and grasped his warmly, and the tears in her eyes rolled down her cheeks.

"Forgive me for speaking to you as I did, forgive me, please," she said, "I — I understand."

She watched him go down the steps, touched by his strong, unselfish, elementary feeling, and assured of its reality by that sympathetic sense of perception which her own sorrows had accentuated.

All night she lay open-eyed and anxious, feeling like one caged in her narrow walls. She had grown accustomed to sleeplessness, having spent many weary, wakeful hours in that same little white and gold room — which long ago had been her bridal bed-chamber — listening to the soft breathing of the small form at her side, and waiting aimlessly for the dawn.

As soon as it was day she rose, having thought of a thing to do. She dressed quickly and went forth noiselessly from the house.

Near the doorway of the Blair homestead she met Uncle Scip. The old negro was just coming around the corner of the house. A glance into his good-humoured, untroubled countenance revealed that she was not too late. He was in search of the morning newspaper. She intercepted it, catching a glimpse of the bold, unpleasant headlines as she hid it away under her coat. He peered into her face with respectful surprise.

"You sho is up early dis bright mornin', Mistis," he said without suspicion. "I is jes come out," he added deprecatingly, looking from side to side, "to git track o' dem outlandish chillun what throws de papers in. Dey don't keer whar dey throws it. You jes lemme git my han's on 'em. I'll fix 'em — foolin' 'roun me wid dey tricks an' monkey-shines." And then in reply to Myra's inquiry:

"You'll find him feelin' right smart dis mornin'. He's a-settin' in thar befo' de fire in de liberry readin' de Specletater."

With her hand on the door Myra hesitated and paled, shrinking from the task before her. A feeble cough fell upon her ear. She turned the knob and went in.

When Blackburn entered the room half an hour later he found the two sitting there talking peacefully together. Myra had flung aside her wraps. She had taken a low seat, and one hand was resting on his father's arm chair in affectionate familiarity. Her eyes were upturned, and the look in them was serene and steadfast. Her lips were parted, and her breath seemed to come quickly, as of one stirred by exalted emotion.

Blackburn paused. He looked searchingly toward his father, and all the blood forsook his face. A spasm of pain contracted his features. His hands were suddenly clinched. The two at the fire rose. Then a slow, beautiful smile broke over his cousin's face, and he knew that the dreaded moment was over, and that he had been spared it through her gentle ministration.

Judge Blair came forward and grasped his son's hand. The old man could not speak. But he bore himself like a king. There was a moment's silence, when his strength seemed suddenly to fail him; and then the frail form that had weathered so many of life's storms straightened itself proudly, and without a word he turned and went softly from the room.

Myra watched him with glistening eyes. "Blackburn, it is the grandest moment of his life," she said simply. "I wanted to be the first to tell him."

She busied herself with her wraps as he stood, tall and white and still, looking dumbly toward her. All at once he crossed the room to her side.

"I will not try to thank you," he broke forth at last in low, tense tones.

She let him hold her jacket for her as if that were the supreme matter. "Now I must hurry," she cried. "That glove over there, Blackburn. No—on that chair."

"Myra, must you go?"

"My poor little boy! Imagine his indignant surprise if he should have to eat his breakfast alone! Good-by, dear. I have planned to spend a part of the morning with Cicely, but I must first make my peace with that small tyrant at home."

He followed her to the hall door, a lump in his throat. On the steps she turned and put forth her hand.

"Do you remember a promise I made you once?"

"It was about — her," he answered, looking quickly away. But a sudden illumination broke over his features. Presently he turned to her with moist, grateful eyes.

"Yes; it was about her," she said. "I told you that through everything I would be her friend and yours. Trust me — if the time should come. Good-by."

CHAPTER XII

BLACKBURN AND CICELY

The night was moist and threatening, and every wet little gust of wind brought down a melancholy shower of withered leaves, and sent a depressing chill to the heart. As Blackburn crossed the street in the direction of the Trotter home the sudden flare of an electric light showed his face white and haggard. He had not seen Cicely. Three days had passed since the night of his ordeal, and he had not been able once to look into her eyes, or to receive from her an assuring word. He had gone again and again to see her. Always the same denial had been sent to him from Mrs. Overton, who commanded that he be informed that her daughter was seriously ill, unable to see anyone, or to endure the smallest strain. He had written. But there had come no response. As he went up the steps of the house his features grew sternly determined.

Old Ben answered his ring. The respectful countenance of the kind old negro, who had been a secret ally in the pranks of the two when Blackburn and Cicely were children, and who had ever kept a soft place in his heart for both of them, looked anxious and uncertain.

"I must see Mrs. Overton, Ben," said Blackburn, firmly, advancing into the hall.

Ben stood a moment scratching his woolly head in extreme perterbation.

"De Cun'l in de liberry," he suggested tentatively, and in a kind of appeal.

"No; I want to speak to Mrs. Overton. Ask her to come to me for a moment, please. I will wait here."

The old servant went off muttering strangely. A long time passed. A tall clock at the head of the stairs ticked loudly. The house was very still except for an occasional, suppressed footfall on the upper floor from time to time. The lights were lowered, and a sense of gloom and unnatural quiet was over everything. Blackburn rose and began to walk up and down the long hallway with impatient, restless strides, baffled, conscious that he was being trifled with, yet resolute.

Presently Mrs. Overton came slowly down the stairs. She was beautifully attired in a soft gray gown, and every hair was in place. She carried herself with a special hauteur, and she moved with the deliberation of an empress. She greeted him coldly.

"Blackburn, Cicely is still very ill," she remarked in an exaggerated whisper, as she withdrew her hand. "I am sorry that you are so insistent. That stupid old Ben blurted it out that you were here, and she declares that she will see you. But it is against my orders — in open defiance of my wishes, I may say."

"I regret it, Mrs. Overton, but I must see her —if she will allow me to do so."

"But you don't seem to realize that her condition has been most alarming. The poor child has eaten nothing, scarcely a morsel, since — since your unfortunate encounter, and she has slept only when under the influence of an opiate. I was compelled to send for the doctor twice that dreadful night. She grows no better, and her nerves are in a fearful state of collapse. I confess that I'm at my wits end; and she just moans and sobs and refuses to be comforted by anything I say to her. Really, Blackburn, it was a most shocking occurrence. I myself am completely upset by it. I can't imagine how you can endure such degradation. If there is one thing above another that a woman admires in a man it is courage. I have always taught my boys that they must be brave. I sincerely hope that they will never be forced to kill anybody, for of course if one can avoid taking the life of another, one would prefer to do so. But there are times when it can't be avoided; and a man would better be dead than a coward. I know that in the North these things are regarded differently. But we don't live in the North. We live in Kentucky. And you know that in Kentucky there can be but one opinion for such conduct as yours. You must pardon me, Blackburn, for speaking so plainly to you. You are just a mere boy to me; and I feel that Cicely's future welfare has been very little considered, else this whole thing would have been avoided. It is merely a natural outgrowth of your unwise political stand. It simply comes of being a 'Goebelite.'"

Somehow he managed to keep an outward self-control. But there was a look in his dark eyes that made Mrs. Overton suddenly lose her ease and become painfully embarrassed.

"Cicely is in the little upstairs library, Blackburn, the front room over the hall," she said with sudden suavity and as if they had just been exchanging the compliments of the season. Blackburn went quietly up the stairs.

Cicely was lying in a loose white silken gown on a low couch before the fire in an attitude of complete abandonment to grief. Her long hair hung carelessly about her shoulders. Her eyes were fixed vacantly on the fire. A stillness as of death seemed to cling to her. Her white face against the pillows of soft lace about her looked like a thing carved out of marble in its unfeigned misery. She had not heard his knock. He took a step or two into the room. She saw him and started violently.

She made a feeble little effort to rise, but could not,

and sank back wearily among her pillows. A tall girl sitting in the corner rose with a stateliness of bearing very much like Mrs. Overton's and slipped quietly from the room, nodding in a friendly way toward Blackburn as she passed. Cicely's eyes followed her young sister gratefully. Then a convulsive sob shook her.

Blackburn sank down on his knees beside the couch. His face was drawn and seamed with pain. He looked as if suddenly grown old. His heart was wrung with almost unendurable anguish. He could not speak. His eyes were fixed hungrily, pleadingly, upon the small stricken face before him, and presently a great wave of pity swept him and he gathered her to him as one gathers a suffering child, his whole soul going out to her in unspeakable devotion.

She lay motionless in his arms, but as he bent his head toward her, he felt the sudden shiver and shrinking of the lovely form. He drew back ashen to the lips.

"Cicely!" he cried aghast, "speak to me — *Cicely* —"

The agony in his voice and in his eyes seemed to rouse her. Suddenly she reached forth both her arms and drew him wildly to her in a kind of desperation of expression. She was quivering with sobs, and her tears wet his cheeks.

Presently he lifted her face and looked deep into her eyes. The delicate lids faltered, fell, and her whole being hesitated — and then yielded to him. He kissed her like one frenzied with mingled doubt and relief. "You love me," he whispered, "Cicely, you do love me?"

"Love you!" she cried, "how can you doubt that I love you after — everything." Then she added softly, "You are my deepest joy — and my deepest pain."

He looked at her in silence.

"But oh, the long hard struggle! Blackburn, the last three terrible days!" Suddenly she hid her face from him.

"You have not blamed me —Cicely, you understand!" he asked quickly in a low, tense tone.

She turned wearily on her couch. "I cannot blame you. But I — I suffer. Oh, Blackburn, if only you had struck him once — just once!" she moaned.

A spasm of pain shot across his features. He released her almost roughly and sprang to his feet.

"Then you do not understand," he said sternly.

He stood looking down upon her in a sort of dumb surprise. Never, in the most wretched hour he had passed through had he suffered himself really to question her ability to rise to the plane he had reached. There had come to him the opportunity of one of those splendid, far-reaching acts of heroism that are inestimable in their effect upon a man's character and upon his times. He had had the strength to meet it.

Something in him austerely demanded a like strength and a like elevation on the part of the women he loved. He believed there was no height of comprehension and of sympathy she could not attain to. He believed she was capable of noble, unselfish action. Yet he knew now that in his supreme moment she had failed him utterly. But he was disposed to be very gentle with her, knowing all that she had had to combat. He foresaw that there would be difficulties.

He went over to the mantel and stood a moment looking thoughtfully into the fire. After a time he glanced toward her lying white and prone and helpless, like one felled by a crushing blow. He resisted the appeal provoked by her piteousness and her womanly beauty. Presently he took a chair and sat down by her side.

"Cicely," he said very quietly, "if you are to be my wife, as you have promised, there may be some long, rough roads we shall have to travel over together. But we shall be together. Does your heart fail you?"

She did not answer. But she reached out one little cold hand to him, and his closed over it. His strong sure clasp seemed to steady her, though presently she drew back trembling.

"I'm afraid — sometimes I am afraid," she cried wildly and sorrowfully.

"Of what?"

"Of you."

A short laugh broke from him. "You will learn to trust me."

"You are so powerful, so determined, so resistless. When you are with me you completely conquer and crush me. I have no strength against you. But away from you I lie awake and think and think and think, and then it is I am afraid. Some of your views seem so overwrought and strange. Oh, Blackburn, if you did not feel called upon to make a sacrifice to the public of both our lives! If only you knew how I long for just a sweet simple existence, with only you and nothing public about it."

His face darkened again.

"If you love me, you will love my life-work and the principle that governs it," he insisted gravely. "You may be assured that, as I have told you before, you are not less to me but more because there is a principle. Cicely, do you love me?"

She looked at him, hurt and aggrieved, through her thick lashes.

"More than anything on the earth — as few women who have ever lived know how to love, I am sure," she answered, her voice thrilling him with its passion and its pain. "It is because I love you as I do that I grow cold with terror and sick at heart at thought of what this terrible thing you call principle may do for me. Even now I must stand aside for it. Sooner or later it will absorb your life. You belong to the world — you can never really be mine."

She turned her face away from him. But all at once she looked up with a quick contrition, and her eyes filled with tears.

"Oh, it all sounds so horrid and selfish and contemptible. I never know until I put it into words. I would not have you different. Listen. Let me tell you. I don't mean just that," she broke forth hurriedly. "I know that when the Call once sounds for one of us to do a certain thing we simply have to rise up and go to meet our destiny, no matter what it may be. I know, because I have heard it, too. Sometimes it seems to me to be the one note sounding in the whole universe. And I know, too," suddenly her voice broke and faltered, "I know that feeling as you do. You could not have acted otherwise than you did three nights ago. But, oh, the awful horror of the thing! That he should dare to strike you — a low creature like that!"

A sudden sob shook her.

He flushed painfully. But he could say nothing. All at once he rose and began to walk up and down the little room, scarce able quietly to endure the strain.

"If only you had struck him once — just once," she moaned again.

He stopped short. He came back to her and sank down on his knees beside her, with one hand smoothing away the loose rippling hair about her temples.

"Not yet — not yet," he kept saying over and over to himself like one dazed.

She raised herself and looked half-startled into his eyes. A natural sweetness of impulse seemed struggling for expression, but she could not find the words. She was like one blinded, yet groping toward the light. And dimly there was being borne in upon her a crucial recognition: the recognition of her own weakness and failure.

"I am trying — I am trying to understand. Be patient with me," she implored anxiously. "Some day — perhaps —"

"Some day, sweetheart — the time is not far off," he answered sadly, but very gently. All the tenderness, all the chivalry of a strong, pure nature that knew what it meant to love one woman and her only, was touched by her humility. In that instant it was not hard to forgive any flaw that had been revealed in her. Already he was eager to restore her to a complete supremacy. But his whole being had received a shock. For a moment he bent above her. Then he kissed her reverently on the brow, and went quickly from the room.

CHAPTER I

CONCERNING THE RACE FOR GOVERNOR

The storm of excitement in the gubernatorial race continued without abatement up to the last moment of the campaign. The anti-Goebel wing of the Democratic party as a separate organization was destined soon to drop out of the conflict. On the morning of the election there were but the two great parties involved.

The state waited breathless, the suspense growing hourly more and more intense. At length confusing telegrams began speeding over the wires. Men looked darkly into one another's faces. Still they waited. Both sides claimed the victory!

Then the storm swept with redoubled fury. It was evident that it would develop into a cyclone. Twenty-four hours passed. But who was to be the next governor of Kentucky? Nobody seemed to know.

In spite of the assertion expressed in flaming headlines and sent forth to all parts of the country that the cause of "civil liberty" had triumphed and that a free and noble people about to be robbed of their sacred right of franchise had just been magnificently rescued from the tyrant's hand, the wildest panic prevailed among the Republicans. It was feared that some of the county election boards would attempt to cast out a portion of the anti-Goebel vote. The dread of a "steal" and of being "counted out" seemed likely to throw the state into a revolution.

From the Democrats came the cry that the "secrecy of the ballot" had been violated, and that, tissue ballots having been used in many of the counties, the vote thus cast was illegal and should be declared null and void.

In a certain part of the state notorious for settling its little differences by a prompt resort to the trusty "Winchester," bands of armed men waited outside the Courthouse while the official tabulation was being made, with a look upon their weather-beaten countenances that boded ill for any commissioners that should dare to exclude a single precinct.

But the excitement in the Kentucky highlands — where the haughty mountaineer, who had got a firm grip upon a somewhat indefinite idea, waited in sullen silence, prepared to protect to the utmost the cause of civil liberty as he saw it — was scarcely less pronounced than that which occurred in other parts of the state and particularly in the city of Louisville. Here the feeling was alarmingly intense, and threats of riot and bloodshed and of violent action toward the Democratic commissioners were heard on all sides. On the day of the election, by order of the Republican governor, the militia had been called out. Once before, and for the first time since the Civil War, by this same authority, the military arm had been invoked, pending the election of a United States senator. As then, the Democrats throughout the state were enraged to a man.

The charge of federal interference was hurled defiantly at the Republicans, and the claim that voters and officers of the election had been intimidated to the loss of nine or ten thousand votes was made and believed. It was declared that the election in Louisville was not a civil but a military election; and that by an unlawful and criminal usurpation of power on the part of the republican governor an "overt act of a treasonable nature against the constitution of the state of Kentucky was committed."

To this the Republicans replied that most of the falling off was due to obstruction of negro voters. Back was hurled the reply that the loss was in Democratic voters, that the vote received by the Democratic ticket as compared with the registration showed as much falling off as that in the Democratic vote, and that a free ballot could not "co-exist with bayonets and gatling guns."

Just before the state board of commissioners was ready to convene, and while indignation mass meetings were being held all over Kentucky on the part of the

Republicans to protest against the Democrats, and on the part of the Democrats to protest against the Republicans, an unexpected turn of affairs took place in the death of the representative in Congress from the Ashland district.

At once a number of Democrats were in the field seeking the nomination for the unexpired term. A special election was ordered, as required by law. Life certainly was not stagnating in "the grand old Commonwealth."

Blackburn Blair decided to enter the race.

On the afternoon of the day on which his candidacy was announced Blackburn was returning home rather wearily from his office, for there was much to be done and that in a very limited space of time, when a carriage drew up near the curbing and a woman's voice called to him. He turned quickly, yet with an effort shaking off the thoughts that all day had been engrossing him.

"Ah, how do you do, Mrs. Oats?" he said.

Mrs. Oats extended a daintily gloved hand. She was beautifully dressed in a reception gown of pearl colour and pink and a most girlish hat composed mainly of pink roses. She was looking pale and a trifle worn. Something sadly suggestive of crow's feet was beginning to show in the corners of her eyes. There were unyouthful lines about her mouth which he had never before seen there, and Blackburn noted with regret the first signs of fading beauty. Yet there was something softer, more womanly in her manner, a sincerity of sympathy of which heretofore she had manifested only a well-feigned counterfeit.

"I have just heard the good news, Blackburn," she exclaimed, "and I have come to tender you my hearty support. Isn't that what you voters say to each other? I really am delighted. We have always meant to send you to Congress, don't you know?"

But despite her cordiality and evident kindness there was a note of anxiety in her voice when she added, "I wish it were all over, and you were through with the tiresome electioneering. I should think it would be a horrid bore, with your Mike Conollys and the rest of them."

"Don't say anything against Mike, if you please," said Blackburn, a shadow suddenly showing in his smile. "I have reason to take a special pride in that Hibernian of late. It will not surprise me if in the course of the next few months I shall have him making temperance speeches. He has positively sworn off for good and all, he tells me."

"Has he? Then he will cease to be interesting. His grocery will no longer attract me. When Mike gives up being an inebriate I'm afraid he'll lose his skill in flattery. But, Blackburn, you look tired. Won't you get in and take a little drive with me?"

He hesitated, but Mrs. Oats flung wide the door.

"Do get in," she insisted, "I will bring you back in time for dinner, and I promise not to say a word about politics."

"Aren't you afraid of such rashness? You'll have a broken promise to repent of before five minutes, I venture to say."

"Tell him to drive out in the direction of Ashland," said Mrs. Oats as Blackburn got in.

"No; you do not tempt me to argument — we are on the same side, don't you know? But it's a subject that one does not easily escape these days. It is in the air and one simply breathes it in. I have just been to the Alexander's to a reception, and it was the one topic. But I hear that in Louisville there is a dreadful state of things, and in Frankfort it is even worse; one half of the people are not on speaking terms with the other half. This afternoon there was a sort of nervous tension, don't you know, that no one seemed able to overcome. There were several quite unpleasant little passes. I own up to one. But Mrs. Overton would certainly try the temper of a saint. She appeared with drawn sword. Even if she has no regard for me on account of being a 'Goebelite,' as she calls me, I should think she would have regard for the colour of my hair. Positively, Blackburn, there was not another thing talked about by old or young during the entire afternoon but the election — that and the announcement of your candidacy."

His ear caught the note of embarrassment in her voice in her reference to himself, and he looked quickly away. It was the first time he had seen her since his encounter with Tippleton, and he was touched by her genuine interest. He had been conscious of more than one woman's shrinking and aloofness. In the way that no one so well as a beautiful woman can accomplish, he had been made to feel that his standing was forever lowered; and again and again it had been borne in upon him what he had lost, no less by an exaggerated courtesy than by the notable absence of all those little coquettish arts which are second nature to the women of his state, and which had heretofore been employed in a very marked degree for his sake.

He was silent, and as they drove through the streets of the old town, past the main thoroughfare crowded with vehicles and electric cars, past the Phœnix Hotel, past the major's, past the railroad crossing, on out into the suburbs, the burden of conversation was sustained almost entirely by Mrs. Oats, whose tactfulness, however, seldom had demands upon it which she was more willing to fulfil. Blackburn had always been a special favourite with her, and to-day as she glanced from time to time at his pale, handsome face, while keeping up an airy chatter relative to the commonplace incidents of her social life, something in her own nature which had recently awakened through suffering, made her keenly sensitive to his mood.

When they had reached the well-kept grounds surrounding Ashland, the rambling brick structure, standing like an old English manor-house on a gently rising knoll and plainly visible through the denuded trees, she gave orders to the coachman to turn.

"Do look at that lovely patch of green over there, Blackburn!" she exclaimed with effusion. "If the spirit of Henry Clay ever roams beneath those superb old trees, wouldn't you think he would take pleasure in seeing what cultivation has done for his bluegrass? Do you know, I think it is even more beautiful in the autumn, with that marvelous second growth it has, than in the first spring days? What a pity," she added with a sigh and a laugh that revealed her beautiful teeth, "that the good God is not equally beneficent to all feminine creatures."

"He is to some," said Blackburn, with the ready gallantry that experience had taught him he must needs be supplied with in talking to Mrs. Oats.

She shook her head still laughing. "Don't attempt it, Blackburn, it really is taxing your powers too far. You don't belong to the age of compliments. Your father now is quite an adept in that line. He can turn a prettier speech than one is likely to hear in a twelvemonth, all in that low, pleasant voice of his."

"How about the major?" put in Blackburn, innocently, "I thought when it came to pretty speeches we all had to take a back seat for him."

A change swept over her features. She paled a little and turned her eyes quickly away. "The major certainly is skilled in such matters. It will soon be a lost art. This rapid age we live in cannot find time for such elegances. Perhaps it is just as well."

She shivered a little and drew her wrap about her, and her animation seemed rather forced when she spoke again.

"There is something wonderfully gentle and winning to me about your father, Blackburn. I don't wonder that your mother loved him so. They have handed down a sort of legacy to this generation as a pair of ideal lovers, don't you know? I never get tired looking at that portrait of your mother which hangs in the library — it is not only the portrait of a very beautiful woman, but of a woman deeply loved. Every feature tells one that."

There was something in her voice that made him turn and look wonderingly at her, and in sudden pity.

But she parried the glance and said lightly as the

carriage drew up a few moments afterwards at his door, "Here we are, Blackburn, and I hope I haven't made you late for dinner. Good-by. A splendid race to you and a glorious victory!"

And then as Blackburn stood bowing rather gravely his thanks, she leaned forward quickly and her face paled, as she seemed to nerve herself to a difficult communication.

"Blackburn," she said tremulously, "I think I ought to tell you that from what I heard this afternoon I am very anxious. But oh, dear boy, don't let anything that may happen disturb you, and just remember that the one who has love has everything!"

CHAPTER II

SHADOWS BEFORE

As he turned toward the house a familiar voice called to him from the opposite side of the street, and an instant afterwards Frederick Dilson emerged out of the shadows.

"Hello, there!" cried the young man, coming up breathless.

Blackburn paused expectant. "How are you, Dilson?" he cried, with an attempt at cheerfulness which he was conscious was far from being as successful as he wished. There was a look of pain and weariness in his eyes, and his manner was that of one sore pressed and perplexed, despite his ready cordiality.

However, Dilson did not seem to notice. "By Jove," he exclaimed in his kindly, light-hearted way, "if you aren't enough to make a fellow feel like swearing! Here I've been hunting you over this old town for the last hour and a half, supposing that you were hard at it somewhere, and all the while you've been off hearkening to the voice of the siren, and leaving the other fellows to do the work. Well, there'll be plenty of it for the next ten days, I venture to say. I see that a hurry call has been issued to the Democratic committeemen of the district for a meeting in Frankfort on the twenty-third."

Blackburn assented, but did not pursue the subject further.

Dilson hesitated. He stood in considerable embarrassment tapping the grass that grew near the curbing with his cane.

"Of course you know I'm for you, old man," he broke forth presently, with an affectionate gleam in his eyes, "for everything — from the Presidency down." He was silent again, and then added quickly, "But that's not what I want to see you about just now."

The two had frequently met recently. There were not many persons in whose devotion Blackburn felt a greater confidence than that of this seemingly volatile but very true friend. But Dilson's constrained attitude toward the matter with Tippleton, his silence and nervous avoidance of the subject, above all, his more pronounced expression of friendly feeling on all public occasions, were among the things that had stung Blackburn most since that dark night of tragedy. It was now plainly evident to him that Dilson regarded the congressional race as a blunder — and for the same reason as that of many others who had sought to dissuade him from the announcement of his candidacy, though placing their objections on various minor grounds.

Something of his father's proud aloofness, that peculiar atmosphere of reserve that seems ever to surround the strong but sensitive nature destined to be misunderstood, showed in his aspect.

"Come in and have dinner with us, won't you?" he suggested in an abrupt change of topic. Dilson looked relieved.

"No, thanks, I can't stay to dinner. I'll just state my errand, and then I'm off. I'm the bearer of an invitation to you for this evening from Major Wise — a somewhat impromptu affair. He has arranged for a little theatre party and a supper after it at his house in honour of Miss Gertrude Overton, who is a good deal cut up over not being allowed to return to Bryn Mawr, you know. Deuced fine looking girl, by the way, if she does succeed in making a fellow feel rather small, with that cool little stare of hers. The major has engaged two of the lower boxes. He wants you in the box with himself and several others — besides the guest of honour. Her sister is of the party, of course, also," he supplemented carelessly, looking away.

"I am very sorry — " Blackburn was beginning when Dilson put in positively and with affected gravity.

"Can't take any excuse, my good sir; I have my

orders. I should never dare face the major with a refusal."

"But I have special work — "

Dilson solemnly shook his head.

"You know the major. He never accepts regrets. I'm to bring you to the opera house to-night, dead or alive — and that's about all there is to it. Did you never hear of that jolly old county judge who flourished here thirty or forty years ago who once gave a command like that? It's a rather rum story. I'll tell it briefly. Hear, and be warned: A hog was stolen from one of the judge's neighbors, and was afterwards found in the smokehouse of a very respectable darky who had belonged to the judge's father. The man protested his innocence and declared that he had got the meat from another darky who had sold it to him. Nevertheless, he was arrested and taken to jail. He sent for the old judge to help him out. The judge told him that he'd let him go free if he'd find that thief and bring him into court, but that he was to bring him in, dead or alive — otherwise, the penitentiary. Two days later the darky appeared. 'Marse Ben,' he said, 'I done cotched dat nigger.' The judge told him to bring him in, but the darky waited. He said, 'I wan' somebody holp me tote him in. He's out heah in de waggin'. He wouldn't come, an' I had to kill him.' Well, it's a go, isn't it?" as Blackburn broke into a laugh. "Good-by, old fellow — see you to-night."

"Don't look for me until about nine, then,— explain to the major," called Blackburn after his friend's retreating form, won in spite of himself, and tempted by the thought of Cicely.

He was greatly troubled about her. She was far from well, and he was surprised and even a little hurt, in view of everything, to know that she had accepted the major's invitation. Since that night when she had clung to him in such a desperation of love and grief, she had persistently, and somewhat unaccountably, he was forced to admit, denied herself to him, although he had gone every day, and often twice a day, to her home, hoping for a few moments with her. There had been a number of wild, unhappy little notes — piteous, confusing, yet throbbing with such an outpouring of womanly tenderness, such an abandon of passionate and intimate devotion as thrilled him to the very depths of his being, and made him more than ready to pardon. One that came several days before had burned into his heart and brain. She had written:

"I am still too ill and miserable to see you, dear. Will you be patient—*can* you? How is it possible that you should understand? Oh, if only I could let you look down deep into my soul, as one gazes into a well, and read all—*all*—dearest, I would not keep back anything from you—that is there! And do you know what you would see? Your own face, looking back at you; and if, Narcissus like, you should love it, that would not seem at all strange to me. But I feel as if a great high wall were between us—so high that it reaches quite up to heaven; and when I try to make you hear all at once my voice grows faint and muffled like a frightened whisper, and I fall back startled and helpless and sick at heart. I am groping in the dark. And yet I know that I must find my way out of this all alone. I must not let you guide me. The woman who is to stand by your side must be strong. More and more the thought presses upon me that she must be powerful to endure—a grand, heroic being like yourself, capable of looking life fearlessly in the face. She must not cower nor shrink—even though she should lose all—oh, God—even though she should lose all! This much I have gained out of these long terrible hours alone with my own thoughts. Do not come to me for a little while yet, my beloved. Wait—wait until I am strong enough to bear your arms about me, your kisses on my lips, and not feel my will weakening under yours so that I can no longer see that what the heart desires the brain must needs approve. Bear with me—forgive me. Oh, darling—darling!

"CICELY."

Blackburn's reply to this was to go straight to her home. He sent up his card with a few words scribbled upon it in his own strong and masterful way. But Cicely would not come down, and he was forced to leave, with a tightening of the muscles about his mouth and a great yearning at his heart. *How* he loved her! — with a love that was long-suffering and abiding and that nothing could shake. And she was his — eternally his — in spite of all her fears and pleadings! The thought swept through him hot and resolute as a flame, yet with unspeakable pity as he turned away, baffled yet determined.

There were many reasons why, during the past few days, he had especially desired to see her. He had not wished to write to her of his candidacy, preferring to talk the matter over quietly with her; and as he made his way to the opera house several hours after his conversation with Dilson, it occurred to him that most likely she knew nothing at all of it as yet, being ill and seeing no one, and in consideration of the fact that both her father and mother had been called away from home just before he had made his decision. It was painful to think that anything that so vitally concerned them both should be told her by anyone but himself, and he hoped that she did not know.

As he entered the theatre the curtain was just falling on the third act. He stood a moment leaning against a pillar and looking around at the gay assemblage. Nearly everyone he knew was in evening dress. Every seat was taken. The play was one that had had considerable success in Eastern cities the preceding winter. It was being presented now in the South for the first time, and it had called forth a special enthusiasm on the part of a people ready to patronize almost anything of a scenic nature from a dog show to a Shakespearean drama. The airy, Southern charm that was apt to pervade such assemblies was particularly in evidence.

Blackburn felt a little like "the dreamer at the feast."

Major Wise and his party occupied the lower boxes on the left side of the stage. They were about twelve in all, and the major, immaculate and elegant, sat smiling beneficently upon his guests.

Blackburn's gaze quickly sought out Cicely. She was in white, as was also her young sister — a tall dark girl, with a very calm and stately bearing, who was giving a somewhat indifferent attention to Dilson's good-humoured efforts to entertain her. Cicely was talking to the young man back of her, and her face was turned away. But presently she paused and looked around, a slight restlessness showing in her glance. Blackburn took out his glasses and drew her to him.

She was not looking well. She was very pale, and the usual glittering animation that lent to her beauty a certain starlike effulgence had given way to a manner that was oddly listless and cold. He stood looking at her, wondering, in a man's clumsy fashion, why she felt impelled to put the useless strain upon herself, and feeling a good deal disturbed, when a sudden thought stabbed him to the heart: she was doing it deliberately and through a prompting of pride — a desire to show to the world that she was able calmly to endure their gaze! He knew intuitively that she was looking for him, and that she wished that they should be seen together in this most public way — as if she felt that something akin to disgrace had touched him and therefore set them both apart.

A hot wave of rebellion swept over him, and he half turned as with the impulse to go away. He checked it, and for an instant he stood unconscious of everything save that one bitter, humiliating thought. Then he set his teeth firmly and moved toward the boxes.

The major was the first to see him as he approached, and a very gratified expression stole over his benign features. He motioned to Dilson, and there was a little stir. The intermission had been long, and the audience was growing impatient. It was more than ready for a new sensation of any kind. As Blackburn took the seat left vacant just behind Cicely, instantly dozens of opera glasses were levelled upon the two.

They greeted each other with the high-bred reserve which is the defense of all fine natures against the vulgarly curious; but Cicely's face, although it betrayed by not so much as a shade of recognition that she was conscious of scrutiny, grew startlingly white and still behind her gracious smiling. She spoke a few words to him slowly and calmly, scarcely meeting his eyes. To which he replied with an equal steadiness, and then turned to Dilson, who was tactfully trying to save the situation. She bent her head over her program, and he felt rather than saw she was suffering acutely under the stress of an intense nervous strain. She did not speak again, but as the curtain rang up and attention was again directed to the stage, she all at once turned and raised her eyes to his in a look that transfixed him with its mingled pain and adoration.

He was deeply touched. He could only sit watching her, helpless and with throbbing pulses, longing for a word, and tormented with nameless fears.

But her eyes were turned toward the actors, and he saw that she was listening with a strange, intense absorption—eager, expectant, despite her outward calm. Her breath came short and troubled. Her lips were slightly parted, and she did not stir — as if her whole being were waiting the dénoument.

He tried to catch the thread, but it evaded him; and presently his glance rested upon her again with a shade of inquiry. The play, although fairly well presented, did not particularly interest him, and he was wondering absently, why it so held her attention, when something happened.

The plot had turned upon a difficulty between two men, rivals in love and in kingly favour — one the hero, the other the villain. An insult had been offered, evidently in the preceding act, and was now being resented. A desperate encounter, embellished by satin and gold lace, was enacted, and a duel fought with swords with such exquisite skill in fencing that kept the large audience for fully five minutes keyed up to the utmost pitch of excitement. When finally the villain fell and the hero stood over him, looking grimly down, having sated his vengeance and wiped out the stain of insult with the stain of blood, a tremendous applause broke loose, swept like a hailstorm through the building, spent itself, and then started up anew, ending at last in a number of prolonged calls and whistles from the gallery, like wind-shrieks amid crackling boughs. The play had touched upon a point which Kentuckians of all grades are swift to understand.

Blackburn turned and looked at Cicely. She was sitting absolutely motionless, her face still toward the stage. Her gaze was fixed and staring, and there was that in her look that made his heart stand still. All at once she sank back in her chair, and almost in the same instant the lights in the theatre were lowered, and the orchestra struck up. He leaned quickly toward her.

"Come!" he said in a low decisive tone.

But she did not stir.

A terror seized him. "Cicely — come!" he said again and rose.

There was a moment's horrible waiting, and she turned startled, like one awaking out of a painful dream. Then he felt her move toward him in the gloom, gropingly, forlornly, like a frightened child. He reached down, grasped her opera cloak, threw it around her, and hurried her out of the theatre, reaching the exit just as a blaze of light again flashed forth.

When they started down the long tunnel-shaped enclosure that led out to the street, he felt a sudden violent shivering seize her frame, and her grasp upon his arm tighten.

"It was wrong to come — I was ill," she whispered in a kind of apologetic confusion. "I — I don't know what is the matter with me." She glanced quickly up at him. "Oh, I have frightened you so!"

Her voice broke in something like a sob. She paused.

"You will have to take me home," she said more calmly, "and you have forgotten your hat and overcoat. Please go back for them."

He hesitated, and she forced a wan smile to her lips. "Please go," she insisted, "I am not going to faint. I wouldn't know how."

He left her and returned quickly. He stood a moment looking round for her carriage as the outer air blew moist and chill against their faces. She divined his thought.

"No — it is only a step — let us walk," she cried moving on; "the cool air helps my head."

He looked down at her feet in their thin slippers. "I can't let you walk," he replied positively.

She looked at him wildly and a strange smile broke

over her features. But she did not answer. She let him help her into one of the waiting carriages without further protest. She sank back wearily in the corner of the vehicle, and neither spoke. Once she reached forth her hand to him and his closed over it instantly. Something in his strong sure clasp seemed to steady her. Her voice sounded sweet and tranquil when the carriage paused at her door.

"Dear, will you go back now?" she pleaded almost humbly, as they went up the steps together. "The major will be so troubled — and poor Gertrude. Try to explain to them that it is nothing."

But he only held her more firmly for an instant, and then followed her on into the house.

Everything was very still. There was only a dim light in the drawing-room, and the fire had burned low, but it lay a great bed of smouldering embers which sent forth a soft red shimmering, most grateful after the night's autumnal mists. In the center of the room she paused, breathing quickly, and again that wild, strange look crept into her eyes.

He crossed the room and took her in his arms.

"My beloved!" he cried. "My poor little girl!"

A sudden spasm of pain swept through her like the convulsive quivering of a wounded bird. She turned desperately, as if meditating flight. Then a storm of weeping; and her head fell forward on his breast, and she sank into his arms, broken and helpless and shaken with heavy sobs.

He stood stroking her cheek, looking down upon her, vainly trying to comfort, and almost beside himself with distressful fears.

"Cicely, are you ill? — what is it? — oh, tell me!"

Presently the sobbing ceased, and she lay for an instant very white and still, neither resisting nor yielding to his embrace. She raised her face.

"I — don't — know, dear. I hope not," she answered wearily. "Leave me now. I shall go upstairs and try to sleep, and maybe — maybe when the morning comes — "

"But I can't — I *cannot* leave you like this!" he cried miserably. "You will let me call some one —"

She shook her head.

"I would rather be alone, and I don't need anything."

All at once she reached up both her arms, and clasped them closely about his neck in a complete abandonment of reserve.

"Kiss me!" she said in a voice that pierced him with its sweetness and roused him to a fearful joy; for in its disclosure of a more intensely passionate devotion than she had yet revealed to him there was a note that rang in his ears like a far off funeral bell.

He kissed her again and again, at first gently, then

with the unrestrained ardour of one whose soul is torn and tortured with dread, whispering disconnectedly all the burning words of love that rushed in a kind of frenzy to his lips.

Presently she put him gently from her, and moved toward the door. Then she went slowly up the stairs.

On the landing she turned and stood a moment looking down at him.

He was standing at the foot of the stairs, and was gazing up at her as one stunned. Even in the dim light she could see that his face was drawn and seamed with an anguish of suspense.

She put forth her hands to him.

"Blackburn —oh, Blackburn!" she cried.

He made a sudden leap toward her, taking the stairs three steps at a bound. But she waved him back.

He paused abruptly, and a smile ineffably sad and tender stole slowly over her features.

"Good-night," she said softly. "Dear, good-night."

CHAPTER III

A CANDIDATE FOR CONGRESS

"I think I can see, Professor, that you are not very favourably disposed toward the idea," said Blackburn, tapping with the fingers of one hand on his office table. "I am very sorry, for I always want your approval. But I feel constrained to make the race."

Professor Kennedy looked troubled. His kindly glance rested a moment upon the stalwart form of the young candidate before him, and then wandered uneasily toward the window and the street below. It was four o'clock of a November afternoon. The scene was dull and dispiriting. An express wagon rumbled noisily by, and the professor watched it until it was out of sight in a kind of absorbed indecision. On the corner of the Courthouse square a group of lawyers were standing talking very earnestly. He thought he could guess the tenor of their conversation. It was Saturday, and he had spent part of the day in a neighbouring town talking to just such groups as that. He was not encouraged. He believed that, owing to his special skill and discretion, gladly exerted in behalf of his young friend, he had obtained an accurate knowledge of the situation so far as the county of Woodford was concerned. For the professor was strongly of the opinion that if fate had not designed him for a staid instructor of Greek and Latin, he would have become something of an expert at the game of politics. As a matter of fact, he was about as well fitted for such work as he would have been successfully to conduct a class in dancing; and Mike Conolly could have taught him in the first round a thing or two that would have made him open his eyes. But he had come back from his exploration a good deal disturbed.

"My boy," he said at length somewhat timidly, "I wish you had consulted with me before you decided to announce your candidacy. I think I would have sought to deter you from making the race at this time."

Blackburn smiled a little grimly. "There were enough to deter me, Professor. But I thought it advisable to make the race."

The professor turned quickly. "Then you are aware that there is — that there is a good deal of uncertainty as to the result?"

"I am aware that there is very little uncertainty as to the result."

Professor Kennedy was confused. Was this confidence of success, or confession of failure?

"The Ashland district is more to be relied on than any in the state," he remarked presently, seeking refuge in evasio "It gave a majority of over four thousand to Mr. Goebel, I am informed, and it has been called, and correctly called, the Gibraltar of the Kentucky Democracy. Nevertheless —"

"Nevertheless, you think I am not the man to carry the district. You are not very flattering, Professor."

"On the contrary, my dear boy, it has long been a cherished dream with me that I should one day see you fully launched upon your career in the Lower House of Congress. I have always sincerely believed that not even the sage of Ashland himself achieved there a renown more splendid than would be yours. Far be it from me to seek to dissuade you — except for the present, except for the present."

"But it was decided among my friends that I was to run in a year from now. The death of the incumbent at this time —"

"The death of the incumbent at this time was inopportune, sir, I may say very inopportune," put in the professor, resentfully. "The state is involved in a most unfortunate turmoil. Never saw the like of it. My advice to you would have been to wait until some of the present excitement had blown over, and then announce yourself next year as previously planned."

Blackburn's features became suddenly set. "It is a kind of test case, Professor," he said at length. "On next Thursday I will know definitely just how I stand with my own people. It is a discovery that I greatly wish to make."

Again the professor's eyes wandered to the window and to the group of men on the opposite side of the street.

"I am told that at the meeting of the congressional committee, which convened under the hurry call of the state executive committeemen, a convention to take place next Thursday at Frankfort was decided upon."

Blackburn assented. "On next Tuesday precinct mass conventions; on Wednesday mass meetings to elect delegates to the district convention; and on Thursday the convention at Frankfort. That is the program, I believe. It allows, of course, only a minimum of time. But six weeks ago I think that few of my friends would have questioned that I would go into such a convention with the largest number of instructed votes of any of the candidates now in the field. It would have been conceded, I think, that, given these same candidates, I would have carried over any one of them the solid vote of Fayette, Woodford, Bourbon —"

Professor Kennedy interrupted. "But it is not six weeks ago, it is not six weeks ago. These are history-making times. I realize that your course with regard to Goebel has made you strong friends as well as strong enemies. But your enemies, though they be legion, will have little control in this matter. As I have said, the district gave a majority of over four thousand for William Goebel; and I have discovered that the party is very grateful to you for standing by it as manfully as you have done. There was nothing half-hearted nor equivocal in your course. You did not try to curry favour with both sides. *Duos qui sequitur lepores, neutrum capit.* Your stand was one to respect; and if some fail to grasp the true principle that animated you, and do not recognize that it was not Goebel, nor even Kentucky, that you fought for, but the nation, it is assuredly not because you haven't told them. You have been hammering away at it long enough to convince the veriest numbskull of your meaning. If you are to be defeated, it will not be because of matters growing out of the present political situation, but upon other grounds — upon other grounds."

Blackburn leaned his elbow on the table and his head upon his elbow. He was silent a long time. When he looked up his face had taken on a sudden hardness.

"I think there need be no hesitation between us, Professor, in mentioning what these grounds are," he said calmly. "You have reference to that affair with Tippleton."

A very pained expression was in the professor's eyes. But it was too late to retreat. He leaned forward quickly and held out his hand.

"My boy," he replied very gently, "the misconception of you in relation to that affair will certainly cause your defeat. I would not be the friend I am if I refrained from telling you. I am not easily misled in matters of this kind. In this one day I have seen enough. You haven't a ghost of a chance for the nomination, I am sure. It is this damned Kentucky sentiment —"

The professor caught himself up with a start. It was one of the few times in his life that he had ever felt tempted to accentuate his remarks by language so questionable. He was completely abashed.

Blackburn smiled a little quietly over this outburst, at the same time hoping that the Recording Angel would deal as gently with his old friend as in the case of My Uncle Toby. His hand closed warmly over the professor's.

"I knew," he said, after a moment, "very little of the precise state of feeling toward me when I entered the race. It has been clearly revealed since I announced my candidacy."

"You are — you are reconsidering?" suggested Professor Kennedy, tentatively.

"It had been my plan," responded Blackburn, staring straight ahead of him, "to make the race next year. The vacancy that has occurred precipitates matters merely. Nothing has altered my resolution to offer myself at the first opportunity for this place. I may not receive the nomination. But I will know, and the state will know, the grounds on which I have met defeat."

"Then you will not draw off?" demanded the professor, with an eagerness he could not conceal. His face had undergone a sudden transformation. He was thinking very rapidly.

Blackburn shook his head. "I am very sorry, Professor, but I will not draw off. I'm in to the finish."

Professor Kennedy sat a moment wrapt in deepest meditation. All at once he rose and grasped his cane. "Then

'Up with the bonnie blue bonnet,
The dirk and the feather and a',' "

he exclaimed, brandishing his stick nobly; "and it's a fine spirit you have, if I do say it myself, who taught you all the Greek and Latin you ever knew, whatever those Princeton fellows may have to say about it."

CHAPTER IV

IN WHICH BLACKBURN SUFFERS DEFEAT

It was four days later, and nearly five o'clock, as Major Orlando Wise had just assured himself for the twentieth time by a consultation of the ancient timepiece he carried.

His thoughts were nervous and disturbed, being focused with considerable anxiety upon his young friend Blackburn Blair — to use his own invariable designation. The major had just got back from a short hunting trip, and he was now, after partaking of a slight repast, impatiently awaiting the returns from the various precinct and county conventions held that day throughout the district.

His library fire was blazing merrily, and a volume of Thomas Moore lay open on the table by his side; for the major was not only an historian and a political economist, but an ardent reader of the poets as well. He had made several futile attempts to divert his attention; and once more he picked up the book and turned to a favourite page.

> "There's a bower of roses by Bendemeer's stream,
> And the nightingale sings round it all the day long,
> In the time of my childhood 'twas like a sweet dream,—"

He gently closed the book. It was utterly useless. For a few moments he sat gazing into the fire. Then he rose and went to the window.

Suddenly he started and pricked up his ears: he thought he had heard a newsboy's whistle in the distance. Immediately his handsome countenance was eagerly expectant.

When the whistle became a certainty, he turned quickly and made his way to the front, as agitated as if Blackburn had been his own son. Once in the doorway, it occurred to him that he could wait just as well at the gate.

The major hurried down the path. Not even the rarest of rare old volumes in his library had ever been so ardently desired as was "The Daily Leader" in that moment.

When the paper was finally handed to him his face was white and his hand was trembling. "Bless me!" he said to himself as he dropped his glasses, shattering them, "who would have thought I'd get myself into such a fidget!"

He had expected that the race would be close, knowing a little of Blackburn's decline in popular favour; and he was of the impression that the convention to be held in Frankfort on the morrow would be one of the most exciting that had ever occurred there. But he was destined to a surprise.

His glance ran quickly down the column. He rubbed his eyes. All at once the paper fell from his hands.

"Great God!" he exclaimed aloud, "the boy has failed to carry even Fayette County!"

Blackburn was alone in his office for the first time after the hard day. Professor Kennedy, the last of his callers, had left him some time before, the look of amazement upon his broad Scotch countenance blending with an expression that was most touching in its distress and father-like devotion.

Long after the last sound of the halting steps in the corridor had died away the young man sat thinking — until the twilight began to gather and the room was filled with skulking shadows. The professor had not brought him anything startling. Thoroughly cognizant of the state of public feeling toward him, the result, which he already knew, was expected. He was not shocked.

He had for some time been an object of envy to certain aspiring ones of his own party, who saw in his cool judgment, his gracious charm of manner, and above all his scholarly and fervid oratory those qualities that make for leadership among their own people. For whatever opinion the rest of the world may hold on the subject of supremacy, the Kentuckian at least will probably never cease to bow before the statesman capable of expressing his ideas with eloquence and passion. It were well then to destroy this new and brilliant figure in the political horizon, and that right speedily. Therefore, it was these persons in particular who found themselves wholly unable to overlook the conduct of young Blair in the affair with Tippleton.

Those who resented his oratory as applied to the recent campaign were more than ready to echo this view. On all sides his courage was questioned, the general verdict, even of the most charitable, being that the young man simply was lacking in those high-spirited and manly qualities which mark the Kentuckian's superiority over all other men. The "damned Kentucky sentiment" was doing its work.

To Blackburn its force had been manifested not only in the averted glance, the coldness and the constraint of those who sought to avoid, but in the artful insinuation of newspapers inimical to him, and in the rough but kindly reference of those who really thought to please him by denouncing Tippleton.

A realizing sense of the moral blindness and slowness of heart that made it a well-nigh impossible thing for those about him to conceive of a course of action not in harmony with their traditional prejudice and natural impulse filled him with the momentary discouragement that comes to all strong, far-seeing natures that have made a brave fight in the face of tremendous odds.

But there was no regret, no shadow of turning, no lurking weakness of character to be revealed by the touchstone of defeat. He was looking the situation, as was his wont, sternly in the face, and with the look of a conqueror. He had climbed the mountain height — *Über allen Gipfeln ist Ruh* — and he had found rest. But the clear air of the lonely summit, to one still longing for the warmth of the human, is cold. The whole structure of his life seemed tottering before him, and he felt he could only stand like a paralytic and see it fall. Time? —Not even time could establish what was lost. He felt that there was little hope that he should ever be understood. Such a revolution of public opinion as he must appeal to could only come slowly, through the gradual upward trend of civilization, or by one of those mighty upheavals of universal awakening brought about by some stark and terrible tragedy that would rouse the commonwealth to its center. Would it ever come to Kentucky?

But as he sat there in the dim light of the November afternoon, again and again Cicely's lovely face had come before him with a passionate insistence. He saw her grieved piteously for his sake, yet proudly resentful of everything that had brought about his defeat; and stung to the heart by this added humiliation. Everything in him cried out in protest against her pain. His head throbbed at the thought of it. That he must hurt her so! — he whose mighty love and tenderness would shield her from the prick of every thorn! Hard and unrelenting toward himself, demanding always that he bear the thorn pricks bravely, he was yet all gentleness and apology toward her; and he was now, as he had ever been, the same blinded, boyish, chivalrous lover whose dream had begun in a rose garden some eighteen years before. Immaculate — flawless as her beauty, with its witchery and softness and poetic appeal —she must ever be to him, let others think of her as they would. The blow of his defeat upon her just at this time seemed to him like the hand of a ruffian upon a suffering child.

For she was seriously ill. Since that night —that ever memorable night, he had not seen her, and there had been no word to lighten the dark hours through which he had been passing. At her physician's orders she lay in a perfectly quiet room, with only a trained nurse and her mother about her. Blackburn had been forbidden the smallest communication. He was hard pressed with anxiety and cares. And there were moments, like the present, when a sickening sense of loss, of something coming, enwrapped him like a pall. Today the very air seemed to breathe calamity. What if she should be worse! The suspense was maddening. He felt that he could not bear it longer.

He started up. In the same instant a step sounded on the stair — an aged step climbing the long flight slowly. There was a knock at the door. Ben entered.

The old servant stood a moment decorously, twirling his soft hat in his hands, and peering with blinking eyes into the shadowy office. "Hit's de second time I done clumb dem sta'hs," he remarked in rueful recollection.

"I'm sorry Ben, that you missed me," said Blackburn, kindly, "Why didn't you take the elevator?"

"Ain' got no use foh dem helevators. Dunno whar dey gwine tek me," answered Ben, fumbling in his waistcoat pocket. He was slow.

"You have a note for me? She is better?" asked Blackburn, quickly.

Ben shook his head mysteriously. "She lookin' mighty white an' still. Her ma, she say dey ain' nothin' much de matter wid her, but me an' de jedge an' de cun'l is con*trary*. I ain' seen her but oncet sence she took sick, an' dat's to-day. She sint foh me, an' she gimme dis, an' say I musn't let nobody have 'em ceptin' yo'se'f."

The old negro walked across the room in a stately fashion and solemnly deposited a small oblong envelope and a tiny box wrapped in white tissue paper on the table.

Blackburn's face suddenly blanched. He grasped

the rounds of his chair tightly. He could not speak.

But the old negro was standing in respectful silence. "Does you wan' me to wait foh a' answer?" he suggested presently, seeing that Blackburn only sat staring at the note and the tiny package like one bereft all at once of his senses.

Blackburn roused himself. "No — Ben — no. I think, that is — there is no answer," he managed to say at last. He searched for a coin, found it, and handed it forth mechanically. The door opened and closed. He was alone.

Many moments passed. The office grew darker. Still he did not stir. Presently he reached out a hand and touched the box, gently, reverently, as one touches a sacred thing. But there was something sinister in the glitter of the small object inside. The ring lay for one instant in his palm and then fell to the floor; and for a moment the room swam before him. Then there came a picture of moonlight and the sound of low sweet laughter, and of a woman's soft breathing as his lips were pressed to hers. Other scenes pressed upon him. A terrible smile hovered about his features; and presently a laugh like a maniac's broke from him and echoed hollow and despairing through the large room. He put up his hand quickly to his head. Was he going mad? His eyes fell upon the note.

There must be some meaning, some explanation.

He tore it open wildly. There were only a few words.

But they were enough. He flung out his arms upon the table and his head sank like a leaden weight upon them.

The blow had fallen heavily.

CHAPTER V

MICHAEL BROOMER AGAIN

It was eleven o'clock of a very cold January day more than two months later. Myra, who loved warmth and sunshine and balmy flower-scented breezes, shivered a little in disgust of the biting air as she drew her furs closer about her. She was on her way to Cicely, though with scarce a hope of seeing her, Mrs. Overton's queenly presence rising continually before her mind's eye in elegant but strenuous opposition. However, Myra was in the mood to be equally strenuous, urged on by an instinctive sense of danger, and her sweet face expressed a resolution not to be thwarted save by a point blank refusal, when she finally pulled her friend's door bell.

She had not seen Cicely since the latter's illness, which had proved to be serious enough to demand absolute quiet, though not so serious as to be alarming. Still, there was no question that she had been really ill, and Myra, as was her wont when anxious about people she cared for, had given herself up to a sort of brooding watchfulness which, Mrs. Overton, for reasons of her own, found slightly oppressive.

To Myra it had gradually revealed many things. For instance, she was entirely sure that it was not at Cicely's direction that she had been steadily refused admittance, even after permission had been given for others to call. Nervous exhaustion might account, she admitted, for a good deal, but it could scarcely account for everything. She was convinced that Mrs. Overton secretly resented her influence.

As she was ushered into the drawing-room two people sitting talking in very earnest conversation near the window turned quickly. A clumsily built, dark-haired, dark-moustached young man rose as Mrs. Overton — looking slightly flustered and surprised, out of her usual self-command by the interruption — took a step forward.

"Oh, Myra, it is you, my dear?" she cried in ill-concealed constraint. "I didn't hear you come in. How good of you to come so often! Cicely is better to-day — much better. She took a drive yesterday, and she came down last evening for several hours. Mr. Broomer has proved himself wiser than the doctor. He thinks she needs nothing so much as fresh air and variety and pleasant companionship. Of course, you have not forgotten Mr. Broomer, my dear? Mr. Broomer," turning with a grand sweep of her flowing skirts to the awkward young man, who had been waiting in considerable confusion for the introduction, "this is Mrs. Mallory whom you doubtless recall."

For an instant Myra looked steadily into the shrewd, kindly eyes bent upon her. Despite his heavy features and sallowness of complexion, his face was not lacking in a certain attractiveness; and there was about him a sort of ponderous dignity that seemed the outward expression of some inward force. But the prosaic, the practical, the commonplace were written upon him with indelible brand. He seemed the natural product of an all-engrossing commercial idea. In his excessive shyness there was something appealing. She held out her hand.

"I am sure that I have not forgotten Mr. Broomer," she said, "but he has had ample time in which to forget me."

"I remember you perfectly, Mrs. Mallory," he answered in his slow, thick voice, as he pushed a chair forward for her. "But you were scarcely more than a little girl when I saw you last. I recognized Miss Overton also at once from my recollection of her as a child. You were both very constant frequenters of my father's shop."

Myra studied him a little thoughtfully, noting the trace of self-consciousness that was revealed in his mention of Cicely's name, and his straightforward reference to his past, with a sudden sharp misgiving. She was not an ordinary person, and she was not to be swayed by the pretty feelings that govern most, but loyalty to Blackburn forbade her to like him. It is a woman's way.

"It was not every one who could offer such inducements," she observed kindly, but with rather distant courtesy.

Mrs. Overton's face darkened. She changed the subject abruptly.

"We have been discussing among other things, Mr. Broomer and I, that disgraceful contest now going on before the state Legislature," she said irritably. "Could anything be more high-handed and contemptible than William Goebel's refusal to acknowledge himself beaten even after the state commission has given the certificate of election to his opponent? The present condition of things in Kentucky is a farce — a perfect farce."

Myra looked her questioner in the face without the smallest evidence of annoyance. She had already had repeated experience of Mrs. Overton's aggressive method of attack in that direction, and she was fully aware of her resentful attitude toward everyone who happened to differ with her.

"It seems that we are less in danger of a farce than of a tragedy, Mrs. Overton," she replied gravely. "But is Mr. Broomer interested in the subject of who is to rule over us as governor of Kentucky?"

she added, turning toward the young man her still, high-bred face, lit with a serene graciousness of expression.

"Does a Kentuckian ever cease to be interested in such a subject?" he asked.

"So you still regard yourself as a Kentuckian?"

"Once a Kentuckian, always a Kentuckian. Isn't it like that?" he queried.

"Yes, I believe it is like that with most persons."

"I am sure I don't know why," remarked Mrs. Overton, with a shrug. "Kentucky has not made for herself a very enviable reputation in recent times."

Myra thought it well to ignore this. "I have been wondering, Mr. Broomer," she said, "before expressing myself too strongly, what your party affiliation is — to use a phrase that must have made a strange confusion in the mind of one of our poor, bewildered darky voters recently, when questioned at the polls. I don't know just what *party affiliation* suggested, but the reply was unique. He said: 'Boss, *I* is a mah'ied man.'"

Michael Broomer laughed. There was a painful return to self-consciousness, a simpering expression about the mouth when he replied, which Myra was disposed to resent. "I'm afraid that I can't make the darky's answer, Mrs. Mallory," he said, "but I wish very much that I could say the same."

The same! Myra would have found it a difficult

matter to forgive him that, even if he had not been doing his best, as she knew, to supplant her dear cousin in Cicely's affections.

"Perhaps, like an acquaintance of Mrs. Overton's and mine, you are an *Honest Democrat*," she suggested, smiling toward Mrs. Overton with a composure that the latter was disposed to resent. "Do you remember Mrs. Bellows, Mr. Broomer?"

"Mrs. Bellows? I certainly do remember Mrs. Bellows. When I was a small boy she once boxed my ears."

"It is not necessary to be a small boy to merit such distinction at her hands," returned Myra. "Metaphorically speaking, at least, there are not many of us who have escaped such punishment. It is the penalty of her acquaintance."

"I venture to say that she doesn't get the better of Virginia Oats," remarked Mrs. Overton, dryly. "It is Greek meet Greek just now whenever those two come together. Mr. Oats is strongly Republican, but that doesn't at all deter his wife. There is nothing I dislike so much as to see a woman opposed to her husband's views. It puts a man in an awkward light before the whole world. Above all things, I admire a *womanly* woman. I tell Cicely all the time, 'Now whatever you do, my dear, don't meddle with politics.'"

Myra was unable to suppress a smile and even

Michael Broomer had to take refuge in a sudden fit of coughing. The picture of Mrs. Overton posing in the rôle of a womanly woman was a little too much for even his phlegmatic sensibilities.

"Virginia Oats is positively rabid," continued Mrs. Overton, imperturbably. "She will not admit that there is a flaw in the whole Democratic party from Bryan to Blackburn Blair. Now it always seems to me that it is possible to discuss these matters without losing one's temper or good-breeding. No one could have a worse opinion of another than I have of Mr. Bryan. I regard him as the greatest demagogue and charlatan in existence, a veritable fire-eating anarchist, a mountebank who would destroy the sacred rights of property just as his low follower, Goebel, has been seeking to do in overturning the will of the people by destroying their sacred right of franchise. I think these things, and therefore I must express them. But when I did so at an afternoon reception the other day several persons immediately left the room. Virginia Oats flew into a rage. Nothing is so difficult to combat as prejudice. It makes a person wholly intolerant of another's opinion, and it is always very bad form."

"I think the main interest in the present political situation in Kentucky so far as the gubernatorial contest is concerned," remarked Michael Broomer, still struggling with his cough, " is its relation to the presidential election next autumn. If the General Assembly should decide in favour of Goebel —"

"How can you question how it will decide?" put in Mrs. Overton, sharply. "Isn't it ridiculously par tisan?"

"Perhaps the recent visit to Frankfort of more than a thousand Republican mountaineers armed with Winchester rifles and sullenly defiant may have had somewhat the effect of intimidation," coolly suggested Myra, staring straight ahead of her.

"Then I sincerely hope it will, I hope it will. When matters come to the pass they have, revolution is the only remedy," replied Mrs. Overton, who had picked up a loose newspaper phrase and was inclined to make the most of it. "If an upstart like that William Goebel, a man sprung from the lowest round of the social ladder —"

She suddenly caught herself and crimsoned painfully. But Mr. Broomer's good-breeding seemed in that instance superior to her own. He gave no sign of making a personal application. He turned to Myra very quietly. There was something fair and kindly in his manner, without being in the least conciliatory.

"You spoke of my party affilation," he said. " Until recently I have always been a Democrat, as my father was before me. But I am opposed to the present policy of the party for the nation and also to Mr. Goebel in Kentucky.

"I cannot condone the appearance at the capital of armed and threatening mountaineers," he added, "if they were brought there, as it is claimed, by Republican officials for the purpose of intimidation; and I am opposed to the reorganization by Republican authority of the militia, and of everything that would suggest a resort to violence. But the determination of Mr. Goebel to lay claim to an office he failed to be elected to is a thing unjustifiable, it seems to me, on any moral grounds."

Myra listened graciously. "My party affiliation," she said smiling, "is scarcely a matter of interest under present conditions, but it is true that I am strongly in favour of the present Democratic policy for the nation; and for that reason, if I had a vote, I should have given it to Mr. Goebel in the state."

"My dear," cried Mrs. Overton, maliciously, "the strange prejudice you speak of may be sufficient explanation of why you are a 'Goebelite,' but I should think that even it would scarcely make you justify the present disgraceful contest."

"I shall not attempt to justify it. I am not in a position to know whether Mr. Goebel was or was not legally elected. I do know that he is proceeding strictly in accord with the law — the organic law of this state, which has been in existence since the earliest days of the Commonwealth. The action of the state commission proved nothing. It was wholly ministerial. If Mr. Goebel believes and his party believes that his opponent received the certificate because in the election methods unjustified by law were practiced, then it is not only his right but his duty to make a contest before the proper tribunal. The Legislature is the only tribunal in this case. And when it has decided, it seems to me that it will be the duty of everyone to acquiesce. Threats of violence and of bloodshed and of subversion of the government, in case the decision rendered shall not be what is desired, argue a condition of lawlessness scarcely to be believed of a civilized people."

"Mercy! Spare us!" broke in Mrs. Overton, with a tragic gesture. "Mr. Broomer, what will you think of a community where even the young women talk like old politicians and hurl the law at your head? In my day such a thing was unheard of. It was not considered good form to know who was the president, or to care — after the Confederacy failed. Won't you stay longer?"

Mr. Broomer had risen and was standing before Myra, holding out his hand with a sudden return to awkwardness.

"Have I frightened you?" she asked.

He assayed a clumsy attempt at a compliment, but

with considerable shrewdness shied off from the political question. He saw that Mrs. Overton was nettled, and it occurred to him that the conversation would better not be prolonged. He was too excellent a business man not to know a little of human nature; and he was not altogether sure of himself in the matter of argument.

"Will you present my — my compliments to Miss Overton," he said in overwhelming shyness, "and say how regretful I am that I could not see her this morning?"

Mrs. Overton moved graciously toward the door. "Cicely is greatly disturbed over having to miss your call," she murmured elegantly. "I hope, however, that she will have the pleasure of seeing you this evening at dinner. We may expect you?"

The young man's face beamed with anticipation, as he bowed himself out.

"Oh, Mr. Broomer!"

Mrs. Overton followed her guest into the hall, and there took place a hurried, intimate conversation carried on in a very low voice — evidently in continuation of something that Myra had interrupted.

When Mrs. Overton returned she wore a look of complacency that was yet tinctured with apprehension. Myra was standing. Mrs. Overton hurried up to her.

"I am sure that you want to see Cicely," she said,

holding out her hand. "It really is too bad, but she cannot talk more than an hour or two in the day, and she expects to come down again this evening. I was even forced to excuse her to Mr. Broomer, as you saw."

"Is Mr. Broomer especially privileged?"

"One always wishes to be courteous toward a stranger, my dear." Mrs. Overton spoke with a mysterious evasion mingled with a sort of pained surprise. There was a slight pause.

"Cicely has just sent word that she will see me, Mrs. Overton" said Myra firmly, moving toward the stairway.

Mrs. Overton stared. "How did she know you were here?"

"Ben probably told her," responded Myra, indifferently.

"Ben is very officious." Mrs. Overton bit her lip. "Don't you think it would be better to wait a few days longer? I am sure you do not want to take any risks," she added in her most wheedling tone.

Myra was already half way up the stair. She paused and looked down toward the anxious figure below. An odd smile suddenly overspread her features.

"I am quite sure that it would not be better to wait a few days longer; and I don't want to take any risks," she said.

CHAPTER VI

MYRA AND CICELY

Cicely was sitting in a great chair before the fire. Her eyes were closed and her head lay on her pillow in utter languor. Against the deep blue of her loose wool gown her face was white and cold. She was spiritless as a flower on a bruised and broken stem. Her beauty was still unmarred — as if even pain forbore its blight upon anything so lovely; but there was something strange in the alteration in her, for it was not the alteration of illness. The soft curves, the delicate flesh, but slightly wasted by suffering, the poetic brow with its exquisite chiseling, filled one with a haunting, painful sense of something vanished. She seemed to have reached the point where she had slipped beyond the possibility of struggle, and to be in the state that is almost the luxury of exhaustion: the complete stillness of all emotion.

She looked up as the door opened and stretched out her arms in a plaintive gesture that was childlike in its veracity. She was one of those women to whom youthfulness would doubtless cling long after youth was passed; and there was a natural sweetness of impulse that sometimes won the heart when the mind condemned. To Myra, whose broad understanding had been heightened by the sympathetic insight that comes to those capable of the greatest love and therefore of the greatest joy and sorrow, she offered the peculiar appeal of a woman despairingly groping on the outside of her Eden, longing for the light, yet too blind and foolish to discern its steady beams.

"I thought you had given me up," whispered Cicely, sadly, in her ear. But the violet eyes suddenly faltered beneath the long, searching gaze that followed quickly upon her words.

Myra sank down upon her knees before the chair and folded the girl tenderly to her heart. "But I have been coming every day, dear. Did no one tell you?"

Cicely shook her head, wondering. "How strange! I might have seen you at any time in the last two weeks. Have you really been coming every day?"

"Every day."

There was a long pause. "And I was beginning to think that — that you would never come again — that you were not willing to come —ever again."

"Why did you think that?'" asked Myra, steadily.

Again Cicely's eyelids quivered. Her hesitation was painful. But it was only momentary. She grew all at once very still. "I have been wanting you to know," she said in a lifeless voice.

Myra rose and took a chair. "What a long, anxious

time, and how beautiful to have you well again!" she exclaimed cheerfully and in a complete change of tone. "But you are altogether too pale, my lady. I miss the lovely wild-rose bloom."

"All my roses are of the past," said Cicely, with a hard little laugh, not meeting her friend's eyes.

Myra was silent for several moments. Presently she leaned forward.

"Cicely, Blackburn is very unhappy," she said, going straight to the point.

A swift crimson suddenly mounted to the girl's brow, receding, however, quickly, and leaving her white and apathetic as before. Her head drooped.

But Myra was unrelenting. "Will you let me speak to you of him for a few moments?" she asked. "I must not stay long."

"I have been wanting you to know," repeated Cicely, in the same dull tones. "I thought of sending for you. But I — I couldn't make myself care enough even to try to tell you."

Myra put forth her hand. "I understand," she responded very gently. "You have been ill and not yourself, and there has been an unequal combat. But you are stronger than you know." All at once she bent her face, sweet and pitiful, a little nearer. "Cicely," she said softly, "there has never been a moment when I have lost faith in you."

"I have lost faith in myself," replied Cicely, shrinking.

"He has told me," said Myra, after a moment, "simply the bare fact. Beyond that I know nothing. It was not possible for him to say anything; and there are some things too sacred and too terrible to be touched upon by even the closest friend. I do not mean to hurt you, dear. I can guess only a little of the chill and the darkness of the sad waters you have been wading through. But I know, and I want you to know, that Blackburn is very unhappy."

Cicely's face was quickly averted. She withdrew her hand. "Have you seen him recently?" she asked. There was a faint eagerness, but there was a coldness also that drove Myra to silence. She sat thinking, with a very troubled look in her dark eyes.

"I have not seen him many times since this — this misunderstanding arose," she replied at length.

"There is no misunderstanding," said Cicely. She waited a moment. Then all at once she raised her white face. "There is no misunderstanding. Everything is at an end between us. He sees — I am sure that he sees — now — that it could not have been different. It was not because of the opposition, as you think. I was strong enough to resist the opposition, but I am not strong enough to be his wife. I would have been wretched, and have made him wretched, and there would have been no hope. I cannot, even now, share in the aims that are always before him. How could I expect to do it in the crowded future years, which would only remove him further and further from me? I loved him. I could not love his work. It was always between us. In time it would have become a mountain of separation."

"If you loved him you would have loved his work, for his work is himself," said Myra, firmly.

"I loved *him,*" persisted Cicely, with her eyes on the fire.

"And you love him still!"

Cicely flinched.

"But there is a nobler love," said Myra, gently, "than you have ever yet reached to. I believe that it is in you to reach to it in all its fullness. It means the complete sacrifice of every selfish thought, it means —"

"I am not a coward," broke in Cicely, hurriedly, "there are not many things in the world I am afraid of. But there is one thing I am afraid of, and that is the horror of an unhappy marriage. I could not slip easily into the contentment of the commonplace. I feel too deeply, too terribly. My heart does not beat in the slow and patient way. I should not be mildly unhappy. I should be distinctly wretched. Oh the helplessness, the utter helplessness of a woman who loves a man whose life is given over to something that has taken the awful hold upon him that his aims have taken upon him! I have seen that kind of misery, and I know that I must not risk it for myself. Anything, anything on earth would be preferable to such a fate."

"Would it be preferable to marry a man you do not love?" asked Myra, abruptly.

Cicely did not answer at once. "At least I should keep my dream," she said, slowly, at length.

Myra turned, startled out of her usual calm.

"Child, you cannot, you dare not do this thing!" she cried, in stern alarm.

"I am so tired. I only want peace," said Cicely, sadly, looking away.

"But would you find it through a lowering of your womanhood?" Myra's gentle manner had changed.

"Once, when I was quite young," said Cicely, with her eyes still on the fire, "I knew a woman who was loved by an artist. I met her while we were abroad. She was living in Paris, and I knew her well. She was a beautiul woman of a proud, sensitive type, with a capacity for feeling that used almost to frighten me — it was so still and so reserved, and yet so deep. The artist fell violently in love with her at first sight. She was not equally attracted, and she tried to avoid him. He pursued. At last he won her. She married him, and for a while they were as happy as mortals can be, I suppose. For six months she was everything to him. He was completely infatuated. Then he went back to his art. It was a poor little art, but he didn't know it. He thought himself great. He was determined that his genius should be recognized. He had had a hard struggle with adversity, but he believed that he was strong enough to overcome every obstacle. He did overcome a good deal by a patient perseverance. She tried to help him — to throw herself into his work. But she knew nothing about art in a technical way. She only bored him by her poor attempts. She saw that he was slipping away from her. But in her great pride she could only suffer in silence. She was wounded to the very heart's center, she —"

Cicely suddenly paused. "It is no use wearying you with the story," she said, "but the end of it all was such unhappiness as I had never seen before. It was something I could not forget. It has haunted me ever since. Often in the last eight months that woman's face has come before me. It was like a warning. Sometimes it was a menace."

"But there is not the smallest similarity," cried Myra, quickly. "It is a nightmare, a hideous dream that you have conjured up to torture yourself with. If he had loved his art, this man, in any true and noble sense, can't you see that he must have only loved her the more because of it? You say it was a poor little art. I can well believe it. And his aim was the purely selfish aim of personal distinction, of an ambitious success. What possible analogy is there between his case and the case of the man you love?"

Cicely put out her hands. "Don't — please — I must ask you not —"

Myra took both the cold little hands firmly into hers.

"Cicely," she said, unyieldingly, "you know it is not ambition. You know it is as high a motive as ever swayed a man. You know it is a call to duty that he hears and dares not silence. And yet —"

She caught herself up for an instant, frightened by the girl's pallor.

"I must not make you ill. But even at the risk of it I must say these things. He does not wish you to play any minor part in his life. He asks you to share in every plan, to go every step of the way with him. I think, I am sure —" a sudden mist gathered in her eyes — "I am sure that if you did not already know that he is beyond any thought of a merely personal gain, you would have known once for all what he is if you had seen the way in which he took his defeat."

"His defeat?" Cicely was bewildered. She was trembling in every nerve. It was the first moment when she had become completely roused.

"His defeat for Congress — for the nomination for the unexpired term."

Cicely leaned quickly forward. "When?" she asked breathlessly.

"In November. I thought you knew."

Cicely sank back into her chair. She turned her face quickly away.

"Can you tell me for certain on what day he knew he would be defeated?" she asked after a long time, with trembling lips.

"He knew it," said Myra, "on the twenty-ninth. The convention took place on the thirtieth."

Cicely quickly put up her hands to her heart. "I didn't know," she whispered, "I didn't know."

Myra rose and bent down above her, seriously alarmed. "But you will tell him," she said very gently, "you will tell him that you didn't know."

Cicely looked at her for a moment without speaking. All at once she sprang up. Her eyes were wide and staring. Her hands fell limply at her side. There was the stillness of a statue about her.

"I can't," she said huskily at length, "I can't. I have promised to marry Mr. Broomer."

CHAPTER VII

THE ASSASSINATION OF WILLIAM GOEBEL

It was the thirtieth of January. The last year of the century had dawned dark and threatening for Kentucky.

The Board of Contest, composed of members of the state Legislature, which had been engaged for a fortnight in hearing the evidence relating to the gubernatorial matter, had reached a decision, and was about to make a report of its findings. According to this tribunal, William Goebel was the legally elected governor of the Commonwealth — William Goebel and not his opponent who, some six weeks before, surrounded by a glittering array of Kentucky colonels appointed by his Republican predecessor, and with an enthusiasm tinctured with anxiety on the part of his adherents, had been duly inaugurated in front of the gray historic Capitol, while the band played, as is its wont on such occasions, "My Old Kentucky Home," and the crowd cheered.

As required by the picturesque oath of the Kentuckians, the new governor had solemnly sworn to support the Constitution of the United States and the Constitution of the Commonwealth, and to be faithful and true to Kentucky, and to execute the office of governor according to law; and he had further sworn that he had not fought a duel with deadly weapons within the state or out of it, nor sent nor accepted a challenge to fight a duel with deadly weapons, nor acted as second in carrying a challenge, nor aided nor assisted any person thus offending, so help him God.

But the glory of the day was slightly dimmed by the dread of a contest.

In the one hundred and eight years of Kentucky's statehood such a contest had never occurred. When it was finally decided by the Democratic organization that the fight should be made, the rage of the Republicans and of the anti-Goebel Democrats knew no bounds.

Friends were estranged. Business was neglected. Hourly the tension grew. Although it had been declared that William Goebel himself had not been eager for the contest, and in filing the notice was acting only in accordance with the wishes of the party as expressed through the regular organization, the feeling of venom against him in pursuance of this last step amounted to a madness.

The Republicans were convinced that they had little to hope for at the hands of an overwhelmingly Democratic Legislature.

Ten days after the first session of the Contest Committee was held a strange company invaded the capital

— a band of mountaineers a thousand strong, clad in their uncouth garb, and armed with Winchester rifles, shot guns, pistols and bowies. These they boldly proceeded to stack in the Executive Building, prior to being regaled at a breakfast furnished them by Republican leaders on the Statehouse grounds. The visit of the Kentucky highlander to the capital of his state was one to be remembered. It was said that he had come to see that *justice* was done. Possibly as a means to this end he proceeded at once to fortify himself with a goodly number of drinks of Kentucky whiskey, the effect of which was to heighten his already picturesque speech, and to lend to his bravado a sort of freedom that was somewhat terrorizing to the good people of the usually quiet little city.

Of these "intimidationists," as they were called by the Democrats, the majority returned to their mountain fastenesses the following evening. About sixty remained as a body-guard about the acting governor, and were quartered in the Executive Building.

In the midst of all this disorder William Goebel, with his splendid nerve, walked like a man of iron, undaunted and apparently undisturbed.

"If they assassinate me," he said with strange prophetic insight, "it will mean to the Democratic party in Kentucky what the blowing up of the Maine meant to Cuba." Threats of his enemies, precautionary counsel of friends — nothing that was anywhere said of him or to him seemed able to provoke in him the smallest evidence of apprehension. His strong will never for an instant relaxed. His mysterious calm was unbroken.

But the thirtieth day of January was to mark a culmination. To the state capital it ushered in a reign of lawlessness unprecedented in the history of Kentucky, and such as made the previous exciting incidents seem tame. There was to be a joint session of the Legislature and it was known that the Contest Committee was ready to report. There was no uncertainty as to what this report would be.

It was a bitterly cold morning. The little town of Frankfort looked gray and cheerless. The Legislature was already in session, but the guiding spirit, the man about whom the whole machinery moved had not yet arrived.

Up the square toward the old Statehouse, with its six tall Grecian columns, a striking figure moved, a dark compactly built man, with a smooth face, and a cool, somewhat impassive mein — a member of the General Assembly on the way to his senatorial duties. Two men were with him, and he was walking a little hurriedly. He had passed the fountain about sixty feet in front of the broad steps of the Statehouse, and was pressing forward when a shot rang out, seemingly a rifle shot that came from the Executive Building on the right.

The man groaned, clutched at his side, and fell — almost at the foot of the steps of the Capitol. There were other shots. But the first had done its work. Soon the cry spread. It grew louder and louder, until heard throughout the state and the nation —

WILLIAM GOEBEL HAS BEEN ASSASSINATED!

Old Judge Trotter came slowly down the steps of his home and made his way feebly toward the heart of the town. The click of his cane on the sidewalk as he moved along with all the impressiveness his small stature would allow, sounded ominous. Anxiety and indignation had resulted in a state of excitement such as made him anything but an agreeable person to encounter. It was nearly mid-day, and his impatience to hear the latest news from the capital — where William Goebel, harassed by the tramp of soldiery, was making his last desperate fight — could no longer be restrained.

The shot had not proved instantly fatal, as at first believed. The victim had rallied, and spoken, and had then coolly questioned his physicians regarding the nature of his wound, and inquired whence the shots had come. Though there was little hope of recovery, those attendant upon him had stood awed in the presence of as magnificent a display of will power and of heroic force as was probably ever witnessed. It was to be a battle with Death; and before even this last enemy the man's valiant spirit did not quail.

Friend and foe watched the struggle with a tension and a secret trepidation that had its root in very opposite emotions.

It was decided by the Democrats that, through a speedy action of the Contest Board of the Legislature, they would declare him governor at the earliest possible moment. But it was a thing not easy to accomplish.

When the Legislature attempted to asssemble at the Statehouse twenty-four hours after the shot had been fired, a strange spectacle met their eyes. Soldiers with fixed bayonets—long lines of infantry drawn up on each side of the hall — the stairway completely blocked!

To each member as he came up there was handed a copy of a proclamation from the acting governor. The proclamation declared that a state of insurrection prevailed in Kentucky, especially in Frankfort, the capital thereof, and that therefore the General Assembly was adjourned, to meet in London, Laurel county, Kentucky, seven days later.

London! The heart of the mountains — the nearest railway station to the county of Clay notorious for its recent feuds and murders and general lawlessness. London, the stronghold of Republicanism!

Thwarted in their attempt to meet at the Statehouse, the lawmakers rushed pell-mell through the streets on their way to the Opera House, pursued by soldiers, who outstripped them in the race, and again drove them back at the point of the bayonet. From one public building to another they sped, only to be blocked at every turn.

Knowing that the Contest Board would on this day make a report and that the decision was in favour of the contestants in the case of both governor and lieutenant governor, it was determined by the acting governor that a resort be made to military interference to prevent a meeting of the General Assembly. Warrants were sworn out for the arrest of every Democratic member of the Legislature, and word was sent to the leaders that if any meeting were held by them at the Capitol Hotel where William Goebel lay, the hotel would be entered and every man who had engaged in the conference would be taken from it by force of arms. The entire militia of the state was being ordered out. Armed men stood guard about the Executive Building, and the civil authorities were forbidden to enter it.

Nevertheless the Democrats were not to be outdone. On the evening of the thirty-first of January, in the year of our Lord nineteen hundred, the Legislature of Kentucky, with seventy-five members present, met in secret session at the Capitol Hotel in Frankfort, and declared William Goebel governor of the Commonwealth of Kentucky.

And thus, propped up on pillows, with the dew of death already gathering on his brow, the intrepid leader signed his name to his first proclamation.

"Now, therefore, I, William Goebel, governor of the Commonwealth of Kentucky, do hereby command the first and second regiments of the Kentucky state guard, and each and every officer and member thereof, to return to their homes and several vocations, and there remain until lawfully called into service."

The old judge had just been going over that portion of the proclamation, muttering it to himself as he proceeded down the street. He was eager for a combat with any Republican whatsoever. One of the first persons he chanced to meet was old Matthias Oats, who came moving ponderously along in the direction of the Courthouse square.

The judge paused abruptly, bringing his cane down with emphasis.

"What is the latest bulletin, sir?" he demanded, surveying the burly form before him with a scowl.

"*Senator* Goebel is still alive I believe," grunted Mr. Oats, with a shrug. "You can't kill him. No such good luck."

The judge straightened himself grandly. "I was already without doubt, sir," he said with great dignity, "that *Governor* Goebel still lives. The foulest conspiracy that was ever planned against mortal man has come to naught. The victim of the plot has outwitted the perpetrators of the crime. He will not die."

"Why won't he?" growled Mr. Oats.

"The Almighty will not permit it, sir."

Mr. Oats was silent, his dull countenance maintaining a stolid calm which he was in that moment far from experiencing inwardly.

"I believe the President has decided that he will not send Federal troops," he remarked presently.

"Federal troops be damned!" roared the judge. "Let him dare to send Federal troops into Kentucky, and it will mean to the Republican party the loss of every Southern state. The rule of the carpet bagger is not to begin among us again. What is needed in a time like this is a man at the head of the nation like Old Hickory, with his 'by the Eternal,' and his strong will. The marvelous exhibition of self-control displayed by the Democrats, in spite of the egregious insults they have received, would illy warrant the sending of Federal troops into this state."

"Sir," cried Mr. Oats, growing suddenly black in the face, and raising his arm defiantly, "sir, if the leaders of your party had their way they would cut the throats of such as I."

The judge wheeled.

"Sir," he said gravely as he tipped his hat, "there are no cut-throats nor assassins in our party."

For an instant the fire of youth leaped from the aged eyes. The two looked each other in the face. There was a pause. And before the patrician the plebeian quailed.

The next person the judge happened to encounter as he proceeded on his imperious way was Colonel Leonidas Johnstone who had allied himself with the anti-Goebel Democracy. The colonel being younger and keener-eyed, caught sight of the quaint figure bearing down upon him before the latter was aware of who it was that was approaching, and with the instinct of self-preservation, was preparing to beat a hasty retreat, when fate intervened in the person of an indiscrete toddler who had just slipped up on the icy pavement, and whose equilibrium the colonel's kind heart felt constrained to restore. The few seconds that were involved in the action were sufficient to bring the old judge and himself face to face.

"Good morning to you, sir," said the judge, turning a scrutinizing glance upon the small object disappearing around the corner. "Good morning to you, and what is the latest news from Frankfort?"

"I'm afraid there is little chance for him now, Judge," replied the colonel, magnanimously. "I'm told that rather serious complications have set in. For my part," the colonel looked away rather sheepishly, "for my part I should be delighted to hear that he would recover. The man has made a gallant fight for life."

"He has made a gallant fight for the Democracy, sir. History does not furnish a parallel for such an atrocious crime as has just been perpetrated in our midst. He has been hounded to the death. Not even General Jackson himself, sir, was a target for a bitterer animosity than has been hurled against him."

The colonel looked grave. He stood a moment with his eyes fixed thoughtfully on the ground. "I was, as you know, Judge, one of those who were strongly opposed to William Goebel and all he stood for," he said at length. "I believed that his election to the office of governor of the Commonwealth ought to be prevented by every honourable means. I have only contempt for this contest, and think it cannot be justified on any moral grounds. But I will say to you here, and I am willing to say it from the housetops, that this assassination is a thing that meets with my heartiest condemnation. I am sure that it will be so regarded by all right-thinking men."

"You're a true son of the South, sir! I honour you, sir, for such sentiment," remarked the judge, drawing nearer and unbending slightly.

"There can be no excuse for assassination — not even the Goebel election law," continued the colonel, with his eyes still on the ground. "I for one very much regret that I ever took part in an opposition that was to develop into a persecution — after I realized the violence of the feeling aroused against the man. It became inhuman and utterly vicious. The assassin's bullet has brought more than one of us to our senses. The Lord knows Kentucky had crimes enough to answer for already. This is one too many. It will call such a halt on the Republicans in Kentucky as will utterly destroy their future chances in the state; and the worst of it is that a whole party will be held responsible for what was the work of only a few."

"And yet look at us to-day," cried the judge, waxing more and more indignant, "at the mercy of this Usurper, with his army about him — this man who has broken his oath of office and violated the law of the land! He should be reminded that for no worse crimes than his Charles I. was beheaded, sir. He should be made to realize that it is no slight matter to fill the capital with armed and reckless men, bent upon mischief. He should know that the militia is not to be called out at his bidding, and the General Assembly excluded from the Legislative halls, and prevented, at the point of the bayonet, from meeting to transact the business of this Commonwealth."

"There is no constitutional authority for this adjournment of the Legislature," admitted the colonel. "A power to convene the Assembly is not a power to adjourn it when in session. Under the constitution there may not be a meeting of the Legislature at any place other than the state capital except in case of war, insurrection, or pestilence. I am convinced that there has been no insurrection —"

"The only insurrection and the only pestilence, sir, has been occasioned by the presence of the mountaineer with his Winchester on his arm, who has been parading the streets of our capital, and who, under the mandate and authority of the acting governor has been quartered in the Executive Building, there to await his further command."

The colonel suddenly held out his hand. He was growing a little restive under the conversation. But he had been greatly sobered by the condition of things. His conscience was not altogether satisfied with his own course; and a kind hearted impulse led him to deplore the untimely taking off of the man he had opposed.

"Well, well, Judge, it is a wretched state of things, but let us hope there may be no more blood shed before we get to the end of this business. I will say this much for your man Goebel: he is dying like a king, and I'm glad they crowned him."

"Spoken like a man and a gentleman, sir!" declared the judge, returning the hand grasp warmly.

In the judge's own home also there had taken place something of a revulsion of feeling, so far as his son-in-law at least was concerned. Colonel Overton was greatly disturbed. Being essentially a man of peace, the dark tragedy that was everywhere the theme of discussion, to one of his temperament was particularly painful in its significance.

Four days after its occurrence he and Mrs. Overton were sitting in the library. Dinner was just over. Mrs. Overton was idly turning the pages of a magazine. The colonel's face, as he sat looking into the fire, betrayed an anxiety that he was far too wise to express in speech. Out in the street the cries of the newsboys were coming nearer, calling attention to a special edition of the daily paper that had just been got out. The colonel knew what that meant.

He rose and began to move restlessly up and down the room, his hands behind him, his head bowed.

But the newsboys were coming nearer. All at once he hurried out into the hall, turning a nervous glance upon the calm, elegant figure by the fireside as he passed. The hall door opened.

Mrs. Overton looked up and listened to her husband's agitated tones asking for a paper.

It was some time before the colonel returned. When

he did his face was very white and the hand that held the paper was trembling.

"Well?" she demanded rather irritably at length.

"It is all over," he said in a low voice.

Mrs. Overton glanced down at the jeweled buckle on her slipper. Presently she tossed her head.

"It is a righteous retribution," she said, standing her ground firmly.

But the strange being whose power had been great enough to call forth so many and such conflicting opinions had passed beyond the tribunal of the human.

William Goebel lay dead at Frankfort.

CHAPTER VIII

MOTHER AND DAUGHTER

A few moments later Mrs. Overton tapped softly at the door of Cicely's bedroom, inspired not only by a universal and particularly feminine impulse in her desire to be the first to impart an exciting piece of information, but bent also on another errand more personal and of considerably more importance to herself.

There came no response, and she drew her light scarf about her, shivering a little as she threw an impatient glance in the direction of a window that rattled loosely at the far end of a hall. She knocked again, this time a trifle imperiously, and then she coolly turned the knob and entered.

"Oh, I supposed you were asleep!" she exclaimed rather ceremoniously at length. She moved toward the chimney corner, and reaching down grasped the poker in her usual prompt and decisive manner and stirred the coals into a cheerier blaze.

Cicely turned wearily. Her couch was drawn up in front of the fire, and she had been gazing into the great bed of embers and writhing flames in an abstraction as complete and isolated as if her soul were actually absent from her body, wandering forlorn and solitary amid unfamiliar scenes. She slowly raised her eyes to her mother's face in a vague and somewhat uncomprehending look, like one dazed, and waited.

Mrs. Overton settled herself comfortably in an armchair opposite and stretched her feet toward the fender.

"I knocked," she said in a tone of displeasure rather than of apology. It had been her practice to hold always a tight rein, and she had no mind to relax in such assiduity now that her children were grown older and inclined even more than in youth to resist her restraints. And she always insisted minutely upon the obeisance compatible with her queenly dignity.

"I knocked twice," she persisted, her eyes roving intolerantly about the room, and resting upon no object in particular.

"I am sorry," said Cicely, with quite the proper deference.

Mrs. Overton rose elegantly and drew her chair nearer the fire.

"How cold it is!" she said. "Are you warm enough there in that light blue thing? I can scarcely recall such weather — and these old Southern houses of ours, with their imperfect system of heating, are about as well prepared for it as a little row-boat for an ocean voyage! I have just been telling your father that before another winter comes a new furnace will have to be put in. That old one is simply unbearable. I'd have had it done this winter but for the expense. It is the thing that always stops me. Poverty is a very sure curb. And we are most uncomfortably straightened just now. The whole house is getting miserably out of repair. It is particularly trying to a person of my temperament. I should like to know just how it would feel to have plenty of money once more."

She broke off with a sigh and a quick glance in the direction of the very still figure outstretched at her side. But Cicely was silent. Mrs. Overton began again.

"I have come to tell you the latest news of William Goebel," she said.

Cicely's face reflected a sudden interest.

"How is he?" she asked quickly, raising herself on one elbow.

Mrs. Overton stared curiously. There were moments when Cicely was an enigma wholly beyond her ken.

"He has just died," she responded indifferently.

Cicely sank back on her couch.

"Oh, is he *dead?*" she cried.

She lay perfectly motionless. Two great tears slowly welled into her eyes and fell in a moist splash upon her cheeks, white and rigid as marble. Then, all at once, to her mother's infinite amazement her tense features suddenly relaxed, softened, quivered, and she broke into a perfect paroxism of weeping, violently intense —as if some secret spring of feeling had been touched and the sealed fountains of her whole being were gushing forth in uncontrollable emotion. Great heavy sobs shook her that seemed to come up out of the very depths of her inmost nature.

Mrs. Overton turned startled. She was not skilled in the understanding of complexities, but as she sat watching and wondering, in some dim fashion it was slowly borne in upon her that the outburst she was witnessing was not all an expression of grief for the man that lay dead at Frankfort, and whose magnificent fight for life was the one thing in which Cicely had shown the smallest interest since her illness. A sharp apprehension, recently quieted, started up anew. She was beginning imperfectly to see that, in her delight and self-congratulation over the accomplishment of her wishes, she had overlooked one thing: the strength and the majesty of real feeling; and as she slowly grasped the idea that a human being is not a puppet, a sudden fear woke in her soul, and she realized that though it may be possible to control another's acts, it is seldom possible to control another's thoughts.

"Well, you are certainly your father's own child," she remarked at length, with a shade of annoyance. "I left him a moment ago with his head in his hands looking as if he had just lost one of his own sons, and completely forgetful of the fact that death may sometime be only a happy riddance. I'm sorry I told you. There now — there, Cicely, don't cry any more, child; you will make yourself ill again, and the man really isn't worth it. For my part, I think he only got what he deserved."

She sat for some time quietly awaiting the calm, looking thoughtfully into the fire and planning her method of attack. She had thought to lead up to the subject which was the real cause of her visit by a slow and tactful process considerably at variance with her usual mode of procedure; and she was, therefore, completely taken aback when Cicely said presently in a composed voice:

"You wished to speak to me. Is it about my engagement to Mr. Broomer?"

Mrs. Overton coloured violently — Cicely surely was a creature of surprises — and bit her lips. For days she had been nerving herself to this decidedly unpleasant ordeal, some force, unintelligible to her and which she secretly rebelled against, in her daughter's composition, causing her to hesitate to touch upon the theme now constantly uppermost in her thoughts. When she actually found herself face to face with it, so to speak, a certain element of cowardice in her nature made her shrink.

She turned, however, very deliberately.

"I do wish to speak to you — and about your engagement," she said.

Cicely's eyes were lowered. Her face did not move a muscle, and there was that in the dumb apathy that enwrapped her which rendered her a somewhat difficult person to deal with in that moment. But Mrs. Overton was not easily deterred. She had put her hand to the plow, and she was not one to turn back.

"Your father and I have decided that it is highly proper that your engagement should be announced at once," she began. "It is not as much as it should be the usual Southern custom to give immediate publicity to an engagement of marriage, but it is always the proper thing, I think —" she suddenly caught herself up —"that is, when a decision has been reached as final as yours in the case of Mr. Broomer. Of course, if it were a merely sentimental affair that should never have been, as is too often the case, it would be altogether different."

She paused a moment in some confusion, and then went boldly on with her eyes on the mantel, as if addressing someone or all of the various objects that caught her glance, a pert little Dresden shepherdess with her crook, being apparently in special honour.

"Your father, with his usual way of borrowing trouble, was at first inclined to delay matters on account of his anxieties about your health. He seems to think you are on the verge of a decline — at least, he talks like that. But I am convinced that there is nothing at all serious the matter with you. You are merely in need of change, excitement, a new interest in your life. And when you realize the amount of happiness you will be able to bring into other lives, Gertrude's in particular, through this marriage, I am sure you will be able to take an unselfish view and wish to enter upon it at once. Poor Gertrude," and Mrs. Overton heaved a little motherly sigh, "has really had a horrible winter — the life here does not interest her — because of her disappointment at not being allowed to return to college. I never dreamed I would not be able to manage it, else I would not have let her come home last autumn after her visit to the seashore with her brothers. I'd have sent her on straight to Bryn Mawr, and her father would have had to find the money for her expenses somehow. But I let her come back, and she is here and likely to be here for the rest of her life, if you do not alter things a little for her. I thought it possible that you would wish to take her abroad if you and Mr. Broomer decide upon the trip after your honeymoon is over."

Cicely's silence was becoming oppressive, and a trifle ominous. Mrs. Overton glanced at her in a sort of nervous apprehension and rushed wildly toward her climax.

"Mr. Broomer tells me that you have not yet made any definite plans," she said, with attempted composure. "I am sure that he has been everything that is considerate and kind, and very patient. It really is touching, the awe in which he stands of you and the feeling he has. This morning I suggested April, and his face looked as if one had suddenly managed some way to drop a lighted candle back of his eyes. I —"

She paused abruptly, and half rose from her chair startled and really alarmed by her daughter's aspect — the piteous shivering that shook her form, the look that had all at once traced itself upon her features.

"Are you cold?" she asked quickly. She stood a moment by the couch. "It is nothing," she said to herself reassuringly, "only a slight chill." She crossed the room and found a silken coverlet.

"There!" she cried, "there! I feel as if you were a little girl again and I was tucking you in bed after you had said your prayers."

"Did you use to make me say my prayers?" asked Cicely, in a hard little voice. It jarred discordantly upon her mother's ears. She turned sharply.

"Now Cicely, don't say that I didn't try to make you religious. You know perfectly well that I tried to make all my children religious. I used to make you read two chapters in the Bible every Sunday afternoon, and when you were disobedient, as you often were, I always insisted upon four — that is, until I found that you knew all the Old Testament stories by heart and really delighted in them; and then I had to find something else."

She had not resumed her chair. She went over to the mantel, and stood gazing into the fire, pondering deeply, her expression reflecting a variety of surface emotions. All at once she turned. Her face had grown resolute.

"There have been times," she declared slowly and in very even tones, "during the past week when I have feared that you were going to prove yourself a weakling after all, in spite of your high spirit. Frankly, Cicely, I have doubted that you were equal to the rare opportunity that has come to you. Most girls would jump at it. Well! I have only wished to do my duty in this matter. But I should like you to tell me before I leave you now if you really do intend to go through with this thing, or not?"

Cicely rose and stood looking her mother in the eyes.

"I shall go through with it," she said.

Mrs. Overton's gaze suddenly faltered and fell.

"Then I may give the announcement to the Sunday newspapers?" she asked quickly, vainly trying to suppress the eagerness that would creep into her voice. "Shall I say April? Or if you should greatly prefer May —early in May,— the month is always so particularly beautiful here —." But Cicely interrupted.

"Let it be April," she responded firmly.

Mrs. Overton lingered a moment over a very affectionate good-night. The door closed. As soon as she was alone Cicely turned quickly.

A strange new alacrity seemed to possess her. In feverish haste she moved about the room, searched for a match, found it, and then lighted the little wrought-iron lamp on her desk.

As she sat down the face of Blakburn Blair, pallid, miserable, accusing, rose like a specter before her. The pen fell from her grasp. She waited a moment in a sort of terror. Her breath came through her parted lips in painful, soblike gasps. Her eyes were wide and staring. She rose and took a few turns about the room, moving in soft slippered feet up and down her narrow confines like some wild thing encaged. Then once more she took up the pen.

"I had thought never to write again," she began, without other preliminary; "I have not felt myself privileged to write, even of the one thing concerning which there could be any excuse that I should. For in what I have done and am about to do I feel that I have forever put myself out of the pale of your friendship—possibly of your respect. It is difficult to analyze motives—the thousand springs that compel us to any special course. And I do not wish to seem to extenuate anything. I am simply throwing myself on your mercy. Will it fail me? Possibly some day when much that is now hidden from your comprehension shall be, through your own sufferings, revealed to you, you will understand. '*Tout comprende, c'est tout pardonner.*' This much at least I trust you will believe—that one thing and one thing only has controlled with me, and that is the surety I have that marriage between us could only result in failure, a far sadder and more terrible failure than the miserable wrecks of happiness we see about us all the time. It is not any one thing—will you try to believe that too? Oh, will you *try?*—that has brought me to this conclusion? It is everything—above all, I myself. I know that I have no right to your forgiveness. I should not ask it now. And yet I do ask it. If you were standing looking down upon my dead face, would it not plead for me? One day, maybe a less distant day than now seems reasonable to believe, one or the other of us shall first pass to where beyond these voices there is peace. Would there be any bitterness left in your soul if that one should be I?

I want you to know that in April I am to be married to Mr. Broomer.

CICELY."

CHAPTER IX

AN UNEXPECTED GUEST

When Cicely came down to dinner the next evening in a very becoming gown of pink silk and lace with a rose in her hair, Mrs. Overton studied her a moment with a complacency which was as much a tribute to her own wise powers of control as to her daughter's grace and charm of appearance. It was, however, a satisfaction somewhat clouded with anxiety. Cicely did not seem to be ill, and she walked with almost her usual proud and spirited bearing, but there was a stillness, a strangeness in her look which was a barrier against all intrusion. There was an expression in her eyes that Mrs. Overton did not like, and that she thought it prudent to ignore.

"How lovely you look, my dear!" she exclaimed heartily, as Cicely entered the library. "Mr. Broomer will be completely entranced. I never am quite sure which is your colour, pink or blue, until I see you in pink. Ah, that is his step now outside! I certainly am glad that he has the virtue of promptness — added to a great many others. Your father is always behind time, and you can't think what a trial his habitual tardiness used to be to me in the early days of my married life. It is still, but such things are always harder to bear at the outset. The most difficult year of all is the first one. Afterwards it is, comparatively speaking, plain sailing for most persons who have any tact. Every married woman will tell you that. Your father never was known to keep an engagement to the minute in his life. He was actually late at our wedding. I wanted to be married precisely at nine o'clock, but I couldn't because he didn't appear, and I was all in a panic, and they were fanning me and holding salts to my nose and trying to reassure me when he did at last arrive. He was perfectly cool and unconcerned. I don't know of anything that more acutely jars upon the nerves of a high-strung woman than the constant evidence of lack of energy in the man to whom she must necessarily look for everything. Now Mr. Broomer —"

But Cicely had turned away.

"I think we have settled it," she said with a hard little laugh, "that Mr. Broomer is quite beyond criticism. Won't you go into the drawing-room and receive him — by way of proving yourself equally as prompt as he is? I heard Ben answer his ring."

As she moved toward the door the slight uneasiness upon Mrs. Overton's features gave way to the smiling condescension with which she usually approached Mr. Michael Broomer. Everything was going well, she told herself with persistent refusal to admit the contrary. The natural shrinking and indifference of a girl just upon the brink of matrimony ought not, she argued within herself, to be at all disconcerting to a woman of her experience and knowledge of life. The day would surely come when Cicely would thank her for the sensible, motherly counsel she had given throughout this whole affair; and in the proud consciousness of duty, faithfully performed, she could afford to bide her time.

At dinner the conversation lagged. The colonel, who was apt to be mildly reminiscent on occasions of this kind, was scarcely in his usual mood, although struggling heroicly to put at ease his rather difficult guest. The old judge was in a huff, and Gertrude whose recent experience at Bryn Mawr had rendered her a somewhat superior young person, seemed to have little to say to her future brother-in-law, whom she considered a very dull specimen of humanity, indeed. However, Mrs. Overton rose valiantly, and with secret scorn, above all such deflection on the part of her household.

There were .several rather brilliant flashes from Cicely. She talked a good deal — in a kind of reckless abandon. Once Mrs. Overton turned with a start when the girl's laughter rang out. There was something wild and desperate in the sound of it as it fell upon her ears. "I am positively growing nervous," she said to herself in indignant disapproval of such weakness. On the whole, it was rather a relief when the coffee was brought in, and when, a few moments later, she watched Cicely's trailing garments as they swept across the hall, followed by Michael Broomer.

There was a blazing wood fire in the drawing-room. Cicely stood before it several moments after the two had entered the room. Her gaze was absorbed and fixed, and she was completely unconscious of the fact that Michael Broomer, with his arm on the mantel, was watching her with the slow, devouring look of a lover.

Presently she looked up and met his eyes. She drew back with an involuntary gesture and motioned him to be seated.

"Do sit down," she commanded in haste, moving quickly toward the sofa. "I quite forgot that I was keeping you standing. Did you ever see such an absent-minded person in your life?"

"You looked as if you had completely forgotten *me*," he replied rather ruefully, as he took a nearer chair than the one she had indicated.

She watched him as he settled himself comfortably with a certain odd hitch of the body suggestive of the movements of a big Newfoundland dog.

"Did I? I was only thinking. I am always falling into a brown study like that, just as if I were quite alone. That is one of the many idiosyncrasies you are yet to become acquainted with. Aren't you appalled at the prospect?"

He didn't answer at once, and she shrank further back among the sofa cushions when he turned his broad, kindly face toward her, lit with real feeling. If only he wouldn't look at her like that!

But he had no poetry of expression with which to woo her, and his reply was as matter-of-fact as if he had been pronouncing approval on a pair of shoes. "I am, as you must know," he said slowly, "one of the happiest people on the earth. I am not appalled at anything. Not a bit of it. Since you have promised me your hand —"

"My hand?" queried Cicely, with a shrug and a quick arching of her delicate eyebrows. "What funny old-fashioned terms you do use! What you mean to say in plain English is simply that I have promised to marry you. Isn't that it?"

"That's about it," he answered smiling indulgently. He reached forward and took one of her hands in his. "Why it's as cold as a snow flake!" he cried aghast, "and you are trembling all over."

She tried to take it from him, but he held it firmly.

"See here, now, you aren't afraid of me, are you? I'm not an ogre, even if you are pretty enough and sweet enough to eat."

She drew herself up a little proudly. "I am not the least bit afraid of you," she said, "but until I have actually given you my hand, as you call it, I believe I prefer not to dispense with that portion of my anatomy. Do let us talk about something else.

He released her and sat silent for a moment looking thoughtfully into the fire, conscious of having blundered, but considerably at sea. Perhaps in some vague way he was clumsily reaching toward the diplomacy expressed in the Shakespearean advice, "Win her with gifts, if she respect not words," when he spoke again. But he began rather cautiously.

"I was talking with a real estate man to-day about that pretty old country place out on the Harrodsburg road I've often heard you speak of, and I find it can be bought. It's now for sale. How would you like it as a sort of bridal present? I came near closing for it then and there. You see this is the way I figured on it. Your people have always owned a good big part of Kentucky, and it stands to reason that you'd want to have a little of this blessed soil along with the rest of them. That's the way it looked to me, but I wasn't sure, and I thought I'd better wait and ask you first."

Cicely's face had grown strangely white. Her eyes were fixed on the hearth rug, and her hands were tightly clasped.

"I am very glad that you did ask me first. I — I

should not care for it," she whispered huskily at length.

"Rather have a house in town, would you? It would be rather more cheerful, perhaps, especially in winter. Now you know I don't care a straw for balls and dinners and receptions and all that sort of thing, but I know that most ladies do, and of course you can go to such things more comfortably if you live in town, not that you won't have carriages in plenty. Well, I'm glad I asked you. So that place is done for, and I must look out for another one."

Cicely rose and began to move softly up and down the room. For some time she did not speak. Finally she paused and forced herself to meet his eyes.

"I do not want a house here, either in town or in the country," she said steadily; "I do not want to see Kentucky — ever again — after I have once left it."

He indulged in a long, low whistle. "Well!" he declared in complete astonishment. "That certainly is a surprise. But it suits *me*. I didn't exactly see how I was going to manage it, but I was thinking that I would have to pull up stakes. It never occurred to me that you'd be willing to live outside of Kentucky. That's the way most people around here feel — most of the old families I mean. It's rather different with a Kentuckian of my stamp, not that I wouldn't enjoy owning one of these big bluegrass farms as much as anybody. But my business interests are largely in New York. I should in any case have been compelled to spend a good deal of time there. There isn't anything the matter with New York, is there?" he added quickly.

"If you prefer it I should like it quite as well as any other place."

He had been watching her as she moved softly to and fro with an almost savage sense of proprietorship, but he knew her fineness and delicacy and he was keeping a restraint upon himself.

Presently she came back to her sofa and sank down wearily.

"I — I am very ungracious," she said, "try to believe that I really am grateful for all the kind, thoughtful things you would do for me." There was a slight tremor in her voice, "I've been ill, and I am not yet strong, and it — it may be some little time before I shall be able to be to you all that a dutiful wife should be — but I shall do my best. Wait — be as patient with me as you can —"

There was something in the plaintive appeal of her voice, in the words themselves that touched and thrilled him and swept him completely off his feet.

All at once he rose and came toward her, reaching out his arms to her and calling her by name.

She turned a startled, almost terrified look upon him as he took the seat by her side. Her heart was beating wildly, but she could not stir nor cry out.

With resistless strength he drew her closer and closer to him. A sharp shiver went through her, but she lay helpless in his arms. There was a sudden gleam in his eyes. He bent down his head toward her lips.

In the same moment a slight noise reached her ears — the turning of the door knob. With a desperate effort she freed herself and sprang to her feet.

Everything swam before her, but she knew that some one was standing in the center of the room, silent, motionless as a statue. The stillness was intense save for the spasmodic sputtering of the blazing wood back of the brass andirons — like the on-rushing sound of a mighty forest fire in her ears. For a moment her gaze was downcast.

Then slowly, miserably, she raised her eyes and beheld the white, deathlike face of Blackburn Blair.

CHAPTER X

IN WHICH BLACKBURN IS SHOT

It was eight o'clock of a mild March evening. Already there was something more than a hint of spring in the air. The maples were sending out their first tender green. Crocus and violet, lilac and syringa! Soon the earth would blossom again. Colonel Overton, settling himself comfortably in the ancient coach which had been brought out at his direction, sniffed the shy, sweet odours complacently as they floated in to him, and assured himself that the long, dark winter was at an end.

The occasion was important, and the colonel had showed his appreciation by donning his evening clothes, and by sticking a spray of lily of the valley in his button hole. He was on his way to the Phoenix Hotel to make a call upon an old Confederate friend whom he had first known as a young man at the University of Virginia, and whom he had not seen since the close of the Civil War. The friend was accompanied by his wife, and the telegram which had been received a few hours before implied only a brief visit. The colonel was completely scandalized. To come all the way from Virginia to Kentucky and not make his house their home! The thing was preposterous. He had come prepared to take them back bodily, bearing a cordial assurance of welcome from Mrs. Overton (which the colonel proposed to amplify in case there should be the smallest hestation) and bent upon having his own way.

But though his thoughts, as he drove along through the quiet streets of the old town, were occupied mainly with the past, the present desperate condition of affairs in his beloved state kept intruding upon him; and it was with a kind of shame and instinctive shrinking that he anticipated the meeting.

Matters relating to the gubernatorial questions were still far from being adjusted.

Although, immediately upon the death of William Goebel, the young lieutenant governor had been sworn in by the Democrats and formally declared governor of the Commonwealth of Kentucky, the Republican claimant was steadily refusing to abandon the office to which he insisted he had been elected. Surrounded by armed men, he held sway with a persistence that was mediaeval in its defiance. The Court of Appeals had been virtually driven from the Capitol; the writ of *habeas corpus* had been defied; martial law had taken the place of civil law. Furthermore, the darkest rumours were afloat.

To a man of the mildness and good taste of the colonel it was indeed a melancholy state of things.

But out of it all there was one clear ray of hope. The

mob had not triumphed! There was to be the re-establishment of law. By agreement, it had been finally decided that the question as to who was entitled to the governorship should be settled by the courts. In the complete shaking up of old ideas which the assassination of William Goebel had brought about, Colonel Overton, like many others, had awakened to a new appreciation of the value of patience and obedience to constitutional authority.

In view of subsequent events, many things took on a clearer significance. Among these, the course of Blackburn Blair some five months before seemed to stand out as if revealed by a sudden flashlight of truth. The colonel was beginning dimly to understand. The young man's blighted political career and shattered romance had given him no little pain.

"Poor Blackburn — poor boy!" the colonel sighed softly to himself, as the carriage finally drew up in front of the hotel.

He was descending from the carriage in his quiet, gentlemanly way when he suddenly became aware of the fact that there appeared to be a special commotion in that end of the town. A crowd was gathered about the hotel. People were hurrying to and fro and talking in excited whispers. There was a look of awe on every face.

Just as the colonel was about to move forward, Frederick Dilson dashed wildly down the steps of the hotel and made his way toward the quaint old coach.

"Great God, Colonel," he exclaimed, "let me have your carriage for a few moments. Blair has just been shot."

Colonel Overton had stepped aside and Dilson was in the carriage giving his orders to the coachman before the elder could get his breath. He touched the young man gently on the arm.

"One moment, my boy. Who —"

Dilson leaned out. "That devil Tippleton, Colonel. Desperate fight between him and one of the Goebel men. Blair rushed in. You never saw anything so magnificent and so utterly quixotic in your life. Tippleton, damn him, escaped with just a scratch. Three other men are killed outright. Blair can live only a few hours. I'm going for Mrs. Mallory."

The colonel stood a moment on the sidewalk like one stunned. The crowd was still moving anxiously to and fro. But he felt disposed to ask no further questions. Dilson's few disjointed words had told everything. The colonel had been a soldier himself and a brave one. He felt roused as by a sudden blast of martial music. The splendid courage, the sublime nobility of the man who had thus saved the life of the enemy who had so foully wronged him thrilled him through and through. He stood perfectly still with bowed head. His heart yearned with pity and with self-accusation toward the pure young spirit whom he too had once misjudged. All at once he put his handkerchief to his eyes, withdrew it, and then softly entered the hotel.

Cicely was moving up and down the long drawing-room — a graceful figure in her white wool gown. She was expecting Michael Broomer. But her beautiful face did not wear the look that is pleasing to a lover. She seemed wearied and impassive, and the violet eyes, robbed of their piquant mirth, held an expression in their depths that was strangely unfamiliar. She walked slowly, her hands hanging limply at her sides.

The clock at the head of the stairs struck nine. She paused, and a look of faint surprise flitted across her features. It was not often he was so late.

Presently there came a loud, quick ring at the door bell. Then a hurried step in the hall. Cicely turned, startled, her nerves not having yet become strong since her long illness. She sat down, smiling a little at herself, in a low chair near the fire. In the next moment Michael Broomer entered the room.

But at first sight of him she sprang up, her hands clasped involuntarily at her breast.

"What is it?" she gasped, all at once white and trembling.

His heavy, kindly face was ashen. He was deeply agitated. He did not answer. But he crossed the room swiftly to her side and stood looking down upon her with a look she could not fathom.

"Something — something has happened!" she cried again, her eyes wide and staring.

He seemed slightly to recover grasp upon himself, though he still hesitated.

"Yes; something has happened," he said at length in a low voice. "I have just been told that Blackburn Blair has been shot and mortally wounded.

The stillness of death followed upon his words. She stood motionless, white as a lily. Suddenly she tottered like a flower bending beneath the scythe.

He reached out his arms quickly to her. But she drew back with a gesture that cut him to the heart.

"I am not going to faint."

He stood helpless, watching the battle between will and bodily weakness, and unable to speak a word.

She sank down on the sofa against the wall. "Now," she said.

He took a chair and drew it nearer to her. Not once had he withdrawn his eyes from her face. There was something piteous and desperate in his dumb appeal.

"Tell me—everything," she commanded in a voice that sounded almost stern.

He began slowly as if reciting a thing by rote.

"There was a pistol fight at the Phoenix Hotel between Tippleton and one of the Goebel men, a man named Sprague. Just as the first shots rang out, Blair, by the merest accident, happened to enter the hotel. Sprague was a staunch friend of his, and it is said that his influence over the man was something remarkable. Blair seemed to grasp the situation instantly. Before the crowd could run to cover, suddenly he dashed across the room and threw himself in between the two men, thrusting himself in front of Tippleton as a shield, and reaching backward in an effort to grasp the revolver. By this time Sprague was completely beside himself. He yelled to Blackburn to stand back, circled a little to the left and fired again. The first shots had missed. Beyond this nobody seems to know anything. Both men emptied their revolvers. But after some of the smoke had died away three men lay dead in the hotel lobby, and Blair had fallen."

He paused a moment. "It was the brave act of the bravest man I have ever known," he said simply and steadily.

Cicely still sat motionless, wrapped in her icy calm. Presently she rose. Her lips moved, but her voice was barely audible.

"I must go to him," she whispered, not meeting his eyes.

Michael Broomer stood up. Then he said very gently a single word.

"Yes."

"Where?" she asked, still looking down at the ground.

"They have brought him home."

A sudden spasm of pain swept over her. She slowly lifted her eyes to his. "Will it be possible for you, after a long, long time to forgive me? Everything must be at an end between us."

His face grew deadly pale again. For one moment he bent with a great yearning above her. Then he reached down and took one of her icy hands in his and held it to his lips in a last farewell.

"I will take you to him," he said.

CHAPTER XI

CICELY

Small groups of people were standing in the hall and in the large rooms of the Blair homestead as Cicely noiselessly turned the knob and entered.

A shadow had fallen across the threshold. Death's footsteps seemed to be drawing near; and already the old house had taken on the solemn and majestic aspect that ever pervades the dwelling, even the humblest, that awaits his kingly coming. All of the lower floor was open, and the chandelier in the great drawing-room where in times past had gathered many a merry throng was dimly lighted and now shone upon faces pallid with awe and wet with tears. Persons of all ages, friends of Blackburn or of his father, drawn thither on hearing of the tragedy, watched with profound anxiety for the slightest news that should come down to them from the bedside of the wounded man. Men stood about in silence or spoke to one another only in low, grave tones. Several near the doorway drew back as Cicely approached and made way for her. Like a statue in her whiteness, she passed through their midst, blind to their presence, and moved onward toward the stairway.

On the upper floor a complete stillness reigned. For a moment she paused irresolute. At the rear end of the hall there was a room — a sort of nursery of other days — in which as children she and Blackburn used to play, a square, spacious room, with a big four post bedstead and other massive furnitiure and a most delicious old fashioned paper on the wall, overspread with landscapes and gorgeous flowers. Some instinct which she did not seek to define caused her to turn toward this room as a place of refuge and waiting.

It was empty, as she expected, save for the childish echoes that seemed all at once to break upon her ears as she softly pushed open the door and moved toward the center of the room. The light in the hall shone in, but was not sufficient to make the various objects distinct. She could place them, every one. From memory she knew with perfect accuracy just where everything was, or should be, and finally she groped her way to a chintz-covered couch near the window, and sank down, cold and trembling, and with piteously throbbing nerves.

For a long time not the faintest sound broke upon her ears — just that same leaden stillness disturbed only by some slight movement from below, the same silent anticipation of a Presence. Presently a door opened — his door. She started up.

There were a number of footsteps in the hall coming

in the direction where she was. In a moment several persons entered the next room, and there began a low hum of men's voices, and her heart stood still. The surgeons holding a consultation!

As the thought penetrated her heightened consciousness something like a madness possessed her brain. She felt as if his life hung a mere arbitary in their hands — that they could save him if they would. Perhaps they would let him die. What if they should not realize the sanctity of what they had to do, its deep and terrible import; if they should be in the smallest degree negligent or obtuse; if —

She tried to rise, to go she knew not where, and then sank back among the pillows on the couch, distracted and helpless, unable to move.

There was a door between the rooms, which was slightly ajar, and occasionally she could catch a word. The men spoke in cool, professional tones that seemed callous to her unreasoning emotion. She sat with wildly staring eyes, quivering as in an ague, strained and breathless. All at once she sprang desperately to her feet. What was it they were saying — oh, what was it? "If he should live through the night." She lost the rest. The suspense was sapping her vitality moment by moment. It was torture.

After a while there came a hush, as if they were deliberating, each man taking counsel with his own thoughts. Then they began again. This time there seemed to be some slight opposition. A feeble ray was lighted in her heart like a taper in a tomb. They talked long and earnestly. At length there was a movement, and she knew that they had arisen — and that they were agreed. The taper flickered a moment, and then went out. There was no hope.

She turned her face to the wall. A numbness seemed to be stealing over her, and she felt as if a part of some hideous dream in which there was something to be done, something that she might do, yet could not, because of the paralysis that held her. In her great longing to free herself, with a mighty effort she struggled to her feet.

They tottered beneath her. With a low moan she flung out her arms, and her whole being appeared suddenly to give way, and she sank down on her knees beside the couch, as if felled by a mortal blow.

But it was from something greater even than her grief. It was as if Truth had looked her in the face.

It was indeed one of those large and pregnant moments before which the soul seems to bow in a kind of awe. It was fraught with a deeply sacred meaning; for through the vision thus received, startling, terrific in its might, she was to rise to a totally new consciousness of life and self. Slowly all the years of her past existence seemed to pass like a procession before her, and she saw herself the central figure, as it were for the first time, and with a stranger's eyes. Thus viewed her life seemed to her a weak and almost worthless thing, dominated by thoughts of self and disobedient to all heavenly promptings. Alone with her remorse and her despair she was learning to the utmost what it means to wake to Love too late, as gradually there stole into her mind and heart the profoundest of all convictions: the recognition that the spirit of love cannot exist without the spirit of sacrifice.

Had she loved him until that moment, she asked herself in the surprise of a complete self-revelation? Was it love that had driven him from her, refusing to share his life on account of the high purpose back of it, the Call that had come to his strong soul? The pure unselfish scheme of his existence spread out a beauteous thing before her startled eyes. How surely, could but his love be given back to her, she felt that she could trust him now; how gladly follow him into every trial, every strife; with what zeal would she throw herself into his great design, believing at last, what he had so often vainly tried to make her see, that he would not be less to her because of it, but rather more.

With the finer perception that had come to her, her contemplated marriage with Michael Broomer seemed a hideous, an unholy thing. She had reached, as in a single bound, to a new conception of the sanctity of the marriage relation. In grasping the thought of sacrifice, she was able also to grasp the thought of unity, and thus to struggle toward some dim appreciation of the vastness of the system that links humanity, the idea of solidarity, and to regard a loveless marriage not only as an individual desecration but as a blow to the whole social structure. But all this, alas, he could not know! Could she let him die not knowing? The thought that he would never know that she loved him rushed upon her in an anguish.

> "Is there none
> Will tell the King I love him tho' so late?
> Now—ere he goes to the great battle? none:
> Myself must tell him in that purer life,
> But now it were too daring. Ah my God,
> What might I not have made of thy fair world
> Had I but loved thy highest creature here?"

The lament of Guinevere kept up a dirgelike sounding in her ears. She felt as if dashed against the rocks and then borne onward into a mighty maelstrom of resistless feelings. She closed her eyes. Prayer? In her desperation the thought came to her as it comes to all when the breakers roar and the tempest threatens to destroy. But could she pray — she? Would Christ listen to such as she, He the type and the symbol of all sacrifice?

Her lips moved—at first very humbly, very falteringly, like a little child's lisping its first request. A sense of divine nearness and comprehension, a great unspeakable pity hovering over her began to enfold and bless her. For an instant her heart almost ceased to beat. Then she felt herself being lifted up; and with the consciousneess she awoke to a new realization of Omnipotence and of Love, and her soul leaped to heaven's throne in one single, voiceless cry.

The clocks of the town were sounding midnight. Still she did not stir. She had lost all sense of time. But from the travail of her soul there was coming a new birth. It was the hour of her apotheosis. Henceforth she was to be different. For self had been crucified.

It was after two when his door opened again. She rose, instantly roused. Myra and Judge Blair came forth, the latter walking feebly and with bowed head. Her heart bled at sight of him. A sudden impulse to go to him, to speak to him, to try to comfort, swayed her for a moment, but all at once she drew back into the shadow under a painful sense of guilt and of separation. They went slowly down the stairs, Myra speaking a few words softly and in womanly tenderness. After a little while she returned alone, and Cicely heard her quietly enter the room again. And once more the thought of her own aloofness pierced her through and through.

Presently she crossed the hall and dropped down trembling outside his doorway. If only she dared to enter! Everything was still. Again that strange numbness was beginning to steal over her. Her lips were dry and parched. She was very cold.

She was uncertain whether moments only or hours had passed, when all at once she knew that something had happened. There were a few hurried words within. She crouched nearer, flighting off by a tremendous effort of will the threatening collapse. In the next instant she realized that some alarming change had taken place in him, and knew that his breathing had become laboured. There was a distinct rattle in the throat. The attendants were moving rapidly about the room.

An icy hand seemed suddenly to grasp her heart. She put up her arms wildly and tried to reach the door knob. She heard Myra's voice and then the physician's giving an order to the trained nurse — and then a sudden blackness, and she knew no more.

In the cold gray light of the dismal March morning Myra, coming out on an errand for the doctor, found her there almost a lifeless thing.

CHAPTER XII

SUSPENSE

Twenty-four hours later Blackburn Blair was still hovering on the verge of death. And for many weeks thereafter his life hung upon a slender thread. Although in due time his wound appeared to be healing, pneumonia had early set in, followed by a low, intermittent fever that further undermined his strength, and that threatened at any moment to take a fatal turn. The one chance for him seemed to rest upon his stupendous powers of will supported by a notably strong constitution, which had been unimpaired by evil habits. At length all hope began to fade away.

The deep interest which from the first had been manifested in his condition only waxed stronger as the days went by. His last act of heroism had thrown a new and startling light on his character. There was a complete reaction of feeling toward him. His fellow Kentuckians, violent, autocratic, almost as haughtily resentful for another as for themselves of the slightest personal affront, yet as swift to pardon as to condemn, and always generous, were undergoing one of those unlooked for transitions which are intensely moral in their meaning.

The state went wild over the splendour of the deed, and the papers rang with eulogy of the manly young life just entering upon a useful and brilliant political career that seemed destined to come to an untimely end. Men who had condemned him for a former forbearance now wholly forgot their disapproval of the past in their admiration of the present; those of opposite political opinion were stilled; even Tippleton had been moved to come out in a card in which he acknowledged himself as having been entirely in the wrong in the encounter which had brought discredit upon the man whose magnanimity had just placed him on a pinnacle above his fellows.

There was nothing in their gift as he lay thus stricken down, that the directors of his party in the state, convinced of his high courage and sincerity, would not gladly have bestowed upon him, not only through a spirit of enthusiasm inspired by his recent act, which was the immediate occasion of the change of feeling toward him, but a sudden and somewhat tardy recognition of the inherent force that could turn failure into victory. His enemies had shown themselves powerless to destroy. Since his defeat he had borne himself with a calm that was plainly undisturbed by rancour or resentment. Such a man would likely prove himself strong in the science of political preferment. Sooner or later the true leader is recognized. The individual who cannot be crushed is invariably crowned: from the days of the barbarous people of Melita, he who does not succumb to the viper is apt to be thought a god. In one form or another tribute is surely paid to him. It was being paid in full measure to Blackburn Blair — now when it was too late.

However, it was beginning to dawn upon the minds of many that it was something more than office that he sought. In only a dim and imperfect way, it is true, yet vitally, it was discerned that the underlying thought of his whole life had been the idea expressed in the voluntary surrender of individual privilege for the sake of the good of the many, and that, therefore, there had been a distinct method in his earlier course with Tippleton. By one of those unexpected turns of events, by means of which a new conception is attained to, public opinion in regard to him was reversed, and he was seen as an altogether different being, one of profound and unswerving purpose, and of giant strength. He was wholly vindicated.

But if Blackburn Blair had proved himself a prophet and an apostle to his people upon the one subject concerning which they stood most in need of instruction, it had indeed been his also to know the loneliness and the suffering that are ever attendant upon all great souls. Such people are seldom fully understood. The breath of the wilderness and of the solitary mountain height seems ever about them, hiding them behind a veil of remoteness from the coarser minds.

Nevertheless, a long step in the state's social evolution had been accomplished. A new ideal of manhood had been held up to view. Already men saw in him the hope of the state. They waited with increasing solicitude all through the budding April weather.

But there was that in nature's smile that seemed to mock. It was evident to all that he was to die — not by any rapid process of dissolution, but slowly, steadily, and almost as it were unnecessarily, in view of his complaint. But the mighty power of will that hitherto had battled so valiantly now seemed to be yielding to the gradual encroachment of disease and to be on the point of surrender.

For hours he would lie in a lethargy, gazing with eyes that scarcely seemed to note its promise on the beautiful old elm outside his window as it swayed and beckoned toward him in the pride of its tender green. Again he would start up in a kind of frenzy and in the attitude of one listening at the first stroke of the great clocks of the town or the sound of church bells. When their solemn pealing revealed that it was not a bridal they sought to proclaim, he would sink once more into the apathy out of which he could only with difficulty be roused. The watchers as they moved softly, Myra, with her soothing sympathy and countless little gentlenesses, his father even, with his haggard apprehension and his deep, unspoken love — all, all were shadows only in the dawning of that springtide that spoke of naught but death.

It was May before any decided change came. It came suddenly. He had been more restless than at any time since the first weeks of his illness, but no immediate alteration in his condition was looked for. All morning he had tossed uneasily, but at length he had fallen into a deep sleep. Myra who had given up hours out of every day and every night to him since his illness, was alone with him in the room. He had slept for a long time. Finally she had sent both of the jaded nurses away for a brief respite, and she was sitting, with her hands folded in her lap, looking sadly out of the open window when all at once she heard him call her name in a voice that startled her.

She went quickly to him. But as her eyes fell upon his face she paused spellbound. Her heart stood still for an instant, and then began to beat with a rapidity that was almost pain. He had raised himself slightly on one elbow, and he was looking toward her with a look that was unmistakable. For it was the look of life, of will, of returning strength — as if all the forces of his being had rallied, put forth one last and mighty effort, grappled with his foe, and conquered!

From that hour his recovery was a sure thing.

With the lifting of the terrible tension under which she had for so many weeks lived, Myra's thoughts returned to Cicely with something like self-reproach. The large compassion with which she was wont to enfold all suffering, caused her to look with special tenderness upon the agony she had witnessed of one to whom repentance had seemed to come too late. Since that bleak March morning, she had grown to stand somewhat in awe of the dumb grief that Cicely from that moment had worn as a garment. There was that in the icy calm that enwrapped her which had caused no little apprehension. There had been a week's dangerous illness at the first. Then, day by day, a mere shadow of her former radiant self, Cicely had come and sat down outside his doorway, quietly, patiently, and with an unobtrusiveness that was touching in its self-abasement. Sometimes Myra was able to give her only a few moments. But again there were long talks together, when Myra felt herself powerless to comfort, and when Cicely would lapse into that strange silence which from the first had aroused her friend's fears. At these times Cicely's relation to Blackburn, her broken faith, her engagement to Michael Broomer and the subsequent ending of it also, were never even indirectly touched upon. But one day, and that during the week when death had seemed nearer even to her than to Blackburn, Cicely had drawn Myra's pitying face down to hers and entrusted a brief message and farewell.

And in the long days and nights that she had sat by him, not once had Myra heard Blackburn voluntarily speak of Cicely. Only in his delirium had he made mention of her, her name breaking in a madness from his lips. But as the time fixed for her marriage had drawn nearer, this had ceased.

Fearing to excite him too greatly, Myra had also kept silence. But Cicely's whiteness and stillness were giving her a good deal of alarm. While the thought of Blackburn's condition was paramount, it had not been so difficult to ignore, and even to harden one's heart a bit. Now it was impossible to do it.

One day several weeks later when Cicely had climbed the stairs looking especially pale and worn, Myra came to a prompt decision. She felt that she could not send her away again with that look in her eyes. She left her a moment in the hall.

"Blackburn," she said bending over him, "there is someone here who would like to speak to you. May she come in?"

Something in her tone made him look up quickly. An expression of poignant pain followed the look of surprise that for an instant traced itself across his features. His lips suddenly grew dry and stiff.

"Who?" he gasped, with an effort at self-control that sent the blood rushing into his pale face.

Myra looked away.

"Cicely," she replied very softly.

For a moment he did not answer.

"I thought," he began huskily, "I thought —" All at once he broke off, and again the look of suffering in his eyes was something that she shrank from.

"You thought that she was married one day last month to Mr. Broomer. She was not. She is not going to marry Mr. Broomer. She is here, and she wishes to see you."

Blackburn looked a moment searchingly into his cousin's face. But her eyes were downcast, and her expression was deliberately unrevealing. There was a long silence.

"I think you are making a mistake," he said coldly at length, turning his face away.

Myra busied herself with some flowers on his table. There was a serenity in her aspect that was telling him more than she felt privileged to disclose. He watched her hungrily.

"No; there is no mistake," she said presently in a perfectly natural voice. "Cicely is here. She has been coming every day at this hour, and we have sat and talked in the old nursery where long ago you and she used to play."

Blackburn's face was quickly turned to the wall.

Myra came to a swift resolution at variance with her former policy.

"She is looking wretched," she said. "All through that first terrible night she was here, alone, in that room. No one knew it. I found her the next morning, unconscious, outside your door. Afterwards she was very ill."

She came nearer and stood a moment smoothing the pillows back of his head.

"I think you ought to see her, dear," she insisted.

Still no answer.

She bent down her head.

"The anxiety is simply killing her. She will not believe that you are out of danger. Oh, Blackburn, Blackburn, I am so glad for you!" she whispered low under her breath.

He tried, but he could not speak. For a long time he kept his face away. But she knew that his lips were moving, and that he was alone with God. Then he reached out a hand in silent gratitude to her, and Myra, with another wholly perfunctory smoothing of his pillows, turned and slipped softly from the room.

CHAPTER XIII

O BRAVE NEW WORLD!

A low cry broke from him when he saw her face. She stood a moment, half timidly, just inside his doorway, scarcely daring to raise her eyes toward the strangely altered visage and gaunt form outstretched on the great bed before her. She was trembling, and her white gown fluttered tumultuously with her quick breathing. There was the look of a great humility upon her — a humility so profound and noble as to invest her with a kind of lofty pride. She did not speak, and he called her name — softly, reassuringly, and in the old tender way. She slowly raised her eyes to his. But as his deep cavernous gaze sank into her own, she started as if a spear had pierced her, and drew back — aghast and quivering, at sight of the terrible change that had been wrought. She took a hurried s'ep or two in his direction, and paused. Then a stifled sob shook her from head to foot, and her head sank on her breast.

"Cicely!" he said again quickly, reaching out to her eager, inviting arms, "oh, my beloved, come to me — come!"

She went swiftly to him like a troubled bird seeking

its nest and mate, and sank down on her knees beside him and folded her arms about him, not speaking a word.

A long time passed. Soft, delicious sounds of the sweet May morning were borne dimly to them from a far-off world that had suddenly receded from them. The odour of locust came in through the open window, and from the garden just below there floated up a quaint negro melody familiar since their childhood, as Uncle Scip, in infinite contentment, busied himself among hs flowers. Now and then, a low, ecstatic love-making going on in the ancient elm broke upon their ears. All at once he lifted her tearful face and looked long into her eyes. The veil of her inmost nature seemed to fall away, and suddenly he drew her to him, and their lips met in the confirmation of a joy complete and long-delayed — the seal of their perfect oneness.

"At last!" he cried, "at last! Oh, Cicely, how *could* you!"

The waxen eyelids drooped. A spasm of pain swept across her pale face. She was trembling in every nerve.

"Blackburn," she whispered huskily, "he never — kissed me once — not once." A wave of crimson swept her from neck to brow. She turned away.

They were both silent. Presently she faltered, growing very white,

"How has it been possible for you to forgive me? I can never forgive myself."

A shadow fell over his features. He could not speak, and she drew back frightened and guilty before the acute distress that for an instant in memory merely looked forth from his eyes. Then he put forth his hand to her.

"There is one subject upon which I think that neither of us can ever bear to touch. Let us forget."

She bowed her head. She rose and moved across the room to the window, seeking to hide her shame and confusion, and unable to meet his eyes. She stood for some time gazing down into the old garden, at the roses nodding in the soft air, at the fall of the brilliant sunlight shimmering upon the well-kept plot of blue-grass. Other days came crowding upon her. The thought of her childhood was like the sweet strain of some unforgotten lullaby. The present faded, and almost as an actuality she saw a small figure beneath the trees —a noble looking boy, and with him, near him always, her gay laughter ringing out like a challenge from time to time, a little auburn haired girl, wilful, wayward, teasing!

The tears gushed into her eyes. How she had tormented him from the first! A great longing to atone, to make it all up to him, stirred her heart to its utmost depths. She turned and looked quickly toward him — worn and altered with the unmistakable marks of that order of suffering that leaves a far deeper impress than disease or mere bodily pain. Then she came and stood beside him with a great yearning in her eyes — the rapt, maternal look that seems at times an expression of the chief element of a woman's love.

"My poor little boy!" she exclaimed softly as she took his face in both her hands, "I will — I will be good to you!"

He lay looking up at her, and smiling in a contentment that scarcely sought to translate itself into speech.

"It will take me just about three days more to get well and out of this," he broke forth presently in boyish glee. "Cicely, there is no mistake?"

Her face wore the hurt look for an instant, and she moved away. Her glance fell upon a low chair near the chimney corner. She brought it to the bedside and sat down.

"I am not the Cicely you used to know," she said gravely.

He refused to be serious.

"Aren't you? But I don't want any other Cicely. That one was altogether lovely.

She smiled a little sadly toward him.

"Dear, how am I to make you understand? You have always had so much to forgive — so much. I — I can never be like that again. Everything became plain to me in that terrible night. Before that I never knew what awful waves and billows can sweep over the soul. I thought I knew. But oh, Blackburn, the cold dark waters that surged around me then — the anguish, the horror of it all!"

His hand closed firmly over hers. Her face had grown white and tremulous again. Suddenly she raised her eyes to his. It was one of those luminous, rare moments in which the soul seems to stand revealed in all its naked beauty. He gazed at her in wonderment and in reverential silence; and as he studied her more closely, and saw how wasted with anxiety and remorse and illness she was, how robbed of her soft bloom, his soul knelt in adoration before her, and he knew that she had indeed deeply suffered, and that she was his at last.

Something in his clasp seemed to steady her, and she began once more. "I knew then that it is only in hours like those that we really find ourselves, and awake to the knowledge of what we are and what our lives must be; and I felt that if God would but give you back to me, as long as I lived I must belong to you, and not only through this little life, here, but forever and forever. I seemed to believe that, in spite of everything, you would love me and forgive me and want me still."

"Ah, you knew that I would want you still!" he exclaimed under his breath.

She turned to him, and the look on his face thrilled her through and through.

"One thing," he said at length, as again the shadow fell, rested an instant, and vanished, "one thing at least I think you can have never seriously doubted: my love for you."

Her expression changed. A lovely light seemed to overspread her features. She was beautiful, with something new and startling in her aspect.

"It was not you I had been doubting," she responded slowly; "it was I. I saw it all then. And I wanted to give myself, all of me, absolutely to you. I wanted your life to be my life — your hopes, your dreams, your plans, all, all to be mine, I —"

"Oh!" he cried breaking in upon her with a quick cry of amazement. Then he added fervently, and in a low voice, "Thank God — thank God!"

She did not speak. For some time she sat in a sort of dreamy quietude, as if listening to the music of her own thoughts. Her hands lay clasped in her lap. She seemed unconscious almost of his presence; and there was a stillness, a serenity in her attitude as of some marvellous white bird that had folded its wings in peace.

But suddenly there came a flash of the old mischievous spirit.

"Blackburn," she said, with soft, subdued gayety, "I have changed about so many things — so many things. Among them politics. I know of nothing that so much interests me. Will you believe it? Let me give you proof. What day was yesterday?"

"It was the twenty-first of May, wasn't it? Why?"

"It was the day on which the Supreme Court of the United States was to hand down a decision in the case of the Kentucky governorship. It has handed it down. Your father and Myra thought they would best not tell you for a little while yet. I am so glad. I want to be the one to tell you. I am going to tell you — now!"

He looked a little puzzled. "I have lost touch with everything. I feel as if I had slept as long as Rip himself."

"They thought they would best not talk to you of anything that might possibly excite you. So you don't even know, you poor dear, that the Kentucky Court of Appeals affirmed the decision of the Jefferson Circuit Court, and that the Supreme Court of the United States reached a decision yesterday! You knew it was agreed that the case might also be taken to the Supreme Court, didn't you?"

"Yes. But the decision — the decision?" he put in eagerly.

"Wait a minute. Let me break it to you mildly."

She looked at him with sparkling eyes. New life seemed throbing in the lovely form. She was radiant.

"I don't believe I know how to break things mildly," she confessed drolly at length. "I'm just going to tell you. Now listen. Blackburn, it was a complete victory for our side! All along the courts have decided that the judiciary cannot go behind the acts of the Legislature. The Democrats, therefore, have proceeded strictly in accord with the law. In Frankfort there were wild rejoicings. Bells rang and people paraded the streets. The militia on guard at the state-house was dismissed. A great many people went to the cemetery and covered the grave of Governor Goebel with flowers."

Blackburn was silent for a moment. "Poor Goebel!" he said very softly at length.

He lay for a long while looking at her in a kind of dumb thankfulness — thankfulness not only for the news she had brought him, but for her own changed attitude toward all such things.

"Now Kentucky is at peace," she announced presently.

All at once he reached forth his arms and drew her quickly to him.

"And so am I," he whispered, out of the depths of his great joy.

CHAPTER XIV

A NEW GIDEON

It was four months later. For weeks the local newspapers had been calling attention to a grand Democratic rally which was to be held in the Lexington Opera House on an evening toward the last of September. The spirit of enthusiasm which already was running high on account of the approaching state and national elections, received a special impetus when it was finally announced that young Blackburn Blair would be the sole speaker of the occasion.

At once the affair took on the nature of a personal tribute. To the impulsive and generous-hearted Kentuckians it was a welcome opportunity to make public testimonial of their high esteem. For to the more earnest and thoughtful of his people — of whatever belief or party affiliation—in the course that he had taken a principle had been established that was of larger meaning to the state than that involved in any of their political differences. Those of his own party in particular were eager to show to the man whom they had rejected, and who had been suddenly revealed to them, that they recognized him as their future leader — the one who more than any other — to use their own vernacular—"would unite and guide to victory the scattered forces of the Democratic cohorts."

Under a constitutional requirement, Kentucky was again involved in another gubernatorial campaign; but with that characteristic prevision that enabled him always to sink the interest of the state in the interest of the nation, Blackburn Blair's first thought during the months of his recovery had been turned toward the matter of the presidential election. And it was with the hope that he might direct the attention of his fellow Kentuckians to the larger view that he had consented to address them.

The evening of the speaking had at last arrived.

It had been decided that the exercises should not begin until half after eight o'clock, but long before the appointed hour the building was crowded to its utmost capacity, the stage even, far as the eye could see, being black with politicians, sitting like crows in conference, and impatient of the delay.

The vast assemblage of men and women waited, keyed up to a flutter of amiable anticipation on account of the marked interest, romantic as well as political, which hovered about the central figure. His engagement had just been announced, and even the oldest and roughest of those present, touched for an instant, and young again by that strange alchemy which is the result of a perennial human feeling, felt a certain quickening of kindly emotion toward the young man whose life had recently been so nearly cut off, and whose star now seemed so gloriously in the ascendant.

All of the boxes were filled. In the one on the right of the stage were Judge Blair and Myra and Cicely, the latter in her cool white gown sitting a little in shadow.

Presently the band struck up a lively air. Fans waved more vigorously. The night was warm and the crowd was growing restless. Calls for the speaker were coming from the galleries. He was not visible, and a slight uneasiness was beginning to make itself felt.

All at once the music ceased. There was a sudden hush. Two men in evening clothes were standing before the footlights, and one of them was trying to make himself heard in a few words of introduction. He paused. And then, as from a single throat, a mighty cheer went up from the great audience, and Blackburn Blair, pale still from his long illness, but powerful and resolute, took a step forward.

For an instant the storm subsided, and then the applause broke loose again, and there was a prolonged shout that could scarce be quieted.

Cicely was leaning with one hand on the box railing. In spite of her high-bred calm she had grown suddenly white, and her eyes glowed like stars. She was breathing quickly, and the rose on her breast fluttered tumultuously, like a thing alive. Her gaze was riveted upon the tall, still figure on the stage in a complete unconsciousness of any other presence save his own. He turned slightly, and for the briefest space he looked into her face; and then she saw him raise his hand and knew the opening words of the speech were being spoken. But it was several moments before she had recovered herself sufficiently to listen clearly.

"In times past," he was saying in a voice vibrating with the deep earnestness that strove to direct the attention of his hearers from himself to the great issues before them, "in times past the people of America were called upon to meet two supreme crises in their civil life. But to-day they have reached a crisis that is more solemnly portentous than any they have ever before approached — a turning point that shall lead to the life or to the death in their midst of popular liberty, human freedom, and human fraternity."

A low murmur of approval went through the crowd but the rich, ringing voice went on.

"If we were standing at the close of the eighteenth century and looking back over the hundred years of that period, discerning judgment would declare that the greatest event they had accomplished was the establishment of the idea of political freedom as set forth in the Declaration of Independence in 1776. As we stand to-night at the close of the nineteenth century — the century that has been greater than any other in social and economic achievement — and look back over the hundred years of this period, I think we may say with all confidence that the greatest event they have accomplished is the establishment of the idea of human freedom as set forth in the Abolition Proclamation of 1863. For in that far-reaching event of the eighteenth century, and in this further reaching event of the nineteenth, the manhood of the race was asserted.

"But potent," he continued, "as was the idea of political freedom and national indepedence, which our forefathers of the eighteenth century accomplished, and vital as was the idea of human freedom and national perpetuity, which our fathers of the nineteenth established, an idea of profounder meaning far to civilization confronts the American citizen at this hour, which marks the birth of the twentieth century—an idea that is the final sum of the previous ideas that separately foreshadowed it, and that is best expressed by those anciently distracting terms, Liberty, Equality, and Fraternity."

The audience was listening spellbound. Something in his look and manner held them in a sort of fascinated attention. Fans ceased to flutter. People were leaning eagerly forward in their seats, with their gaze riveted on his face. But the powerful, vibrant voice began again.

"It is true that never before in the history of the world have there been evidences of greater selfishness than are about us at this hour — a rapacity that has been made possible by the advanced commercial sagacity which is the shame as well as the pride of our age. It is true that not only in our own country, but in other *civilized* nations, the oppression of capital upon labour has been steadily increasing with the increase of the wealth of the world. The greed for money and the greed for power, with all their corrupting and ossifying influences, have been spreading as a plague through the life of our government, until the souls of men have become dead to truth and to fraternal feeling. But through all this inhumanity of man to man, a power, silent but irresistible, has been accumulating that shall become the destroyer of licensed iniquity: it is that spirit of freedom in its wide-reaching sense which 'adheres,' as Webster says, 'to the American soil,' and which, struggling through the shadowy efforts of impractical social reformers, has at last culminated in the vital principles that are now before us."

The crowd went wild with enthusiasm. The pale face of Blackburn Blair had grown paler. The light of a deep and solemn conviction shone in his eyes.

There could be no questioning his profound sincerity. One by one he took up the various points of the platform.

Finally he said, "The leaders of the Democracy are not responsible for existing conditions because they discern afar their results; and neither do they mean to hasten these results by their warning pleadings.

"Think you," he cried, with suddenly uplifted arm and in a voice that rang like a clarion note throughout the building, "think you that the prophets of old, as they described the inevitable overthrow of the idolatrous Hebrews by the kingdoms of Assyria and Babylon, meant to encourage those heathen nations to destroy the sinful Israelites, or only to urge their brethren to repentance and to salvation? The former supposition is absurd. And so the prophets of to-day, uninspired, it is true, save by a knowledge of truth and the tendencies of man in the past, would, in their lowlier way, point out to their countrymen the evil that menaces this nation, and with all the conviction that is in them urge them to repent, ere it be too late, of the idolatrous greed that is besetting them, and to open their minds to the truth that the perpetuity of a free Republican government depends, not upon the centralization of power and the increase of wealth among a few, but upon the distribution of control among the people, and the advance of the idea of Liberty, Equality, and Fraternity."

He waited a moment for the storm of applause to subside, and then went on gravely.

"Let us not be blinded by sophistry and delusion. The present policy of the Republican party is the narrow policy of aggrandisement. It is the logical outgrowth of that illiberal and exclusive measure, Protection, which is the foundation canon of its creed, just as the positon of the Democratic party is the logical outgrowth of its broad and far-seeing advocacy of the doctrine of Free Trade."

He had spoken for more than an hour. Suddenly Blackburn lifted his hand in conclusion.

"The most vital crisis of our nation is upon us, and our country's call is solemn. Never before in the history of America has there been more need of wisdom in interpreting the principles of free government; never before in the history of the Constitution has it had more need of able defenders. We cannot magnify our present situation. It is too real for doubt and derision, too awful for tears or hysteria. The destiny of our Republic is at stake. With the result of the election in November, the idea of popular government as assayed in the United States shall be thwarted or established.

"The decision may go against us. Nations in the past, in their idolatrous selfishness, have been allowed to work out their own destruction. Athens tossed behind her her ancient principles and reached out her arms to conquest, and Rome dazzled the world with her victories. But Athens and Rome began to decline even with their seeming triumphs. And shall we also go the way to death? Shall America, the brightest hope of civilization, shall America, too, perish? She has not yet reached her highest greatness, has not yet assayed all the principles she came into being to establish: it is too soon for her to degenerate.

"It cannot be that the conscience of America is silenced, that the patriotism of America is dead. Her manhood is only slumbering. Awake then and prepare for the conflict. 'Be strong and courageous, be not afraid nor dismayed.' The attractions of selfishness are against us, and the might of wealth is our foe; but it is only 'an arm of flesh' that is with our opponents; 'with us is the Lord our God to help us, and to fight our battles.'"

There was an instant's intense hush, and in the strange silence that followed upon his last words a thrill that was solemnly electric pierced the hearts of his hearers. And then, just before the clash of musical instruments, and the sudden uprising of the great assemblage, in the midst of a wild and tumultuous cheering, Blackburn turned quickly toward the box on his right.

Cicely was bending forward, with parted lips, and

with hands clasped at her breast. He met her eyes, and his face shone.

In the next moment a white rose fluttered softly to his feet.

CPSIA information can be obtained at www.ICGtesting.com
Printed in the USA
BVOW050207250912

301325BV00003B/7/P